Second Edition

Netball

STEPS TO SUCCESS

Wilma Shakespear
Margaret Caldow

HUMAN KINETICS

Library of Congress Cataloging-in-Publication Data

Shakespear, Wilma, 1943-
  Netball : steps to success / Wilma Shakespear, Margaret Caldow. -- 2nd ed.
     p. cm. -- (Steps to success sports series)
  ISBN-13: 978-0-7360-7984-6 (soft cover)
  ISBN-10: 0-7360-7984-X (soft cover)
  1. Netball. I. Caldow, Margaret. II. Title.
  GV889.6.S53 2009
  796.324--dc22

                              2008052162

ISBN-10: 0-7360-7984-X (print)   ISBN-10: 0-7360-8530-0 (Adobe PDF)
ISBN-13: 978-0-7360-7984-6 (print)   ISBN-13: 978-0-7360-8530-4 (Adobe PDF)

The Web addresses cited in this text were current as of March 2009, unless otherwise noted.

Acquisitions Editor: John Dickinson; **Developmental Editor:** Cynthia McEntire; **Assistant Editor**: Scott Hawkins; **Copyeditor:** Patsy Fortney; **Proofreader:** Joanna Hatzopoulos Portman; **Graphic Designer:** Nancy Rasmus; **Graphic Artist:** Tara Welsch; **Cover Designer:** Keith Blomberg; **Photographer (cover):** Hannah Johnston/Getty Images; **Photographer (interior):** Bruce Long; **Visual Production Assistant:** Joyce Brumfield; **Photo Production Manager:** Jason Allen; **Art Manager:** Kelly Hendren; **Associate Art Manager:** Alan L. Wilborn; **Illustrators:** Tim Stiles, Alan L. Wilborn; **Printer:** Premier Print Group

We thank the Queensland Academy of Sport in Queensland, Australia, for assistance in providing the location for the photo shoot for this book.

Human Kinetics books are available at special discounts for bulk purchase. Special editions or book excerpts can also be created to specification. For details, contact the Special Sales Manager at Human Kinetics.

Printed in the United States of America   10 9 8 7 6 5 4 3 2 1

Human Kinetics
Web site: www.HumanKinetics.com

United States: Human Kinetics
P.O. Box 5076
Champaign, IL 61825-5076
800-747-4457
e-mail: humank@hkusa.com

Canada: Human Kinetics
475 Devonshire Road Unit 100
Windsor, ON N8Y 2L5
800-465-7301 (in Canada only)
e-mail: info@hkcanada.com

Europe: Human Kinetics
107 Bradford Road
Stanningley
Leeds LS28 6AT, United Kingdom
+44 (0) 113 255 5665
e-mail: hk@hkeurope.com

Australia: Human Kinetics
57A Price Avenue
Lower Mitcham, South Australia 5062
08 8372 0999
e-mail: info@hkaustralia.com

New Zealand: Human Kinetics
Division of Sports Distributors NZ Ltd.
P.O. Box 300 226 Albany
North Shore City
Auckland
0064 9 448 1207
e-mail: info@humankinetics.co.nz

Second Edition

Netball

STEPS TO SUCCESS

Contents

Climbing the Steps to Netball Success

Netball's great attraction is that it has room for everyone. Netballers love to play and compete. The concentration on the faces of the shooters and the desperation of the defenders are regular features of any netball court. Netballers love devising game plans. Hours are spent developing tactics and analysing how these great ideas fared in the heat of competition.

Netball: Steps to Success is written for all netballers—beginners, social players and those who aspire to the lofty heights of the international scene. It is for all who seek to better understand what good court craft looks like and how it is developed.

We look first to the basics, emphasising the need to do these well because they are the foundations on which success is built. We then begin to challenge you to reach a little higher and expand that all-important level of skill.

Once you have begun to master the basics, we advise you to get on the court and find your favourite position. Don't be in a hurry to specialise. Try them all. You will find that our attacking and defending sections will guide your early steps, and the specialist steps will help you decide which position you prefer.

When you step out on that court, you need to understand strategy. I am sure you have all seen the enthusiastic player who chases everything and ends up being more of a hindrance than a help. Strategies bring order; they allow us to combine our talents effectively so that we use space well and work to our strengths. We believe that the golden rule here is S and S (simple and smart). Understanding just what that means on court will help you to win.

We also want you to understand how a successful team functions. Learn to look inside the team as a whole. Do you see a group of individuals who are somewhat disjointed, or do you see a group that can maximise its talents collectively? Knowing how to adapt your talents to work with those around you is a critical part of being a successful netballer. Remember, the sum of the whole is so much greater than the individuals' talents.

Like many, our first introduction to netball was at school. Netball was our winter sport. We were encouraged to take it seriously, so we joined opposing clubs in Melbourne. After chasing each other around the local courts, we found ourselves teammates, playing for Victoria at the national championship, and then national team honours beckoned. Travelling to England to compete in the first World Championship was amazing. We were the first members of our families to travel abroad. It wasn't just winning that first World Crown that fired our love for the game; it was the whole life experience that we embraced.

Another great highlight was the opportunity to work with Gaye Teede at the Australian Institute of Sport. We had the time to rewrite our approach to training. Working daily with some of our country's most gifted athletes took our preparation to a whole new level. The impact on netball, particularly within Australia, was significant.

Today we find ourselves back in Australia after spending a significant period of time in the UK. Margaret coached the England national team from 2003 to 2007, and Wilma directed the development of the English Institute of Sport (2001-2007). Our love for netball and of sport in general has never diminished since we marched through the winner's colonnade in Eastbourne all those years ago. There have been numerous awards and much recognition. Meeting the Queen at Buckingham Palace would top that list. However, it is the friendships that we have made along the way that matter most and the life lessons that we value.

Netball is a team game, which means there are two aspects of becoming a successful player. First you learn the skills of the game—how to catch and throw, to score goals, and to move in attack and defence. Then you learn to use these skills effectively with other team members to produce a winning team.

The first five steps in this book provide a foundation—a solid base of performance and movement skills you need to attack and defend effectively. Constantly polish these basic skills because, if honed to perfection, they will not let you down. As you progress, you will be able to combine these skills and then test them in match-like conditions (step 6). The next steps make sure that you use space well on court and understand how to use your skills to develop strategies that work. Steps 7 through 9 look specifically at each third of the court to help you appreciate the subtle differences within each one. Step 11 looks at how a winning team functions while the final step suggests ways to improve your fitness.

The drills in each step grow from simple to complex. You should aim to work at maximum intensity on each drill. Honestly score your success at the end of each drill and then total these scores to rate your progress at the end of each step. Make sure that you are competent before moving on. It is much better to take your time and repeat the step than to rush on with poor skills and little understanding. Challenge yourself by tackling a new drill or a more complex version of the one you have just done.

Don't be surprised if you make mistakes. When you start practising new skills, they don't always fall into place. You will need to work hard, so put your best effort into training. When a routine breaks down, return to the basic skill, work it until you are confident, then tackle a more demanding task. Never walk away from a difficult passage—learn to work your way through it.

Once you are really doing well with the basic skills, you will find that training with a partner or a small group is more productive. When you begin team play, most training will be done with your team members.

As you climb the steps to netball success, follow the same sequence for each step:

1. Read the explanations of what the step covers, why the step is important and how to execute the step's focus.

2. Review the photos that show how to execute each basic skill successfully.

3. Look over the common errors that might occur and recommendations for how to correct them.

4. Read the directions and success checks for each drill. Practise accordingly, and record your scores. The drills are arranged in an easy-to-difficult progression, so make sure you can successfully complete each drill before moving on to the next one. Pace yourself by adjusting the drills to either increase or decrease their difficulty, depending on your skill level.

5. As soon as you finish all the drills for the step, have a qualified observer, such as your teacher, coach or training partner, to evaluate your basic technique. By focusing on correct technique, you can enhance your performance. Ask your observer to suggest improvements.

Now, to begin! Read the next section to find out what the game of netball is all about; then take the steps toward becoming a skilled performer and a valued member of a team playing this great game.

Acknowledgments

The late Margaret Pewtress had a huge influence on our playing careers and our professional lives. She taught us that if we aimed high, worked hard and really went for it, then most things were possible. She set a tradition that we have tried to pass to this generation.

In the preparation of this book we are indebted to the generosity of some special friends and colleagues. We were delighted to secure the talent of our photographer, Bruce Long. His expertise and patience have captured the essence of our work. Paul Smith, who has worked with both the Australian and the England netball teams as their fitness expert, guided us through and wrote much of step 12. Chris Burton checked our rules summary, while our models—Jenny, Justin, Megan, Peta, Romelda, Samantha, Sophie and Tamsin—gave their time and talents so generously and the Queensland Academy of Sport (QAS) provided access to their facility.

Finally, we would like to acknowledge how fortunate we are to have families and friends who encouraged us to follow our dreams and were there for us through the great days and those that presented somewhat more of a challenge.

The Sport of Netball

Netball is a fast-moving, high-scoring game that was adapted from basketball to better suit the genteel young women of late-19th-century England.

Netballers must pass the ball within 3 seconds and are allowed to take only one step with the ball before releasing it. The team in possession of the ball aims to attack towards its goal circle to score, and its opponent's role is to defend.

Teams may include up to 12 players, but only 7 may take the court at any one time. Each player has a playing position determined by the areas on the court where she may move.

Only the teams' two shooters are allowed to score goals.

A netball court is divided into three areas of equal size. There are two goal circles (a semi-circle centred on the goal line with a goalpost in the middle) at either end of the court.

A 0.9-metre (3 ft) circle is marked in the middle of the court. Play commences with a centre pass and restarts in the centre each time a goal is scored. The centre pass alternates between the teams throughout the match. A netball match is usually played over four 15-minute quarters; however, a number of local variations are in place across the netball world.

HISTORY OF NETBALL

When Dr. James Naismith invented basketball in an American YMCA in 1891, it is unlikely that he realised that he had also given birth to netball—today the most popular women's sport in Australia, New Zealand, the United Kingdom, the Caribbean, South Africa and Malawi and one that continues to grow strongly with close to 60 member countries in the International Federation.

When the students of Madame Osterberg's College of Physical Training at Hampstead, England, were first introduced to netball in 1895—then known as women's basketball—there were no printed rules and no court lines, circles or boundaries. The goals were two waste-paper baskets hung on walls at each end of the hall. Because the baskets were closed at one end, the umpire had to climb a ladder to retrieve the ball each time a goal was scored. Spectators found this highly amusing. Players surely felt it wasted time.

Two years later the game was first played outdoors. The English students introduced rings instead of baskets and a larger ball, and divided the ground into three equal playing areas known as thirds of the court. The women who played wore long, flowing skirts and leg-of-mutton sleeves. The first recorded rules were published in England in 1901.

From such humble beginnings the game was introduced to other countries by schoolteachers and members of the religious teaching orders, who, at the time, travelled to all the far-flung corners of the British Empire. Netball arrived in Australia and New Zealand at about the turn of the 20th century.

The first national association was that of New Zealand in 1924, followed by England's in 1926 and Australia's in 1927. Although geographically close, New Zealand and Australia continued to alter rules without reference to each other until 1938, as did other netball-playing countries of the

Commonwealth for years after that. Of course, this made international competition difficult.

In 1960 an international code of play was introduced, and within a few years the game was called netball worldwide. The first World Tournament was held at Eastbourne in England in 1963, where Australia and New Zealand established themselves as the sport's leading nations. In a thrilling encounter, Australia defeated its Kiwi rivals by a single goal to claim the first World Crown. Since that time, Australia has dominated, winning 9 of the 12 titles held to date.

In the 1979 series, there was a three-way tie among New Zealand, Australia, and Trinidad and Tobago. An international rule is now in place to determine a winner through a final series.

Netball has two major international events. The World Championships are staged every four years, and since 1998 netball has been part of the Commonwealth Games.

The introduction by the International Federation of Netball Associations (IFNA) of an annual world ranking system means that national teams must compete regularly on the international stage to maintain their ranking.

Today the game is governed by IFNA. There are currently almost 60 member nations of IFNA, most of whom are members of the British Commonwealth of Nations. The member nations are grouped into five regions—Africa, America, Asia, Europe and Oceania—each with a representative regional federation. These regional federations are an integral part of the global governance structure and assist in the implementation of IFNA policies and the development of the sport in their respective regions.

One of the major challenges for the game today is to continue to develop its appeal nationally and internationally; to that end, some interesting programs are emerging. The Trans-Tasman Series in New Zealand and Australia is taking the game to a new international level, allowing top athletes from around the world to be recruited by the various franchises. The Super Cup Series in England provides a platform for talented athletes to compete regularly at the highest domestic level.

Dr. Naismith would no doubt be amazed to see the development of the game he invented. Today this popular game is not played only by women; men are taking to the courts as never before to participate in league play. Besides men's leagues, mixed netball is one of the game's fastest growth areas. Whole new generations of players are being introduced to the game.

The future holds much promise for netball as television coverage and the Internet take it to new audiences around the world. It is well positioned to take its place in the fast lane of corporate and international sport, the hallmark of successful sports in the 21st century.

GAME PLAY

A netball team consists of seven players with specific positions that restrict them to movement within specific areas—or thirds—of the court. Letters worn by the players on their tops identify their positions. This helps the two umpires who control the game to see when players travel outside their areas.

The object of the game is to score more goals than the opposition. Goals are scored by projecting the ball above and then completely through a ring attached to a goalpost. Goals can be scored only by one of the team's two shooters standing within the team's goal circle. The goalposts are 3.05 metres (10 ft) high, and the ring, which has an internal diameter of 380 millimetres (15 in.), has a net attached to it, which makes it easy to see when a goal is scored. Each goal scores 1 point.

The court measures 30.5 metres (100 ft) long and 15.25 metres (50 ft) wide (figure 1). It is divided by lines, called transverse lines, into even thirds: two goal thirds and a centre third. The centre third contains a centre circle 0.9 metres (3 ft) in diameter. At either end of the court (in each goal third) is a goal circle 4.9 metres (16 ft) in radius, and a goalpost centred on the goal line. All lines on the court measure 50 millimetres (2 in.) wide and are part of the playing area.

For the purpose of umpiring, the length of the court is divided in half by an imaginary line across the centre from sideline to sideline. Each umpire is responsible for controlling and

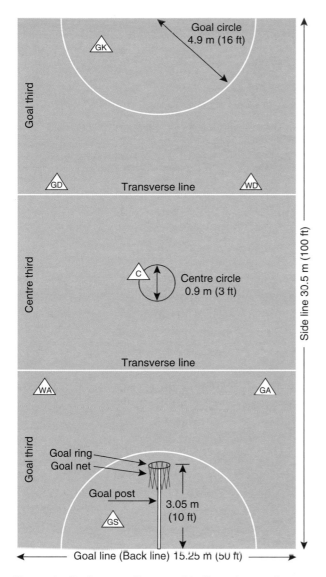

Figure 1 Basic court diagram with dimensions and player positioning.

transverse lines at either end of the court (figure 1). After the whistle sounds, the players enter the centre third to contest the first pass.

Netball is, by design, a passing game; dribbling and running with the ball are not allowed. Through quick and accurate passing, the attacking team moves the ball down the court towards its goal. The ball must be handled in each third of the court as it travels from end to end. Because a player is allowed only one step with the ball and must release it within 3 seconds, proper positioning to receive and deliver passes quickly and cleanly is all-important for the attacking team. The aim of the team in defence is to anticipate and position itself to intercept a pass or to limit the attacking team's shooting opportunities by forcing an error. Netball demands that all team members have sound attacking and defending skills and are able to switch quickly from one role to the other as team possession changes.

Netball is a non-contact sport, and the rules and penalties for defending reflect this. When a player has possession of the ball, the opponent must clear a distance of 0.9 metres (3 ft)—stepping back with a move called a recovery step—before attempting to defend. Attempting to defend within this defined distance is called obstruction and results in a penalty pass or shot being awarded against the infringer. Contact—hitting, pushing or bumping—that interferes with play brings the same penalty.

After the ball reaches a shooter within the team's goal circle, a shot at goal can be taken. Netball shooters mainly use a stationary shooting technique. This sudden stopping to shoot for goal provides an immediate change of tempo from the speed of down-court play. When the ball leaves the shooter's hands, the action starts again. Defenders try to intercept the shot or position themselves for a rebound. If the attempt to shoot a goal is unsuccessful and the ball rebounds into court, then play continues; if the ball goes out of court, then a throw-in is awarded against the team that last made contact with the ball. One goal is scored from each successful shot. A centre pass restarts play after each goal with possession of the centre pass alternating between teams throughout the match. This is in contrast to basketball, in which the team that does not score the goal gets possession.

giving directions in one half of the court, from the centre to the goal line and the whole of the sideline. Both work together to ensure that the game flows smoothly and that players receive clear, concise decisions. At the start of the game the captains notify the umpires of the result of the toss for goal end or first centre pass. The umpires then toss for goal end. The umpire winning the toss will control the half of the court designated the northern half.

Play begins, after the umpire's whistle, with a centre pass from the centre circle. Before the whistle, all players must be in their starting thirds. That means that the only players in the centre third are the two centres. All other players stand behind the

Shaking Up the Rules

For the 2009 World Netball Series, the IFNA modified the rules to speed up the game, challenge the elite players and increase scoring. Although these rules were designed for one tournament on a trial basis, they may foreshadow the future of netball on the world stage. These rule changes added to the challenge for the top six teams in the world—Australia, New Zealand, England, Jamaica, Samoa and Malawi.

Under the modified rules, games consist of four six-minute quarters, with three two-minute breaks. Double points are awarded for shots taken outside the goal circle. Instead of alternating the centre pass following a goal, the centre pass is taken by the team that conceded the previous goal. Teams are allowed unlimited rolling substitutions during game play, and each team may designate one quarter as a power play quarter. During the power play quarter, all goals are doubled. Instead of 1 point, a shot taken from inside the goal circle is worth 2 points during a team's power play quarter. A shot taken from outside the goal circle is worth 4 points during the power play quarter.

It is unknown if these rule changes will catch on, if they will make the game more exciting for players and fans or if they will alter the game too much. What is known is that netball continues to thrill players and fans with its combination of skill, athleticism and teamwork. As the sport evolves and extends its reach around the world, it will continue to win the hearts of its players and fans.

A scorer records both teams' goals, and a timekeeper has responsibility for the duration of play. There are four quarters of even time for an official match. The international timing is four quarters of 15 minutes. When a team plays two matches on the same day, the matches are reduced to two 20-minute halves or an agreed time. Many local time variations are used throughout the netball world. Juniors begin with four 5-minute periods of play. In school competitions 10-minute quarters are popular, and 15- or 20-minute halves are also common.

The rules of netball have been simplified for younger players in recent years. Modified rules are definitely the best way for young players to learn. As skills, tactics and drills are described throughout the book, the applicable rules are discussed.

Like many team sports, netball has some rules that require quick interpretation and judgment by umpires during the game. Of course, this is the area that creates controversy and excitement and allows the fans a chance to air their feelings. The players, on the other hand, should be disciplined and not show any reaction to any questionable calls. Given that the time players can handle a ball is restricted to 3 seconds, their focus should move quickly to the next pass. Besides, a player who brings the game into disrepute can be sent off the court for a period of time at the umpire's discretion.

Netball is played on a variety of surfaces. Sprung wooden flooring is ideal, but often the cost is prohibitive. Grass, asphalt and commercially developed surfaces that add a rubberised component to asphalt such as Flexi-Pave are currently among the most common playing surfaces.

PLAYERS

Although each player must be adept at the skills involved in both attacking and defensive play, the seven positions and their respective playing areas (table 1) determine each player's specific roles and contribution to the team.

Goal shooter (GS): The mainstay of the team's shooting, the goal shooter position requires an accurate shot and the ability to create space for the pass to be taken safely. It's important for the goal shooter to develop a variety of attacking options and, after shooting, get a good position for rebounding.

Goal attack (GA): The secondary shooting role, the goal attack needs a solid shooting technique, an ability to provide attacking opportunities in the shooting third and an ability to assist

Table 1   Netball Positions

Player position	Position requirements	Physical attributes	Areas allowed
Goal shooter (GS)	Accurate shooting Strong body positioning Good timing Varies attacking movement Strong rebound Strong defence of attack third	Balance Good agility Excellent power and elevation Strong holding ability	Attacking goal third
Goal attack (GA)	Accurate shooting Fast, strong attacking play with variation of movement Accurate passing Strong feeding Combines with WA/C/GS Strong rebounding Strong defence over goal and centre thirds	Good change of direction Strong elevation Good vision Speed and agility	Attacking goal third and centre third
Wing attack (WA)	Accurate feeding Explosive off the mark Creative Varies movement Works closely with the attack unit Pressure defence in own area	Balance, particularly around goal circle edge Speed Strong elevation Good vision Power	Centre third and attacking third except goal circle
Centre (C)	Good spatial awareness Reliable passing Accurate feeding Varies movement Links defence and attack thirds Ability to read the game Good timing Tight defence down court	High fitness levels Good vision Excellent power and elevation Speed and agility	Centre third and attacking third and defence third except goal circles
Wing defence (WD)	Smart tactician Contests ball strongly Quick recovery Varies defending strategies Combines with GD/GK/C Strong attack down court	Speed and agility Strong elevation Power Balance around goal circle and attack transverse line	Centre third and defence goal third
Goal defence (GD)	Speed off the mark Quick recovery Ability to channel and deny attacking movement Strong body positioning Controlled rebounds Attacks the ball and keeps contact penalties low Drives ball strongly down court as unit with WD/C/GK Varies defence of shot	Power Strong elevation Speed and agility Quick footwork	Centre third and defence goal third
Goalkeeper (GK)	Reads down-court attacking play early Varies body positioning Good anticipation Powerful rebounding Quick recovery Defence pressure on shot Speed off the mark	Strong Strong elevation Good body control Speed and agility Quick footwork	Defence goal third

in the centre-court attack when needed. The goal attack must be a versatile athlete who can defend strongly in two thirds of the court.

Wing attack (WA): The wing attack needs to have a good feel for positioning of the shooters and accurate passing skills. These are needed to feed the ball precisely for the team shooters. At the centre pass the wing attack is the key player. It's important for the wing attack to develop strong, explosive moves to beat opponents across the line and take the ball.

Centre (C): The racehorse of the team—one who can run all day—the centre must possess good, balanced attacking and defending skills, and a reliable pass. A good awareness of all players on court and the space in which they are working is important. By reading the opponents' down-court play, the centre must be able to recognise where the defensive gaps are and to move into them quickly while always looking for that loose ball to pounce on.

Wing defence (WD): The wing defence is the first line of the players specialising in defence.

The wing defence needs a thorough knowledge of defence strategy to defend the centre third and the top of the goal third and must possess the ability to stick with an opponent. The wing defence should try to out-think the wing attack because to outrun the WA is very difficult. The wing defence also has an important attacking role through midcourt.

Goal defence (GD): The mobile defence player who concentrates defensive pressure in the back third, the goal defence must react quickly to opponents' moves, knowing where the most likely intercepts are. The goal defence must position to direct the attacker away from the play. The goal defence's goal is to restrict the opponent's scoring opportunities.

Goalkeeper (GK): The last line of defence, the goalkeeper tries to counter the opposing shooter, particularly in the goal circle. Goalkeepers must know where the goalpost is at all times and keep opponents as far from it as possible by positioning well. A good goalkeeper defends every shot and jumps strongly for rebounds.

EQUIPMENT AND ATTIRE

The most important piece of equipment in netball is the ball. For senior players, the netball is 690 to 710 millimetres in circumference and weighs 400 to 450 grams. It may be made of leather, rubber or a similar material. Junior players use a smaller, lighter ball.

All players wear positional identification. This is usually a bib worn over the playing strip. At the elite level players tend to wear the letters on a patch that is attached to the uniform. This identification is important for the umpires. It allows them to see that all players are in their appropriate playing areas of the court.

The traditional short, pleated skirt and plain-coloured polo shirt are giving way to body suits, bright shorts and shirts. The new emphasis on colour and comfort is proving very popular

with modern players. Many teams coordinate their warm-up track suits with their playing uniforms.

A number of manufacturers provide shoes that are specifically designed for netball. Players should look for a shoe that cushions the landing; provides solid heel and arch support; and is light, comfortable and durable.

Because netball is basically a non-contact sport, the use of protective equipment for players is limited on court to the padding of goalposts to reduce the risk of injury to players in case of collisions.

For player safety, athletes at the elite level tape their ankles or use ankle guards to reduce the risk of serious injury. Some players use mouth guards as well.

NETBALL RULES

Obtain a copy of the official rule book for a detailed explanation of the game. You can obtain a copy from your local or national organisation or the

International Federation of Netball Associations (IFNA). A summary of the main rules and modifications for beginner players is provided here.

Game

At the local level the game is played over four quarters of 15 minutes each, with a 3-minute interval between the first and second and between the third and fourth quarters, and a 5-minute interval at halftime. At higher levels and international games the interval at halftime is 5 or 10 minutes.

Two umpires control the game. Before the match begins, they toss to determine which half of the court they will control. The scorer records each goal scored and all centre passes. The scorer also calls the centre pass if the umpire asks. The timekeeper takes the time from the umpire's whistle to start play and signals the end of play to the umpire, whose whistle ends play. The timekeeper also ensures that time lost through a stoppage is played in the quarter or half in which the stoppage occurred. During a stoppage other players must remain on court, and no coaching is permitted. To indicate a stoppage, the umpire signals to the timekeepers to hold time (figure 2).

A team consists of up to 12 players, one of whom is designated the captain. Seven players are on court at one time, and there is no limit to substitutions that can be made from the team's bench during the game. A team must take the court if at least five players are present, one of whom must play centre.

The captains toss for the choice of goal end or centre pass and notify the umpires of the result. They also have the right to approach an umpire during an interval or after the game for clarification of any rule.

To start play, the centre who is taking the centre pass has the ball in the centre circle. The opposing centre is free to move in the centre third. All other players are in their respective goal thirds. The umpire's whistle starts play. The centre pass may be caught or touched by any player who is standing or who lands within the centre third. After each goal and each interval, a centre pass restarts play. The centre pass alternates between the teams throughout the game.

Stoppage

When play stops for an injury, the umpire restarts play from the spot where the ball was when play stopped. The team that was in possession of the ball takes the pass from the spot where play stopped as indicated by the umpire.

The first injury stoppage for each team in each quarter or half is up to 2 minutes. For each subsequent stoppage, the injured or ill player has 30 seconds to leave the court. If a player is bleeding, play is stopped until the wound is adequately covered and blood is removed from the ball and clothing if necessary.

No coaching by any bench team official or bench player is permitted during a stoppage. However, the team manager may approach the players at the sideline to provide fluids.

Advantage

The umpire does not whistle an infringement when it would be a disadvantage to the non-offending team. Instead the umpire calls "advantage" by moving her right arm from the right across her body to the left (figure 3).

Figure 2 Hold time.

Figure 3 Advantage.

Contact

Contact that interferes with play, whether it is made by a player or with the ball, is penalised. The umpire signals personal contact on the arm by holding out her left hand and tapping her left forearm with her right hand (figure 4). A penalty pass or shot is given for an infringement of the personal contact rule. If the contact occurs in the goal circle, the penalty is a penalty pass or shot. If the contact occurs anywhere else on the court, a penalty pass is awarded. Any player allowed in the area where the penalty occurred may take the penalty.

Figure 4 Contact on the arm.

Discipline

The umpire has the authority to penalise any action not covered in the rules that is contrary to the spirit of the game. If a player continues to infringe after earlier penalties, or the umpire considers that the normal penalty (including advancing the penalty) is insufficient, the umpire may issue a warning. If a player re-offends after a warning, she may be suspended from a game for a specified period. No substitution may be made for that player or that playing position. The position remains vacant during the suspension unless it is the centre. In the case of very serious misconduct, the umpire may order a player to leave the court without a warning. No substitution may be made for a player who is ordered off the court.

Footwork Rule

The footwork rule states that players cannot reground the landed foot while in possession of the ball. A detailed explanation of this rule is in step 3. The umpire signals stepping by putting both hands out flat and moving them up and down, similar to a stepping motion (figure 5). This rule can be modified to allow shuffling on the spot to gain balance before throwing or shooting.

Figure 5 Stepping.

Free Pass, Penalty Pass or Penalty Shot

A free pass is awarded for all minor rule infringements. A penalty pass or shot is awarded for actions that infringe on the rights of another player. A penalty pass is more severe than a free pass because the offending player is literally removed from play during a penalty pass. The offending player must stand beside the thrower who is taking the penalty pass until the ball leaves the thrower's hands.

Obstruction

Obstruction is any effort to defend a player, whether in possession of the ball or not, from a distance closer than 0.9 metres (3 ft) with arms upraised. A player using outstretched arms to defend a player without the ball and who is closer than the correct distance, or who is using intimidating movements against an opponent, is also obstructing. The correct distance is measured on the ground between the nearer foot of the defender and the landed foot of the attacker. An attacker who lessens the specified distance is not considered to be obstructing; the attacker must accept the disadvantage of moving closer to the defender. Obstruction incurs the same penalty as contact—a penalty pass or shot. The umpire signals obstruction by raising both hands, palms flat, and holding them a small distance apart (figure 6).

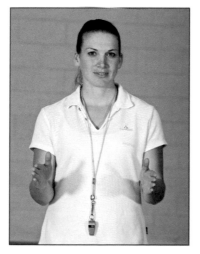

Figure 6 Obstruction.

Offside

Players are offside if they enter any area other than their designated playing area. The umpire signals offside by raising one hand and moving it in an arc (figure 7). Players may reach over and take the ball from an offside area as long as they do not contact the playing area.

The penalty for offside is a free pass to the opposing team. The free pass is taken in the area in which the player went offside. A player who can enter the offside area takes the penalty where the infringement occurred. When two opposing players go offside but neither touches the ball, they are not penalised. If one or both of them are in possession of the ball or touch it, a toss-up is taken between those two players in their own area of play. An exception is when a player who is allowed only in the goal third goes offside into the centre third and an opposing player simultaneously goes offside into the goal third. A toss-up is then taken in the centre third between any two opposing players allowed in that area. The umpire signals a toss-up by raising the right hand, palm flat and turned up (figure 8).

Figure 7 Offside.

Figure 8 Toss-up.

Out of Court

The ball is out of court when it touches the ground, an object or a person in contact with the ground outside the court. It is also considered out of court when held by a player who is in contact with the ground outside the court. The umpire signals the direction of the pass by raising the hand, palm up, to the side of the pass (figure 9).

Over a Third

The ball may not be thrown over a complete third without being touched by a player in that third. Players are considered to have thrown from the third in which they gained possession, even if they step into the next third as they throw. When the ball is thrown over a third without being touched, a free pass is given to the opposing team just beyond the second line that the ball has crossed. The umpire signals over a third by raising an arm with the hand parallel to the ground, palm turned to the right (figure 10). She moves the hand across, parallel to the ground, turning the palm to the left.

Ball Movement

Players are considered in possession of the ball when they have control of it with one or two hands. If they do not catch it cleanly, they may bat or bounce it once to gain possession or to direct it to another player. Once they have possession, players have 3 seconds in which to pass or shoot for goal. If they do not pass or shoot within 3 seconds, the umpire will signal a held ball (figure 11). The held ball rule can be modified so that the ball may be held for up to 6 seconds. Players may not punch the ball, roll it to another player, kick the ball or fall on it. They may not play the ball in any way while on the ground.

Once players have passed the ball, they may not play it again until it is touched by another player or rebounds off any part of the goalpost. A free pass is awarded to the opposing team for any infringement of this rule.

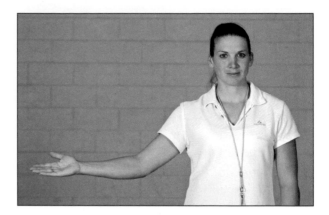

Figure 9   Direction of pass.

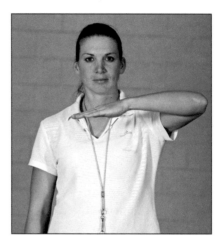

Figure 10   Over a third.

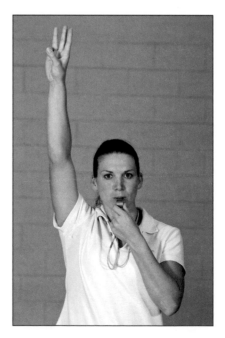

Figure 11   Held ball.

Goals

One of the team's shooters must release a shot within 3 seconds of taking possession of the ball within the goal circle. This rule can be modified to allow 6 seconds for the shot to be released. A goal is scored when the goal shooter or goal attack throws or bats the ball over and completely through the goal ring. Each goal counts for 1 point. If a shot for goal is deflected by a defender but then passes through the goal ring, a goal is scored.

If the shot for goal is unsuccessful and the ball rebounds into court, play continues. If the ball goes out of court, then a throw-in is taken where the ball crossed the line. On the court during the throw-in, there must be room for a third player to move between the hands of the thrower and receiver the moment the ball is passed.

Substitutions and Team Changes

Substitution occurs when a player leaves the court and is replaced by another player. Team changes occur when players on the court change playing positions. Teams have the right to make substitutions or team changes either at an interval or when play is stopped for injury or illness. If substituting during an injury stoppage, the injured or ill player for whom play was stopped must be involved in that team's substitution or team change. There is no limit to the number of substitutions a team can make provided the players used do not exceed the 12 named for the match.

Toss-Up

The toss-up is used when opposing players infringe simultaneously or gain possession simultaneously, or when the umpire is uncertain about who last touched the ball before it went out of court. The toss-up is taken as near as possible to the spot where the incident occurred. Players taking the toss-up face each other and their own goal ends, with their arms straight and hands by their sides. The nearer foot must be no closer than 0.9 metres (3 ft) from the opponent.

The umpire releases the ball midway between both players from just below the shoulder level of the shorter player's normal standing position. The whistle is blown as the ball is released. The ball may be caught or batted, but not directly at an opponent.

Throw-In

When the ball goes out of court, it is thrown in by an opponent of the team that was last to touch it. To throw the ball in, a player stands outside the court, immediately behind the line close to the point where the ball crossed. The player must pass the ball within 3 seconds of standing ready to pass, and the ball must leave the hands before the player re-enters the court. The penalty for breaking any of these rules is a throw-in to the opposing team at the spot where the infringement occurred.

RESOURCES

Information about many regional, national and international organisations can be found on the Internet. The International Federation of Netball Associations (IFNA) is a good source for contact information on international organisations. The organisations listed here are just a few that over see netball around the world. To find information on more countries, go to www.netball.org and go to the list of members.

Netball Australia: www.netball.asn.au

United States of America Netball Association: www.usanetball.com

Netball New Zealand: www.netballnz.co.nz

Jamaica Netball Association: www.jamaicanetball.org.jm

England Netball: www.englandnetball.co.uk

Netball Singapore: www.netball.org.sg

Key to Diagrams

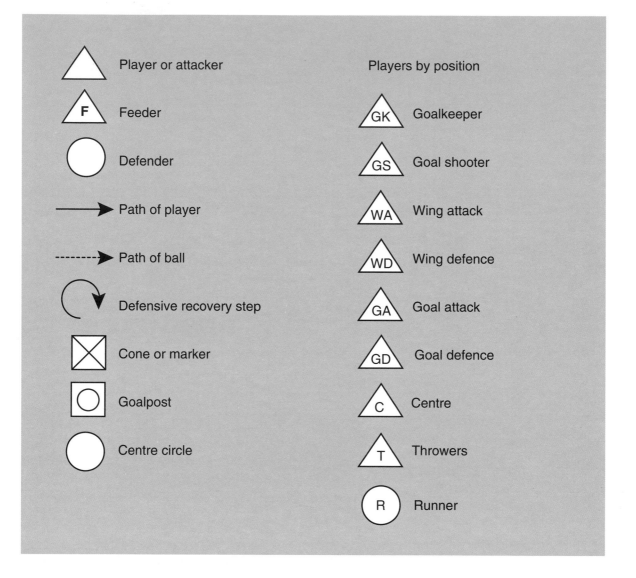

Player or attacker

F   Feeder

Defender

Path of player

Path of ball

Defensive recovery step

Cone or marker

Goalpost

Centre circle

Players by position

GK   Goalkeeper

GS   Goal shooter

WA   Wing attack

WD   Wing defence

GA   Goal attack

GD   Goal defence

C   Centre

T   Throwers

R   Runner

Catching

Catching is the first step in handling a netball, so it is appropriate that this is the first step to practise in becoming a netballer. It is important that you catch the ball consistently. Good netballers let their fingers do the work. Your fingers should drive out to meet the ball, make contact and pull it in quickly because you must move the ball on within 3 seconds.

In this chapter you'll learn the two basic catches in netball: the two-handed catch and the one-handed catch. The two-handed catch is the safest and allows for greater control, whereas the one-handed catch is less safe but gives you greater extension to the ball. We then look at the more advanced skills of using a controlled tap and taking low balls. In match play the correct choice of catch is crucial.

As part of the catching skills we also introduce the toss-up. Today's umpires use the toss-up sparingly because they are coached to make hard decisions and be decisive. We take a quick look at good technique for winning the toss-up

so you are well prepared should the umpire be unable to decide just what has happened and call for a toss-up. Fast, sure hands win toss-ups and possession of the ball.

Players sometimes think that basic skills such as catching and winning a toss-up are really not important, that clever tactics win matches. Nothing could be further from the truth. It is absolutely essential to have the best basic skills you possibly can. Elite players use practice drills to ensure that their hands are safe and sure at every practice session.

The rules of the game penalise a replayed ball. If you have control of the ball and drop or fumble it, you cannot pick it up again until another player has handled it. The penalty for a replayed ball is a free pass for the opposition.

In a very close game, taking a really difficult catch, using a controlled tap or winning that vital toss-up can give your team a winning edge. Make sure you work at these basic skills so your hands are safe and sure.

BASIC CATCHES

Begin with two hands. As your confidence and ability increase, practise the catch with one hand. You will probably find that you'll master the one-handed catch more easily with your

dominant hand—that's natural—but make sure to work hard on catching with your non-dominant hand too.

Whether you're catching with one hand or two, your body must be well balanced. Beginners should watch the ball all the way into their fingertips. To execute the two-handed catch, drive out both arms to take the catch as the ball approaches (figure 1.1*a*). With your thumbs behind the ball and fingers outstretched, take the catch with the fingers (figure 1.1*b*). Pull the ball quickly into your body (figure 1.1*c*).

Figure 1.1   Two-Handed Catch

PREPARATION

1. Keep body well balanced
2. Watch ball
3. Drive out arms to meet ball
4. Bend elbows slightly

a

EXECUTION

1. Fingers spread wide
2. Thumbs behind ball
3. Fingers firmly grip ball

b

FOLLOW-THROUGH

1. Pull ball quickly in towards body
2. Prepare to pass or shoot

c

Misstep
You lose sight of the ball.

Correction
Watch the ball until you take the catch.

Misstep
You don't protect the ball.

Correction
Pull the ball into your body once you have control of it.

When catching with one hand, the fingers and thumb are extended fully as they drive out to take the pass (figure 1.2a). The ball is taken in the middle of the hand, with the fingers gripping it tightly (figure 1.2b). The wrist bends behind the ball to absorb the impact. Quickly pull the ball into the body using your other hand to steady it as you prepare to throw (figure 1.2c).

Figure 1.2   **One-Handed Catch**

PREPARATION

1. Keep body well balanced
2. Watch ball
3. Extend arm to ball

a

EXECUTION

1. Position hand behind ball
2. Outstretch fingers
3. Take ball in middle of hand
4. Firmly grip ball with fingers
5. Curve wrist and hand around ball

FOLLOW-THROUGH

1. Pull ball into body
2. Use other hand to steady ball
3. Prepare to pass or shoot

b

c

Misstep
You don't control the one-handed catch.

Correction
Firmly grip the ball with the fingers. Curve the wrist and hand around the ball. Pull the ball in quickly and steadily with the other hand.

Problems with the catch will be evident immediately; you will drop or fumble the catch. Most errors are caused when players do not grip the ball correctly. Make sure your hands are well positioned on the ball with your thumbs behind it (figure 1.3). Develop a vice-like grip; once the ball is in your hands, it stays there. This will help eliminate most of the problems with your catch.

Figure 1.3 Thumbs behind ball and fingers outstretched.

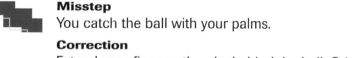

Misstep
You catch the ball with your palms.

Correction
Extend your fingers, thumbs behind the ball. Grip the ball firmly with your fingers.

As you become more experienced, you will be able to feel the catch come in while you scan the court for the best passing option. We call this an automatic catch. When you can take the catch without having to watch the ball all the way into your fingertips, your catch is automatic. If you can consistently take an automatic catch without fumbling or dropping the ball, you are ready to tackle the advanced skills.

ADVANCED BALL CONTROL

The rules allow you to tap or bat the ball once in a controlled manner before you take the catch or move the ball on to a team member. When you are contesting high balls and you are unable to take the catch, you should use this rule to your advantage.

In tight aerial contests you will sometimes find that you are very close to your opponent and in danger of causing contact. The controlled tap allows you to move the ball quickly away from your opponent so that you can pull the ball in without causing contact or overbalancing.

Your arm is at full stretch with your hand under or to the side of the ball, fingers slightly spread (figure 1.4a). Focus on the ball and know where your opponents are. This will enable you to see where the space is to direct your tap or bat.

Your fingers strike the ball quickly, once, to move it away from your opponent (figure 1.4b). You are now able to control the catch (figure 1.4c) and pull the ball into your body. Remember that you can use only one controlled tap or bat, so the movement must be crisp and clean. The umpire should be in no doubt that you are controlling the ball.

Figure 1.4   Controlled Tap or Bat

PREPARATION

1. Keep arm at full stretch
2. See where opponents are
3. Decide where to direct tap

a

b

c

EXECUTION

1. Fingers slightly spread
2. Wrist and hand turned to direct tap or bat
3. Fingers tap ball

FOLLOW-THROUGH

1. Secure ball
2. Pull ball into body

Misstep
You make an inaccurate tap.

Correction
Open your fingers slightly. Your fingers and wrist control the direction of the tap. Direct the ball into a safe space.

Balls that come in low or have to be picked up from the ground often present difficulties. Perhaps this occurs because the player is caught off guard when a low ball is passed. Most throws target the receiver's upper body or the aerial space above her. When a ball suddenly skims in below the knees, the receiver needs to be prepared to handle it competently.

Low balls occur for a number of reasons. Some come from a well-placed bounce or underarm throw, and others may simply be loose balls that others have failed to control.

You will need to focus on the ball; get your weight down and use your body to protect it (figure 1.5a). Reach out with both hands (figure 1.5b), and pull the ball quickly into your body (figure 1.5c).

Figure 1.5   Low Balls

PREPARATION
1. Protect ball with body
2. Bend knees
3. Lower body
4. Watch ball

a

b

c

EXECUTION
1. Outstretch arms
2. Spread fingers
3. Grip ball firmly

FOLLOW-THROUGH
1. Quickly pull ball into body

Misstep
You fail to control a low ball.

Correction
Maintain your balance by widening your base. Protect the ball with your body. Bend your knees and lower your body. Pull the ball quickly into your body.

Practise on the run and stationary, from the hold. Position your hands on the side or under the ball. Try both and see which one works for you. When running to pick up a loose ball, you might find it better to scoop the ball in with one hand before you quickly use both hands to pull it into your body.

TOSS-UP

Stand facing your goal end and your opponent, 0.9 metres (3 ft) apart. Keep your arms straight, with your hands to your sides (figure 1.6). Balance your weight evenly with legs slightly bent and your weight down.

Figure 1.6 Players ready to take the toss-up.

Misstep
You raise your hands before the ball is released.

Correction
Focus on the ball and listen for the whistle.

Watch the ball in the umpire's hand. As the umpire steps forward between you to release the ball, get ready to react. You should feel like a tight spring ready to be released. Make sure you do not move before the whistle is blown. If you do, you will be penalised and the opposing team will be awarded a free pass.

As the umpire blows the whistle, quickly bring your arms forward, taking possession as close to the point of release as possible. Remember to control your feet; don't overbalance.

Misstep

You overbalance as you move your arms.

Correction

Be controlled. Widen your base.

An alternative action that players use quite successfully to win toss-ups is called the top-and-tail grip (figure 1.7). As soon as the umpire releases the ball, shoot both hands forward. Position your throwing hand on top, reach over the ball, and have your other hand ready to grip the ball underneath. Once you have won possession, pull the ball quickly into your body. The fastest hands to the ball will win the toss-up. If you are not having a lot of success when you swing your arms upwards, try this alternate method.

Figure 1.7 The top-and-tail grip.

CATCHING DRILLS

Safe, sure hands are best developed with individual practice. Devote 5 minutes of the day to work specifically on the catch. Set yourself tasks that get progressively more difficult. Watch the ball throughout the practice. As your confidence and your ability increase, begin to practise the catch without looking at the ball all the time. See if you can feel it happen.

Catching Drill 1. *Just Hands*

Hold your hands loosely in front of your face. Quickly open your fingers and thumbs to the catch position until you cannot stretch them any farther, and then close your hands. Open and close both hands quickly 10 times, then each hand separately 10 times.

To Increase Difficulty

- Change the starting position of your hands. Try above the head, on the right side, low near the ground, and on the left side.
- Use both arms and fingers. Hold your arms loosely beside your waist and extend both arms and fingers to the catching position. When using your arms, your target goal is 5 times.

Success Check

- Thumbs almost touch behind the imaginary catch.
- Fingers are fully extended.
- Eyes watch the fingers.

Score Your Success

Open and close hands 10 times = 5 points

Complete 5 attempts with both arms and hands (more difficult variation) = 1 bonus point

Your score ___

Catching Drill 2. *Staying on the Wall*

This drill is designed to speed the hands rather than control the catch. Stand about a step away from a practice wall, facing it. With the ball in your right hand, bat it quickly against the wall, at shoulder height, allowing your fingertips to do the work. If you bat quickly, the ball rebounds back to your hand; that is, the ball maintains the same position on the wall. We say that the ball is staying on the wall when this happens. If you tap the ball too slowly, the ball does not return to your hand; it falls down. Complete 10 quick taps with each hand.

To Increase Difficulty

- Move the ball up and down the wall.
- Move the ball across the wall.
- Maintain ball movement while changing hands.
- Reverse your starting position, putting your back to the wall. Turn your hand so it faces the wall, and turn your head so you can see the ball.

To Decrease Difficulty

- Throw the ball against the wall and catch it one-handed until you establish the speed necessary for tapping.

Success Check

- Fingers strike the ball.
- Wrist and hand move quickly.
- Ball maintains the same position on the wall.
- Eyes watch the ball.

Score Your Success

10 successful taps with right hand = 5 points

10 successful taps with left hand = 5 points

Your score ___

Catching Drill 3. *On the Clock*

Mark a clock face on the wall. Stand approximately one step away from the wall, facing it. A partner stands behind you and randomly calls a time on the clock. You respond by reaching quickly with the nearest hand to touch the hour with an outstretched finger. There is no ball in this drill. Return quickly to your starting position and wait for the next call. Go for 10 seconds, completing as many touches as you can.

To Increase Difficulty

- Use the right hand only. You will have to rotate your body to reach across the clock face.
- Use the left hand only. You will have to rotate your body to reach across the clock face.
- Close your eyes and repeat the drill.
- Your partner calls the hour and minute (e.g., ten past six). You use both arms, one to indicate the hour and the other to indicate the minute. Your hands should touch the clock simultaneously.

Success Check

- Fingers strike the appropriate hour.
- Arms move quickly.
- Fingers are outstretched.
- Body maintains good balance.

Score Your Success

10 or more accurate reactions in 10 seconds = 10 points

7 to 9 accurate reactions in 10 seconds = 5 points

4 to 6 accurate reactions in 10 seconds = 3 points

3 or fewer accurate reactions in 10 seconds = 1 point

Your score ___

Catching Drill 4. *Stationary Catching*

This drill provides stationary catching practice using a wall and a partner. Focus on the fundamentals of controlling the ball and developing safe hands.

- Toss the ball into the air about 1 metre above your head. Extend both hands to the ball so you take the catch quickly and cleanly. Pull the ball in while at the same time bending your knees slightly. Perform 10 repetitions.
- Stand 1 metre from a practice wall. Throw the ball onto the wall and take the catch quickly and cleanly with both hands. Perform 10 repetitions.
- Have a partner stand a few metres in front of you. Your partner begins by throwing the ball to you at chest height. Take the catch quickly and cleanly. As you become more skilful, have your partner speed up the pass. Your partner should vary the positioning and angle of passes to include high and low balls. Perform 10 repetitions.

To Increase Difficulty

- Catch with one hand instead of two.
- Alternate one-handed catches between your right and left hands.

Success Check

- Eyes on the ball.
- Arms fully extended to take the ball.
- Ball pulled in quickly after the catch.

Score Your Success

10 consecutive catches from tossed ball = 5 points

10 consecutive catches from wall ball = 5 points

10 consecutive catches from partner throw = 5 points

Your score ___

Catching Drill 5. *Steal, Don't Touch*

Stand beside your partner, facing the practice wall. Stand three or four steps away from the wall and about half a metre from your partner. Ask your partner to throw the ball hard onto the wall so it rebounds straight back to him. As the ball returns, quickly reach across to catch it, using both hands, before your partner catches it. Your partner should try to beat you to the catch. Neither of you should move your feet—let your hands do the work. To maintain your balance, bend your knees to lower your centre of gravity.

To Increase Difficulty

- Use one hand to take the catch.
- Vary the speed of the ball.
- Take the catch on the move. Start the drill two steps away from your partner.

Success Check

- Eyes on the ball.
- Arms and fingers extended.
- Anticipate.
- Grip ball firmly.
- No partner contact.

Score Your Success

Complete 5 consecutive catches without contacting your partner = 10 points

Your score ___

Catching Drill 6. *Double Catches*

This is a partner drill intended to speed up the catch. It will challenge your vision and control of the ball. Stand about 2 metres away from and facing your partner. You both have a ball. Put your feet about shoulder-width apart, and slightly bend your knees to lower your centre of gravity.

On the command "Go", simultaneously pass the balls to each other using two hands. You throw a straight pass; your partner throws a high pass. Both of you should take the catch quickly and immediately release the same pass. The balls should move quickly between you, with your wrists and fingers extending to catch and then flicking to release. Complete 10 consecutive passes.

For the second phase of the drill, both of you have your arms outstretched to the side with a ball balanced on the right hand. On "Go", both of you release a one-handed straight pass to your partner's outstretched left hand. Quickly catch the ball with your left hand and then throw it back to your partner's right hand. You should throw and catch the balls simultaneously, with speed. Complete 10 consecutive passes.

To Increase Difficulty

- Vary the pass: You use a high pass; your partner, a bounce pass.
- Clap hands between catches.

- Reverse your starting positions so you have your backs to each other. Turn around quickly on "Go".
- Walk and then run while still controlling the ball. Can you reach top speed and still control the catch?

To Decrease Difficulty

- Begin by passing one ball between your right hand and your partner's left hand. When you can complete 10 consecutive passes, introduce the second ball.

Success Check

- Fingers spread wide.
- Ball balanced on the fingertips.
- Fingers and wrist used to flick the ball.
- Good vision.

Score Your Success

Complete 10 consecutive two-handed catches = 5 points

Complete 10 consecutive one-handed catches = 5 points

Your score ___

Catching Drill 7. *One-Handed Catching and Tapping*

In this partner drill, you will practise extending to take the high ball. Your partner stands 1 metre from the wall, facing it with a ball. Stand immediately behind your partner. Your partner will use an underarm throw high onto the wall. Elevate and reach over your partner, trying to pull the ball in with one hand and land with a wide base. Your partner doesn't move but uses a wide base to hold a strong position in front. In taking the catch, you must not contact your partner. After you complete five consecutive one-handed catches, rotate positions with your partner.

To Increase Difficulty

- Vary the direction of the ball, to the left or to the right.
- Both players contest the catch. After the ball is thrown, both of you elevate and contest the ball.
- The player at the back starts in the reverse position so she needs to turn in the air to take the pass.

- Begin the drill again. Take a step away from your partner so you are too far to gain full control without overbalancing. Reach out to fully extend the catching hand. Use a controlled tap to take the ball safely over your partner's head before you pull it in with both hands.

- Finally, try tapping on. Your partner throws the ball high onto the wall and you elevate to tap the ball at full stretch. Direct the tap to your partner who moves to take the catch.

Success Check

- Full arm extension.
- Good body control.
- Wide base on the land.
- Ball pulled in quickly to body.
- Body protects the ball.

Score Your Success

Complete 5 consecutive one-handed catches without contacting your partner = 10 points

Your score ___

Catching Drill 8. *Take the Toss*

Here are two drills to help increase your toss-up speed. They can be easily slotted into training sessions, particularly after very demanding drills. Using an opponent gives you game-situation practice and increases interest in the drill.

First, stand ready to take an imaginary toss-up. Say "Go" to yourself and see how quickly you can bring your hands up to take the ball. This helps develop a fast reaction when the umpire introduces the ball. Complete 10 repetitions.

Now stand facing your partner, 0.9 metres (3 ft) apart, arms and hands by your sides, your body still and tensed. In this position you are ready to react to the umpire's whistle, which signals the release of the ball. Quickly pull your arms and hands up to snatch the ball before your opponent has time to gain possession. Compete with your partner to see who can win three consecutive toss-ups first.

To Increase Difficulty

- Play the best of five toss-ups.
- Win one toss-up; then move to play a winner from another pair.

Success Check

- Weight on balls of feet.
- Knees bent.
- Hands tensed at hips.
- Quick reaction.

Score Your Success

Complete 10 toss-up actions as quickly as you can – 5 points

First to win 3 consecutive toss-ups = 10 points

Your score ___

SUCCESS SUMMARY OF CATCHING

We cannot over-emphasise the importance of safe and sure hands. Catching is critical to a netballer's success and enjoyment. Every ball counts out on the court. Use your training sessions to develop confidence in your catch.

Make sure you really attack the catch. Drive your arms forward to meet the ball. Stretch those fingers so they are ready to grip the ball tightly. Keep your thumbs behind the ball; they act as your safety net. Once you have the ball, pull it in quickly. A strong snatching action really makes a statement about just who has the ball.

Make sure you can handle the catch whether the ball is coming from a well-delivered pass or rolling loosely on the ground. As your confidence grows, challenge yourself to use the tap or change your grip on the toss-up.

Before moving on to step 2, Passing, evaluate how you did on the catching drills in this step. Tally your scores to determine how well you have mastered the skill of catching. If you scored at least 75 points, you are ready to move on to step 2. If you scored 60 to 74 points, redo the drills you had trouble with and then go to step 2. If you scored fewer than 60 points, review the chapter and redo the drills to raise your scores before moving to step 2.

Catching Drills

1. Just Hands	___ out of 6
2. Staying on the Wall	___ out of 10
3. On the Clock	___ out of 10
4. Stationary Catching	___ out of 15
5. Steal, Don't Touch	___ out of 10
6. Double Catches	___ out of 10
7. One-Handed Catching and Tapping	___ out of 10
8. Take the Toss	___ out of 15
Total	___ **out of 86**

Once you have mastered the catch, you are ready to move on to the important step of passing. In step 2 you will learn to move the ball accurately on court to overcome the defence and create scoring opportunities for your team.

Passing

Netball is very much a passing game. To move the ball up and down the court, team members throw it to each other using either one or two hands. This emphasis on passing is one of the factors that distinguish netball from its game of origin, basketball, so it is not surprising that throwing skills have become highly specialised.

Although the leading nations all began with quite distinctive passing styles, today's international players are more similar than different. You will see one- and two-handed releases, high and low balls, speed on the ball when the gap opens and those lovely long passes that seem to float through the air forever. The variety is amazing, and pinpoint accuracy is a trademark.

The purpose of this step is to introduce the basic passing techniques of the game. Of course it does not cover all possibilities, but it does provide you with the ability to play the game effectively. To be most successful, you should develop a repertoire of passes so you always have the element of surprise. This chapter will help get you started.

The aspiring netballer needs to develop three important parts of the skill of passing: the technique of the various throws, the ability to place a pass accurately and the ability to select the most appropriate throw in play. This step allows you to develop the techniques you need to be successful and provides some simple ways to develop accuracy. Selecting the appropriate pass is covered in later steps in which we combine skills.

To play netball, you need to pass the ball. To play successfully, you have to pass the ball accurately. Each time you have possession of the ball on the netball court, you will have to throw it, except if you are a shooter; then you will have to shoot as well.

No matter where you play, whether you are in the midcourt as centre or on the goal line as goal defence, you have to pass the ball. In a netball game, your team will have passed the ball many times down court to your shooters. Netball teams that have good passing skills give their shooters many opportunities to score. The reverse is also true: Poor passing skills restrict your team's opportunities and provide turnovers for your opponents to capitalise on.

When the ball is passed with pinpoint accuracy, it is very difficult for opponents to defend. In netball it is often said that teams that can thread the ball through the eye of a needle are unbeatable. This saying most appropriately sums up the importance of accurate passing in this game.

TYPES OF PASSES

Netball throws fall into two categories: two-handed and one-handed passes. Within these categories are high-ball and low-ball passes that can be delivered with speed or floated into the space that a team member has created. Make sure you are proficient with either hand as well as with both hands. The strong defensive pressure on every pass that can be seen at the top levels of the game has resulted in two-handed passes, particularly the overhead pass, being used more frequently by all teams.

Most of the passes that you are introduced to here can be executed with one or two hands.

These include the bounce, flick, overhead, side or bullet pass, shoulder and underarm. The lob is the one-handed pass that we cover; and the chest pass, the two-handed.

The passes and their advantages are listed in table 2.1. Mastering these basic techniques will enable you to develop a versatile range of throws that will keep your opponents guessing.

If you are a very young player, you might find it easier to use a smaller ball and try two-handed passes first. You will find that using both hands gives you more control and power initially.

ONE- OR TWO-HANDED PASSES

Passes that can be executed with either one or two hands are the easiest throws to begin with. Your hands sit either behind the ball or on the side of the ball. Your wrists and fingers guide the ball, and your elbows, arms and body weight generate speed and distance on the pass.

For the beginner the two-handed version enables a good long throw, even though the player may not have yet developed much upper-body power.

The more experienced netballer should be able to work the one- or two-handed version of the pass. Really good players can pass with either hand and from both sides of the body. Having a broad range of passes that you can use will be an asset in match play.

Remember: The two-handed pass has a built-in safety device. It can be retrieved quite easily at any point before the final release. The one-handed pass, on the other hand, is often difficult to retrieve once the throwing action has begun.

Table 2.1   Types of Passes

Type of pass	Method of release	Advantages
Bounce	One or two hands	Great for confined spaces Useful feed into the goal circle
Chest	Two hands	Accurate pass Long or short pass Easily controlled
Flick	One or two hands	Fast pass Catches opposition unaware
Lob	One hand	High, floating pass Requires pinpoint accuracy
Overhead	One or two hands	Fast pass Used to avoid the arms of defenders who are reaching over the ball
Shoulder	One or two hands	Fast, powerful pass
Side or bullet	One or two hands	Quick, direct pass
Underarm	One or two hands	Short, accurate pass Brings an element of surprise

One- or Two-Handed Bounce Pass

Hold the ball firmly in the fingertips of both hands (figure 2.1*a*). Flick your wrists and fingers to release the ball; you can use either one hand or two hands, as shown in figure 2.1*b*. (The one-handed release is shown in figure 2.2.) For the short bounce, aim to have the ball bounce close to the receiver's feet. For a long bounce pass, generate more speed and power to create a higher bounce. Follow through with the arms, fingers and wrists while relaxing your shoulders and deeply bending your knees to maintain body balance (figure 2.1*c*).

Figure 2.1   Two-Handed Bounce Pass

PREPARATION

1. Elbows in
2. Thumbs behind ball
3. Knees slightly bent
4. Eyes on target

a

b

c

EXECUTION

1. Body balanced
2. Initiate with wrists
3. Direct with fingers

FOLLOW-THROUGH

1. Follow ball with arms and wrists
2. Relax shoulders
3. Keep knees bent

Misstep
Your opponent intercepts your pass.

Correction
Are you seeing where the defender is positioned?

Figure 2.2 One-handed release for a bounce pass.

In a match play situation the placement of the pass will be determined by the defender's positioning. Make sure that when you practise you are able to deliver to a variation of positions—front, right and left sides, and both stationary and moving.

The bounce pass allows an element of surprise because you can disguise the two-handed release so well. It is frequently used in and around the goal circle as attackers endeavour to outwit defenders. However, it is also used to good effect anywhere on the court.

Remember, the ball can bounce only once before it gets to the receiver.

One- or Two-Handed Flick Pass

The flick pass is no doubt the quickest way to propel the ball forward. The ball is quickly controlled and then moved on from the catch-ing position. A flick of the wrists sends the ball quickly to the receiver. Its great strength is the element of surprise because it does not allow the defender time to recover.

Hold your arms in the catching position. Quickly roll your wrists towards the receiver and use your fingers to flick the ball to the receiver (figure 2.3). Make sure that your wrists and fingers not only generate power to propel the ball onwards but also direct the flight. For a short flick, a light touch is required. A longer flick requires more power.

a

b

Figure 2.3 Hand action of the flick pass: *(a)* one-handed; *(b)* two-handed.

Misstep

Your pass lacks direction.

Correction

Check your release. Are you using your fingers? Are you well balanced?

One- or Two-Handed Overhead Pass

The use of the two-handed overhead pass has increased as down-court defensive pressure has increased. Today it is used extensively to counteract the pressure from arms outstretched over the ball. When you raise the ball above your head, you give yourself more room, which makes it easier to release safely.

Hold the ball firmly in both hands, which are raised above your head (figure 2.4a). Hands are to the side of the ball with the thumbs behind. Use your wrists and fingers to propel the ball either in a straight line or upwards to your target (figure 2.4b). Follow through with your fingers and wrists (figure 2.4c).

Once you are confident with the two-handed overhead pass, try releasing with one hand. This pass adds variety to your skills because it can become a gentle, well-placed short ball or a powerful long ball.

Figure 2.4	Two-Handed Overhead Pass

PREPARATION

1. Raise ball above head
2. Hold ball tightly with both hands
3. Grip ball firmly with fingertips
4. Thumbs behind ball
5. Slightly recoil hands to generate power

a

(continued)

Figure 2.4 *(continued)*

b

c

EXECUTION

1. Focus on target
2. Drop ball back behind the head
3. Keep body well balanced
4. Judge distance and speed of ball
5. Use wrists and fingers to propel ball

FOLLOW-THROUGH

1. Follow ball with fingers and wrists
2. Transfer body weight forward

Misstep
Your overhead pass fails to clear the defender's arms.

Correction
Raise the ball higher above your head to begin your throw. Watch your point of release. As you prepare to pass you may need to pull the ball further back behind your head so that you can release the ball earlier. Make sure you are not taking the ball forward into your defender's outstretched hands.

One- or Two-Handed Shoulder Pass

Use the shoulder pass whenever you need a quick, direct pass. Begin with the ball on the fingertips of your throwing hand. Position your elbow at right angles to your shoulder. Hold the ball close to your body at shoulder height. Your throwing hand is behind the ball, and your elbow extends away from your body. For a one-handed shoulder pass (figure 2.5), protect the ball with your non-throwing hand. Your opposite foot to the throwing hand should be forward, and your shoulder should be open.

Figure 2.5 One-Handed Shoulder Pass

a

PREPARATION

1. Hands behind ball
2. Ball on fingertips
3. Ball protected by non-throwing hand
4. Weight down; knees slightly bent
5. Opposite foot forward

b

OPEN SHOULDER

1. Shoulder open
2. Provide speed with arm and body
3. Release non-throwing hand

c

PROPEL BALL

1. Transfer body weight forward as you extend arm to propel the ball
2. Use wrist and fingers to direct the pass

d

FOLLOW-THROUGH

1. Throwing hand follows ball
2. Back foot comes through
3. Weight transfers forward

Misstep
Your pass falls short.

Correction
Open your shoulder or put your body weight behind the pass.

One- or Two-Handed Underarm Pass

The underarm pass can originate from any starting position below the waist and can be executed with either one or two hands. It is most effective when it has an element of surprise and is most commonly used in and around the goal circle.

Balance the ball on the outstretched fingertips of your throwing hand. Pull the ball quickly into your body. Release the ball with one hand (figure 2.6a) or two hands (figure 2.6b) in a forward movement as your hands pass your thigh. Follow through with your fingers and wrist for accurate placement of the ball.

Side and Bullet Pass

Use one or two hands to pass from the side of the body. The one-handed bullet pass is a powerful pass that shoots the ball through space. The side pass is a two-handed throw that moves the ball quickly.

When using two hands, hold the ball to your side, close to your body, at about waist or shoulder height (figure 2.7). Hold the ball firmly with your fingertips and place your thumbs behind the ball. One hand sits to the bottom of the ball, and the other, on the side of the ball. Flick the ball with both wrists and fingers towards your target. Use your body weight to increase power and take your weight onto your front foot.

For the one-handed bullet pass, begin with the ball on your throwing hand at waist level (figure 2.8). Place your feet about shoulder-width apart, with the foot of your non-throwing side forward. Slightly bend your knees and balance your body well. To start the release, quickly open your forearm and wrist. Whip your hand forward to propel the ball in a straight line to the target. Follow through with your throwing hand as you transfer your body weight forward.

The bullet pass is very effective when you need to move the ball quickly into a small space. For example, when you are throwing in from the sideline, at the centre pass or passing into the goal circle.

Figure 2.6 Underarm pass: *(a)* one-handed; *(b)* two-handed.

Figure 2.7 Starting position for the two-handed side pass.

Figure 2.8 Bullet pass.

 Misstep
Your teammate drops your pass.

Correction
Ease off the power. You might be propelling the ball too hard.

LOB PASS

The one-handed lob pass requires a skilful touch to deliver it accurately high over an opponent's head. The lob is a high pass that requires subtle finger control to direct the ball accurately to the target. Begin with the ball on the fingers of your throwing hand at shoulder height with your elbow bent and your throwing hand under the ball (figure 2.9*a*). Your throwing hand should climb in a straight line to full extension (figure 2.9*b*); you release the ball at full extension for maximum flight (figure 2.9*c*). Throw the ball in an arc to go over defenders and then follow through with your wrist and fingers.

Figure 2.9   Lob

PREPARATION

1. Hand under ball
2. Ball on fingertips
3. Elbow bent
4. Weight down; knees slightly bent
5. Opposite foot forward

a

EXECUTION

1. Climb throwing hand straight upwards
2. Release at full extension
3. Propel with fingers and wrist
4. Ball has high arc

b

FOLLOW-THROUGH

1. Point wrist and fingers to ground
2. Relax shoulder, arm and elbow
3. Transfer weight to front foot
4. Move back foot through

c

Players who are leading forward may suddenly drop back, calling for the lob to clear a congested area. Shooters who hold space in the goal circle also call for the lob to be delivered accurately to them. It is very hard for a defender to contest a well-placed lob without causing contact.

CHEST PASS

The chest pass is regarded as the basic throw for beginners. Although it is a useful basic pass to know, its use on court has diminished for experienced players because they seek more powerful and commanding ball skills. The advantages of the chest pass are that it can be executed quickly and it can propel a ball powerfully over distance.

To execute the two-handed chest pass, hold the ball firmly with the fingertips of both hands. Place your thumbs behind the ball, wrists cocked. Hold the ball close to your chest, elbows to your sides (figure 2.10a). Your body weight should be evenly distributed between both feet, which are usually shoulder-width apart.

Flick the ball from your hands, using your wrists to initiate the pass and your fingers to direct the ball (figure 2.10b). The ball can travel either in a straight line or an arc. Use your forearms and body weight to provide more power and distance. Follow through with your fingers, wrists and forearms (figure 2.10c).

Figure 2.10   Chest Pass

PREPARATION

1. Elbows in
2. Thumbs behind ball
3. Feet astride
4. Knees slightly bent
5. Eyes on target

a

b

c

EXECUTION

1. Keep body balanced
2. Initiate with wrists
3. Direct with fingers

FOLLOW-THROUGH

1. Keep body balanced
2. Follow ball with arms, wrists and fingers
3. Transfer body weight forward

Misstep
Your two-handed pass drifts.

Correction
Grip the ball tightly with both hands. Make sure you transfer your body weight forward on release. Follow through strongly.

BAULK AND FAKE

Although technically not passes, the baulk and fake are very useful skills to develop. Because they are used as preliminary movements for passes, it is appropriate to introduce them here.

The baulk is used as a surprise, to trick defending players into reacting to what they think is a throw. The baulk is very useful to create space for passing when defenders are pressuring the pass with their outstretched hands almost over your ball.

The baulk is done with two hands. Both hands are needed to ensure that the ball does not leave your hands. To perform a baulk, hold the ball firmly with both hands and initiate a throwing action with both your forearm and wrist, as if you were going to pass the ball. Hold the ball tightly so that you do not actually release it. Remember that replaying the ball

incurs a penalty, so make sure that the ball does not leave your fingertips. Quickly recoil your hands and reposition to execute your selected pass.

If the baulk is successful, the defender should commit to what appears to be a pass, giving you room to execute your throw. Remember, you have only 3 seconds to pass the ball, so speed is important.

Faking is an advanced skill and requires good peripheral vision and confidence in your teammates. For a fake, look in one direction but pass in another. With a well-executed fake, the defender will think that you are passing where you are looking when you actually are passing to a player whom you are not in eye contact with. This can be very effective because defenders often cue off your eyes.

DRILLS

Netballers need to pass with accuracy, speed and variety. These drills will help you achieve this, assisting you to sharpen your concentration and reflexes. Once you have mastered the

technique of a pass, focus on the placement of the ball. Learn to feel the touch of a pass: the float of a lob; the long, hard shoulder pass; or the quick, short flick.

Passing Drill 1. *Passing Warm-Up*

Here are a few warm-up activities you can do before you start each practice. Choose two from the following list and work each for 2 minutes. To sharpen concentration and reflexes, replace a netball with a tennis ball or use the smaller, lighter balls that are used in the modified game.

- Throw the ball from one hand to the other across the body. Now try it above your head. Make sure you can start with either hand.

- Throw the ball to yourself and catch it. Use two hands and then use one hand and then the other. Throw the ball above your head, behind your back so you have to turn to catch it, to your right side and to your left side. Now clap before you catch it.

- With a ball in each hand, throw and catch them simultaneously, first with the same hand that released the ball, then with the opposite hand.

- Bounce the ball into space ahead of you and sprint to retrieve it. Vary the number of times you allow the ball to bounce before you catch it. Use both hands and then only the right and only the left.

Success Check

- Grip the ball with the fingers.
- Guide the ball with the arms and wrists.
- Direct the flight with the fingers.
- Release the ball quickly.

Passing Drill 2. *Target Ball*

Target Ball is a versatile drill to help develop your aim using a variety of target locations, distances and passes. Remember to practise proper form with your release and follow-through.

Draw five hands at various heights on a wall with a piece of chalk. Take three steps from the wall to begin your practice. Using a shoulder pass, see how many throws it takes to hit every hand in order once. Now use the two-handed chest pass and repeat the exercise.

Mark five chalk lines on the ground at varying distances from the wall. Try to hit one target with one pass from each line. Then try to hit all targets from each line. After hitting all the targets from each line, choose another pass and begin the drill again.

Use targets on the ground for high-ball practice. Mark three or four large crosses on the ground. Release the ball high above your head and see if you can make it land on the targeted cross. Use both one-handed and two-handed passes when practising.

To Increase Difficulty

- Change hands and try passing with the other hand.
- Increase, by 2, the number of steps you take from the wall to begin the practice. Once you are at 10 to 12 steps, you are handling a good long ball.

- Use other throws: chest pass, bullet pass, two-handed overhead and underarm. Always begin close to the wall and achieve your goal before increasing the difficulty by stepping back.
- Repeat the drills from the reverse position. Start the practice with your back to the wall. Throw the ball into the air above your head. Jump to catch it and turn to face the wall as you land. Make sure you achieve your goal at each activity before you move on. If you work hard, you will find that there is no noticeable difference in the speed and accuracy of the pass from a front start and a reverse start.
- Have a partner stand about 3 metres away to your side. Your partner passes you the ball as you are facing her. Pivot to face the wall and then work through the various sequences of the drill before taking the ball on the opposite side and extending the drill further.

To Decrease Difficulty

- Use one target and gradually add others when you master the technique.

Success Check

- Guide the ball with the fingers.
- Open the shoulder before release.
- Follow through with the fingers, wrists and body.

Score Your Success

Hit each hand in order with shoulder pass = 5 points

Hit each hand in order with two-handed chest pass = 5 points

Hit one target from each chalk line = 5 points

Hit each target from each chalk line = 5 points

Hit each large cross with one-handed passes = 5 points

Hit each large cross with two-handed passes = 5 points

Your score ____

Passing Drill 3. *Flick Drill*

Stand facing a partner, about 3 metres apart. Your partner passes to your right hand, about shoulder height. Quickly return the ball by extending your throwing hand to meet the ball and flicking it on as you make contact. As the ball comes in, the wrist and fingers quickly propel and direct it back to your partner. Practise until you can complete six accurate flick passes in a row.

To Increase Difficulty

- Turn to face the opposite direction and repeat the drill. This means that you have your back to your partner. Turn your head to watch the ball coming in, but keep your body facing the opposite direction.
- Vary the height of the pass. Maintain your accuracy as you take high and low balls. Repeat from the reverse position.
- Facing your partner, shuffle quickly across a 3- to 4-metre straight line. Take balls that fully extend you on either side; flick them

back to your partner as you move from left to right. Vary the height and speed of the ball. Now work from the reverse position.

- Shuffle across from the reverse position. When the ball is released, turn quickly to face the incoming pass and flick to your partner, who then places a low ball for you to flick back. Repeat on the opposite side.

Success Check

- Turn the wrist and fingers towards the receiver.
- Snap the wrist quickly.
- Guide the ball with the fingers.

Score Your Success

Complete 6 accurate flick passes in a row = 10 points

Your score ____

Passing Drill 4. *Hit the Hand*

Stand three or four steps away from your partner. Have your partner raise a hand to full extension. Throw the ball to your partner's outstretched hand. If the ball is placed accurately, your partner should not have to move at all to take the catch. Have your partner constantly change the starting position of his hand. Practise until you can complete five consecutive passes to your partner's outstretched hand.

To Increase Difficulty

- Increase the distance between you and your partner.
- Practise different throws.
- Begin with your back to your partner. Throw and catch the ball, turn, and throw.
- Have your partner move to take the ball.
- Try to complete five different passes when both you and your partner are moving. Increase this to 10 successful passes.

Success Check

- Ball travels quickly to target.
- Follow through with throwing hand.
- Move weight onto front foot at release.

Score Your Success

Complete 5 consecutive passes to your partner's outstretched hand = 10 points

Your score ___

Passing Drill 5. *Work Three Passes*

Stand about 5 metres in front of your partner, who has the ball. Offer three different attacking moves (e.g., forward, break left, break right). Your partner must accurately pass the ball to you on the move. After you take the catch, return the pass to your partner. Practise until you complete three successful repetitions with accurate passing and strong catching. Change roles so that you become the thrower and your partner makes the offers.

To Increase Difficulty

- Increase the offers to four and then to five.
- Introduce a defender to contest the moves.
- If the ball is dropped, start again.

Success Check

- Accurate passing.
- Variety of moves.
- Variety of passes.
- Strong hands on the catch.

Score Your Success

Complete 3 successful repetitions = 5 points

Your score ___

Passing Drill 6. *Up and Back*

Stand 5 metres in front of your partner. Have your partner sprint towards you. When your partner is about 1 metre from you, have him stop quickly and sprint away from you. As this happens, release a lob. If the ball is well placed, it will be easy for your partner to jump into the air and take the catch at full stretch.

To Increase Difficulty

- Use the two-handed overhead pass.
- When your partner stops quickly, get him to change direction (e.g., diagonally left or right).
- Introduce a defender to contest the high ball.

- Have your partner stand 1 metre in front facing you. Place the ball to your partner's left or right side. He turns his body quickly to the ball side, steps back and elevates to take the lob.

Success Check

- Eyes are on the target.
- Body is well balanced.
- Ball travels in a high arc.
- Ball is well placed for receiver.

Score Your Success

Complete 5 well-placed lobs in a row = 10 points

Your score ___

Passing Drill 7. *Hands Over the Pass*

The final test for passing is to see if you can maintain accuracy when the pass is being pressured. Go back to the target practice on the wall. Start about five steps out. Throw the ball to yourself to begin the drill. As you catch, have your partner take up a position 0.9 metres (3 ft) directly in front of you and reach forward to pressure the ball. Throw the ball accurately to your target on the wall. When the defender's hands are over the ball, make sure you do not contact her. This is a good time to practise the baulk. Remember that you can always gain space by stepping back away from the defender, provided you work within the footwork rules. Step 3 will provide an in-depth look at the application of this rule.

To Increase Difficulty

- Elevate and release the ball at the peak of your jump, maintaining the accuracy of the pass.

- Add a third player who provides a stationary target by raising her catching hand.
- Have the third player provide a moving target for the pass.

Success Check

- Keep eyes on the target.
- Be aware of defender's hands.
- Choose appropriate pass.
- Shorten follow-through.

Score Your Success

Complete 3 successful pressured passes to the target = 5 points

Your score ____

Passing Drill 8. *Baulk and Pass*

Stand 5 or 6 metres away from your partner. A defender is 0.9 metres (3 ft) directly in front of you with his hands stretched out over the ball. Your partner makes an attacking move. Use a baulk to clear the defender's hands before you pass to your partner.

To Increase Difficulty

- Introduce a second attacking player. You must now select the best option from the two moves being made, and then deliver the pass accurately. Then add a second and third defender to mark the two attacking players. Your aim is to deliver the ball accurately under this pressure.
- Now introduce the fake. Mix it up with the baulk and straight passes and see how

convincing you are. Attempt to complete five successful passes that include at least one baulk and one fake. Can you increase this so that all passes have a baulk or fake?

Success Check

- Baulk is quick and convincing.
- Grip ball tightly for baulk.
- Eyes on target.
- Release ball quickly when opening is created.

Score Your Success

Complete 3 successful passes after a baulk = 10 points

Your score ____

Passing Drill 9. *Throw and Think*

The final drill is used to remind you that once you have made your pass, you must think about the next move. It allows you to use the passes we have learnt in a challenging drill. When you are passing well, try it.

Sixteen players form a 10- to 12-metre square in the midcourt. Players are in four even groups at each corner of the square, standing behind one another. When you pass the ball in a straight line to one of the players on either side of your line, sprint to the back of the line on the other side of you, the side you did not pass to. When you pass the ball diagonally across the square, you can sprint to any line. You must work together as a group to ensure that no line becomes empty before you complete 10 successful passes. Choose the throw you will use and the player to start, and away you go.

To Increase Difficulty

- Vary the passes and the size of the square.

- Increase the number of passes by five until you can do 40 to 50 passes (20 for juniors and 30 or more for seniors).
- Time yourselves and try to go faster the next time you do the drill.
- Place a floating defender in the middle so your pass must clear the defender.

Success Check

- Make accurate passes.
- Move ball with speed.
- Think about the next move.
- Sprint to the next line.

Score Your Success

Complete 10 successful passes with all 4 lines functioning = 5 points

Your score ___

SUCCESS SUMMARY OF PASSING

You have just practised one of the game's major skills—passing. Successful netballers pass with accuracy and use a variety of throws. Knowing how to select the right pass also calls on your visionary and decision-making skills. Once you have mastered the basic elements of the pass, challenge yourself frequently in match-like conditions.

Before moving on to step 3, Footwork, evaluate how you did on the passing drills in this step. Tally your scores to determine how well you have mastered the skill of passing. If you scored at least 90 points, you are ready to move on to step 3. If your score is 75 to 89 points, redo the drills to improve your score before you move on. If your score is less than 75 points, review step 2 and redo the drills before you move to the next step.

Passing Drills

1. Passing Warm-Up	___ out of 20
2. Target Ball	___ out of 30
3. Flick Drill	___ out of 10
4. Hit the Hand	___ out of 10
5. Work Three Passes	___ out of 5
6. Up and Back	___ out of 10
7. Hands Over the Pass	___ out of 5
8. Baulk and Pass	___ out of 10
9. Throw and Think	___ out of 5
Total	___ **out of 105**

Now that you can catch and throw, it is time to look at footwork. Being able to control your feet will enable you to maintain good body balance when you execute the pass and receive the catch.

Footwork

We have already looked at the importance of the basic work that hands do in netball: catching and throwing. Another basic element of the game involves the feet. If you are to master this exciting game, getting your feet under control is essential.

The footwork rules of netball are quite unique and specific, and in these modern times, somewhat controversial. Simply put, the rules state that after taking possession of the ball, the first grounded foot may not be regrounded before the player releases the ball. An infringement of the footwork rule incurs a free pass for the opponent. This rule is further explained later in this step.

Originally the one-step rule was designed to cater to a genteel, ladylike way of playing. It is quite likely that the ladies of Madame Osterberg's College of Physical Training at Hampstead felt it inappropriate for women to run the whole length of the court while dribbling the ball.

Restricting the movement to one step forced players to pass.

Perhaps if the game had appealed only to the genteel, modern-day concerns would not have arisen. Today, however, the game is played by finely tuned athletes, many of whom undertake vigorous training schedules to seek international supremacy. Speed of movement has become a trademark of the leading nations' styles of play.

In a quick-moving, non-contact game such as netball, being able to control your body is an important component of on-court success. The key to sound body control is good footwork. If your feet are under control, guiding your movement, keeping your body well balanced and allowing you to change speed and direction effectively, then you can concentrate on the important on-court decisions to make with the ball—the crucial matters that win or lose games. Players who fail to control their feet have difficulty executing accurate passes.

DEVELOPING BASIC FOOTWORK SKILLS

To be a successful netball player, you need to master the basic footwork skills of the game. Whether you are in attack or defence, you need a powerful movement to generate speed on your take-off; the ability to run fast, change direction swiftly, and jump strongly; and the ability to side-step. Mastering these important skills enables you to move with speed and agility.

Take-Off

The first two steps of your planned movement to the ball, the take-off, are crucial. If you generate a powerful take-off, your opponents will have difficulty staying with you, and your chances of a successful catch will be greatly enhanced.

A powerful take-off involves the whole body. Your weight should be down and your knees bent. It is very common to see players begin their movements with a backward step or a few small steps that tend to go up and down on the spot, taking them nowhere and making it very easy for their opponent to defend.

Make sure that you drive with your legs and arms and that your first step is powerful. Your aim is to be proficient off either foot. You should be able to generate a powerful take-off whether you are starting your movement with feet astride or whether you have one foot in front of the other.

Misstep
Your first take-off step is backwards.

Correction
Use your arms to drive yourself forward.

Misstep
You do not have enough speed on take-off.

Correction
Bounce quickly a few times on the spot before you drop your weight and take off.

Run

You generate more power when you run when you use your arms as well as your legs. It is surprising the number of players who forget to use their arms to help them run faster. The faster you pump your arms, the more speed you generate with your legs. Run with your body weight slightly forward and your arms at waist level, held close to the body. Take the arm back behind the body; then pump it forward quickly. Keep the body relaxed but strong.

Although most of the running you do is forwards, usually at an angle to meet the ball, make sure you can also do a sideways, backwards movement, which requires a crossover step (figure 3.1). For a crossover step, transfer your body weight to the outside foot then cross in front of the outside foot with the other foot. This will allow you to run backwards with speed.

Figure 3.1　Crossover Step

PREPARATION
1. Keep weight down
2. Move with speed
3. Transfer weight to outside foot
4. Use good court vision

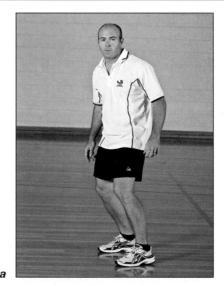

a

(continued)

Figure 3.1 *(continued)*

b

c

EXECUTION

1. Cross inside foot over front foot
2. Keep body well balanced
3. Watch ball

FOLLOW-THROUGH

1. Quickly transfer weight to outside foot

Misstep
Your upper body sways when you run.

Correction
No transfer of body weight. Accentuate your arm movement. Hold a stick or relay baton as you practise your running to help see just what your arms and hands are doing.

Change of Direction

Frequent changes of direction on the netball court keep the opposition guessing. They are never quite sure just what you are going to do next, and that is the way you like it.

Changes of direction should happen quickly, with an element of surprise. From your running stance, quickly lower your body weight at the same time that you plant your outside foot, the foot opposite the direction you intend to go. Absorb your body weight with this foot and then quickly push off in the opposite direction (figure 3.2). The lower your body weight, the more powerful and more rapid the movement will be.

Figure 3.2 | Change of Direction

PREPARATION

1. Get weight down quickly
2. Plant outside foot to anchor movement
3. Absorb body weight

a

b

c

EXECUTION

1. Push off in opposite direction quickly
2. Use arms to help generate speed
3. Watch ball

FOLLOW-THROUGH

1. Sprint off in new direction
2. Stay aware of space

Shuffle

Use the shuffle to move across a short space. Your feet are astride with your weight down and knees bent (figure 3.3). To shuffle to the right, use your left leg to push off while your right leg widens the base. The left leg then shuffles in near the right. Raise your elbows slightly at waist level to counterbalance the movement of the feet.

The shuffle is a quick movement that should be worked from a low base to generate a powerful movement. You can do a shuffle in any direction: sideways, backwards and forwards.

Figure 3.3   Shuffle

PREPARATION

1. Feet shoulder-width apart and astride
2. Weight down
3. Eyes on ball

a

b

c

EXECUTION

1. Keep weight down.
2. Quickly extend outside foot to widen base
3. Use arms to counterbalance

FOLLOW-THROUGH

1. Slide inside foot across space quickly so feet are again shoulder-width apart
2. Keep weight down
3. Extend outside foot
4. Repeat movement at speed

Misstep
You lose balance when executing the shuffle.

Correction
Keep your body moving over a stable base, feet shoulder-width apart. As the outside foot reaches to extend the base, transfer the upper body and quickly pull in the other foot.

Elevation and Jump

To dominate aerial play, you need to be able to elevate strongly to take the ball. Good technique will help you gain maximum extension to the ball.

The power of the jump originates in the legs. Begin a jump with a deep knee bend to initiate a strong movement as you drop your body weight, keeping your elbows tight to your sides. As you push your body weight up, use your arms to assist in the upward driving movement. Keep your body well balanced as you accelerate upwards.

For a standing jump, try to use the two-footed take-off when you elevate. The feet are parallel about shoulder-width apart. You should also practise from a starting position that has one foot in front of the other. This will help you elevate strongly when you are using a mobile start. You can either quickly bring the back foot forward or the front foot back to create a parallel base. Drop your weight and explode upwards. This quick one, two movement (figure 3.4) will give you good body control in the air.

a   *b*   *c*   *d*

Figure 3.4 The quick one, two movement to elevate from a moving start: *(a)* balanced position with one foot slightly in front; *(b)* parallel base; *(c)* drop weight; *(d)* explode upwards.

Misstep
You do not have enough elevation on your jump.

Correction
Separate the running movement by pausing momentarily before take-off. Use a deeper knee bend at take-off.

Experienced players should also practise from a one-footed take-off. The one-footed take-off is more dynamic, however it does propel the body forward so it must be used selectively. The base you elevate from using the one-footed take-off is not as stable as the base in a two-footed take-off, so you will need to work hard to control your body in the air when you use this technique.

Remember the important points of the take-off when you combine the jump with a running movement: A two-footed take-off gives you more power and balance in the air; a one-footed take-off allows you to climb higher and gives you another alternative.

LANDING

Poor landing technique means that your body has an unstable base from which to execute skills. It also increases the chance for injury. Netball demands rapid reactions to on-court action; good landing technique enables you to be in a well-balanced position and ready to respond instantaneously.

For the safest landing, you need to absorb the impact as effectively as you can. A wide-base two-footed landing (figure 3.5) cushions the impact more evenly than a one-footed landing, so use this landing as often as possible. Allow your knees to bend and absorb the force on impact.

Sometimes on court you simply will not be able to use both feet to land and must use a

one-footed landing. The principle for executing the one-footed landing is the same: Allow your knee to bend and absorb the impact. Bring your other foot into contact with the ground as quickly as possible to redistribute your body weight evenly.

The split landing (figure 3.6) is when you land with a wide base with one foot in front of the other. Both feet land simultaneously. This is an advanced landing technique that allows you to nominate your grounded foot. Young players can find it difficult to use without bouncing, so use it only once you have mastered the basic techniques. As you land, be sure to absorb the impact through the feet, ankles and knees.

Figure 3.5 Landing safely.

Figure 3.6 Using the split landing.

Misstep
Your body jerks when landing.

Correction
Land with a wide base. Use a deep knee bend to cushion the impact.

Misstep
You overbalance when landing.

Correction
Widen your base, keeping feet shoulder-width apart, and bend your knees.

UNDERSTANDING THE FOOTWORK RULE

Once you have successfully landed, the footwork rule dictates your next move. The rule states that you cannot reground the first landed foot. While you have possession of the ball, you may not drag or slide your grounded foot or hop on either foot.

The foot that touches the ground first after you catch the ball is the grounded foot. It is important that you are aware of which foot you land on. If you have landed on one foot, this is not a difficult task. When you use a two-footed landing, you can select either foot as the grounded foot. You may then step onto the non-grounded foot, but you must throw the ball or shoot before regrounding the grounded foot.

Once you land with the ball, you need to pass or shoot within 3 seconds. Although the important thing to remember is not to reground your grounded foot, you have the following foot movement options to choose from before you pass or shoot:

- Pivot
- Pivot and step onto the non-grounded foot

- Jump
- Jump and turn in the air
- Step onto the non-grounded foot
- Step onto the non-grounded foot and jump
- Step onto the non-grounded foot, then bring the first leg through, making sure you release the ball before the grounded foot is regrounded

In short, the choice you have ranges from taking no step and simply pivoting, to fully extending the rule and almost taking two steps. Isn't that a complex task? Elite players can do all this and more.

Selecting what to use takes much practice. To begin, apply the rule with the basic techniques of pivoting and stepping on, and then build your repertoire. Remember, you must release the ball within 3 seconds, so your feet need to work swiftly and surely to allow you maximum time to take the ball and pass it safely.

PIVOTING

Often you will take the ball while facing in one direction and want to pass facing another. The pivot enables you to turn quickly on court. Having landed on two feet, select the appropriate side to turn, left or right (figure 3.7a). Keep your weight down and knees bent and pivot to that side so you turn to face the opposite direction (figure 3.7b). Pivot on the ball of the landed foot. Follow through with your non-grounded foot to regain a well-balanced position (figure 3.7c). You are now facing your team's goal third and are ready to pass to a team member.

Figure 3.7   Pivoting

PREPARATION

1. Take catch
2. Bend knees to cushion landing
3. Balance body
4. Know grounded foot

a

b

c

EXECUTION

1. Keep weight down
2. Keep body upright
3. Rotate body
4. Push body around with non-grounded foot
5. Spin on grounded foot

FOLLOW-THROUGH

1. Bring non-grounded foot through
2. Keep body balanced
3. Keep eyes on target
4. Prepare to pass

Misstep
You lose balance as you turn.

Correction
Keep your body upright and weight down and use the non-grounded foot to counterbalance.

Misstep
Your grounded foot lifts.

Correction
Keep your knees bent and your weight down and dig your grounded foot in.

If you land on one foot, simply use it as your pivot foot. Turn in the direction you are heading, and bring the other foot through to keep your body balanced. Remember the golden rule for pivoting: If you land on your right foot, pivot to your right; if you land on your left foot, pivot to your left. If you have a two-footed landing, you may rotate to your right or left.

EXECUTING THE STEP-ON

You need to exercise sound judgment to use the footwork rule to your advantage. The step-on is an advanced skill, so don't rush into it or you might make mistakes. Make sure you have mastered the land and pivot before you try the step-on. It is best to use the step-on when you have outrun your opponent and no one is in front of you to offer a defensive position. The space is open and you step on to gain ground before you release your pass.

Having landed on one foot (figure 3.8a), step forward onto the non-grounded foot (figure 3.8b); then follow through with the grounded foot (figure 3.8c). Release the ball before you reground the grounded foot. If you use a two-footed landing, you can step forward onto either foot and then release the ball before your nominated grounded foot is regrounded. If you need to turn to face the opposite direction before you take the step, simply pivot on the grounded foot; then step on.

Misstep
You lose balance as you step on.

Correction
Check your stride length. Most likely you are overstriding. Check your speed—are you out of control?

Figure 3.8 | Stepping On

PREPARATION

1. Cushion landing
2. Note grounded foot
3. Keep weight down
4. Sight target
5. Keep momentum moving forward

a

b

EXECUTION

1. Step onto non-grounded foot
2. Keep body upright
3. Keep body balanced
4. Watch target

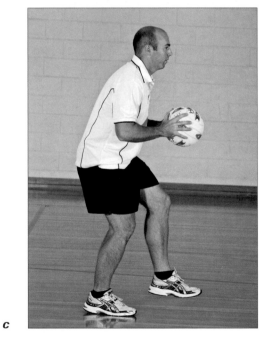

c

FOLLOW-THROUGH

1. Bring grounded foot through
2. Release ball before regrounding the grounded foot

Misstep
Your landed foot drags.

Correction
Keep well balanced and your weight down on your feet. Dig your grounded foot in.

Right-handed throwers normally land on the right foot. This allows them to step onto the left foot and be in a well-balanced position before executing the pass. For left-handed throwers, the reverse applies. However, you should aim to become proficient off both sides of your body.

If you keep your body well balanced, you will be able to deliver your pass accurately.

Misstep
Your landed foot regrounds.

Correction
Speed up the release of the ball. Have you made a poor decision? Should you have used the step-on?

USING THE RECOVERY STEP

Use the recovery step to quickly clear the space between you and your opponent after you have made an unsuccessful attempt to defend the pass. The rules of the game require a defending player to stand a distance of 0.9 metres (3 ft) from the grounded foot of the attacker. The recovery step allows you to reassert yourself and pressure the pass or a shot because you are now in a position to contest.

The recovery step is a backwards jump or step that takes you the required distance from the thrower (figure 3.9). You land facing your opponent so that you can offer some defence on the ball.

As your opponent takes the pass, stop your forward movement, drop your body low, keep your knees well bent, push back from both feet and jump or step backwards to the legal distance of 0.9 metres (3 ft). Now, quickly raise your arms and pressure the ball. Reach forward and pressure the point of release.

Figure 3.9   **Recovery Step**

STOP

1. Stop movement
2. Prepare to recoil body
3. Drop body weight down
4. Focus on opponent
5. Note opponent's grounded foot
6. Watch ball

a

b

c

EXECUTION

1. Push off from one or both feet
2. Jump or step backwards strongly
3. Land 0.9 metres (3 ft) in front of opponent

FOLLOW-THROUGH

1. Raise arms to pressure pass
2. Try to intercept ball on release
3. If unsuccessful, drop arms
4. Keep weight down and block opponent's next move

Misstep

You are penalised for obstruction.

Correction

Your distance is too short. Jump or step back farther. Practise with a stick on the ground that measures 0.9 metres (3 ft) so you become familiar with the legal distance. You may have raised your arms before you cleared the legal distance. Make sure you practise clearing before you raise your arms.

DRILLS

Footwork skills are best practised frequently and in short bursts. Look for quality of movement rather than quantity. This means that in a practice session you should include two or three patterns and spend 2 or 3 minutes on each movement. Begin with a simple action and increase its difficulty as your confidence and ability grow. This step is an area in which you can create your own drills, so don't be afraid to use your imagination.

Footwork Drill 1. *Power Take-Off*

This drill allows you to work on your take-off skills. Focus on keeping your weight down and your movements explosive.

Jog the length of the court, 30.5 metres (100 ft). In each third, the coach will blow the whistle. When you hear the whistle, take three powerful running steps. Aim to be at full speed in three steps.

To Increase Difficulty

- On the whistle, change the movement to a powerful jump. Make sure you are coming from a two-footed takeoff. Use the one, two quick steps to get your feet parallel before you take off. Now take two steps backwards before you elevate.

- On the whistle, take two running steps and a strong jump. Take two steps right; then change direction. Repeat to the left.

- On the whistle, take an imaginary catch, land and pivot. Stop, pitter-patter, then sprint out three strides.

Success Check

- Weight is down on take-off.
- Legs and arms are driving.
- Eyes are up.

Score Your Success

Achieve full speed in 3 steps = 10 points

Your score ____

Footwork Drill 2. *Leaping Around the Line*

This drill helps you develop powerful elevation and gives you a chance to practise safe, controlled landings.

Stand astride a sideline, facing across the court, feet shoulder-width apart. Take a deep knee-bend position and jump as high as you can into the air. Bend your knees to absorb the landing. Attempt to land back at your starting position. Complete three jumps.

Now stand a short step behind the line. Step forward onto the line with one foot and quickly bring the other foot through before you take off. Did you feel that quick one, two rhythm? Can you still land back on the line? Complete three jumps.

47

To Increase Difficulty

- Clap your hands three to five times above your head before you land.
- Scissors-kick your legs twice before you land.
- Use a short take-off of three or four running steps. Make sure you get the one, two steps in before you elevate.
- Introduce the ball. Have a partner throw a ball and leap and catch it as you land.
- Now add a pivot to the run, leap and land. Once you have landed, pivot to face the opposite direction. When you can do this without the ball, include a ball catch and throw.
- Try the step-on instead of the pivot. When you land, take your full step forward and begin the next step before you release your pass.

Success Check

- Take off from two feet.
- Keep the body upright.
- Drive movement with the arms and legs.
- Leap high.
- Bend the ankles and knees to land.
- Maintain body balance.
- Keep the head up watching play.

Score Your Success

3 successful elevations starting and landing on the line = 5 points

3 successful elevations with a short run-up landing on the line = 5 points

3 successful elevations with a short run-up and clapping or a scissors kick before landing on the line = 5 points

3 successful elevations with a short run-up taking the ball at full stretch and landing on the line = 5 points

Your score ___

Footwork Drill 3. *Footwork Cone Circuit*

This is best done in the goal circle, but it can be adapted to other court areas. Place a cone 1 metre in front of the goalpost. This is the central cone. Starting from the baseline, place four cones along the edge of the circle (figure 3.10). Begin the drill by standing next to the central cone. Run to the first cone, change direction and return to the central cone. Run to the second cone and return. Repeat this until you complete a circuit of all four cones.

To Increase Difficulty

- Run to the outside cone, use a recovery step and back shuffle to return to the central cone.
- Run to the outside cone. Jump and execute a two-footed landing before running backwards to the central cone.
- Shuffle out and back to each cone.

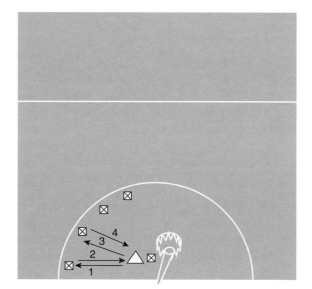

Figure 3.10   Footwork Cone Circuit drill.

- Have a partner start the drill after you reach the first outside cone. Maintain or increase this distance from your partner as you work through the cones. Your partner should try to catch you.

Success Check

- Keep the head up watching the play.
- Move with speed.
- Maintain body balance throughout.

Footwork Drill 4. *Ladder*

The Ladder drill and the Agile Feet drill are designed to help develop foot control. They simply provide a starting point for you to work from. Once you are moving fluently, keep changing the routines; make sure that you make them more demanding to really challenge you.

Draw a ladder on the ground or use cones to mark the rungs. Mark six steps about a stride apart.

1. Face the ladder; then step quickly into the centre of each space with one foot touching the ground between each rung. Now begin with the opposite foot. Repeat, but run through the steps.

2. Use both feet in each rung. After you have stepped into the rung, bring the other foot in to counterbalance before you step into the next rung.

3. Hop on the right foot and then the left up the ladder.

4. Jump low and fast from two feet between each rung. Repeat but elevate high between the markings. This time, once you have elevated, bend down to touch the ground before jumping high to the next step.

To Increase Difficulty

- Turn sideways. Use your right foot to take the quick step and then bring your left foot in to counterbalance before you step quickly into the next rung. Work the left side and then add the running, hopping and jumping movements.
- Go up and down the ladder. Reverse your movement to return. Make sure you maintain your speed and balance as you travel backwards.
- Replace the ladder with low hurdles about 20 centimetres high. Maintain your speed and balance as you adjust your footwork.

Success Check

- Rapid foot movement.
- Body well balanced.
- Head up watching play.

Footwork Drill 5. *Agile Feet*

Set an agility course. Use four cones a step apart at the start of the working area; 10 metres ahead use six cones to mark two 5-metre squares, one to the right and one to the left; and finally, place a cone 10 metres ahead of the squares (figure 3.11).

To commence the drill, go through the first four cones, touching one foot between, then sprinting out to the next cone (10 m). Go right using a side shuffle. Sprint forward to the next marker (5 m); then go left using a side shuffle. Finally, sprint forward to the last cone (10 m).

To Increase Difficulty

- Repeat the drill using the left side of the course.
- Touch two feet between each cone. First lead with your right foot and then with your left.

- Use a quick two-footed jump between the cones.
- Elevate high between each cone.
- Run backwards on the 5-metre sprints.

Success Check

- Quick feet.
- Speed maintained throughout.
- Body well balanced.
- Head up.

Score Your Success

2 successful runs through the agility course in which you move with speed and do not touch the cones = 10 points

Your score ___

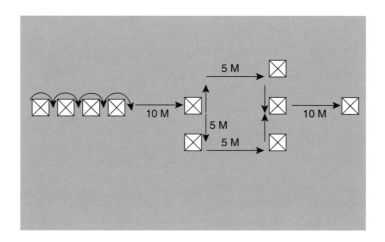

Figure 3.11   Agile Feet drill.

Footwork Drill 6. *Balloon*

Split into groups of four. Mark a small working area 3 to 4 metres wide and long.

Two players (workers) stand in the middle of the working area with three balloons. The pair outside the working area is holding extra balloons. Using rapid foot movements, the workers have to keep the three balloons afloat by hitting them into the air with an underarm, open-hand hit. Once the

three balloons are afloat, another balloon is fed to the working pair, then another, for a total of five balloons. All balloons must stay within the working area.

To Increase Difficulty

- Keep six, then seven, balloons in the air for 1 minute.

Success Check

- Eyes on the balloons.
- Quick footwork and recovery.
- Good spatial awareness.

Keep all 5 balloons off the ground for 1 minute = 10 points

Your score ___

Footwork Drill 7. Two-Ball Drop

Using tennis balls is a fun way to get those feet moving. The next three drills offer a few ideas to try.

To do the two-ball drop well, you will have to use a powerful take-off. Split into groups of three. One player has two tennis balls, one in each outstretched hand. One worker stands 3 to 4 metres in front of the player with the tennis balls, and the third player is resting. The player with the tennis balls randomly drops one ball at a time. The worker has to sprint forward and collect the ball before it bounces twice. Players rotate after the worker collects five tennis balls.

To Decrease Difficulty

- Allow the ball to bounce twice.

Success Check

- Speed off the mark.
- Eyes on the ball.
- Arms drive forward.

Score Your Success

Use a powerful take-off to retrieve 5 tennis balls by the first bounce = 10 points

Your score ___

Footwork Drill 8. Underarm Target

Split into groups of three. One player throws, one works and one retrieves. You will need a bucket of 12 to 15 tennis balls.

Stand in front of a wall 3 to 4 metres apart. The worker has her back to the wall. Using an underarm throw, the thrower rapidly fires balls at the worker, who has to work across a small parallel line to dodge the ball, then quickly push back to the middle to recommence. The third player retrieves the balls and places them back in the bucket. After completing a bucket of balls, players rotate.

To Increase Difficulty

- As the worker, reverse your starting position. Although your body is facing the wall, your head must turn to watch the balls.

Success Check

- Strong take-off and change of direction.
- Quick feet.
- Eyes on the ball.
- Body well balanced.

Score Your Success

Complete a bucket of balls within 1 minute = 10 points

Your score ___

Footwork Drill 9. *Hand Tennis Off the Wall*

Stand 3 metres from the wall with a tennis ball in your right hand. Turn your body sideways before you hit the ball against the wall. You must hit the ball with an open hand (like you are playing tennis). Move after the ball and keep returning it. Make sure to turn your feet and your body around to the side each time you receive and strike the ball. After hitting the ball 10 times with your right hand, switch to your left hand. Make sure your feet and your body turn behind the ball as you work this side.

To Increase Difficulty

- Make the hits consecutive.
- Use alternate sides to take each ball, right side for the first ball and left side for the next one.

- Work with a partner. You will have to move your feet quickly to rotate around each other to hit the ball.

Success Check

- Body turns to the side to hit the ball.
- Feet move quickly to position for the hit.
- Quick recovery and preparation for the next hit.

Score Your Success

Hit the ball 10 times against the wall with your right hand = 5 points

Hit the ball 10 times against the wall with your left hand = 5 points

Your score ____

Footwork Drill 10. *Recovery Step Practice*

Mark a chalk line 0.9 metres (3 ft) from the transverse line. You are in a crouched position with one foot forward on the transverse line and the other a little more than shoulder-width behind. Make sure your weight is down. You should feel like a tight spring ready to uncoil. Push back strongly with both feet and jump back to clear the legal distance, keeping your arms by your sides. If you land on the line, your judgment is just right. As soon as you land, raise your hands to pressure the pass.

To Increase Difficulty

- Try the same recovery action but start by running three or four steps to the transverse line.
- Have your partner stand on the transverse line with a ball. When you have executed the recovery step, your partner releases the ball and you try to intercept it.

- Stand beside your partner on the transverse line. Toss the ball in the air. Both contest the catch. When you are unsuccessful, use the recovery step to defend the pass.

Success Check

- Move weight down to start.
- Push off strongly.
- Clear the distance (0.9 m or 3 ft).
- Keep the arms down while clearing the distance.
- Raise the body and hands after landing.

Score Your Success

Complete 5 successful recovery jumps to the legal distance = 5 points

Your score ____

SUCCESS SUMMARY OF FOOTWORK

Running, landing, pivoting and stepping on form the basic movements for footwork skills. You can easily add a simple jump to these. Ask your coach to check your action to ensure that you are not penalised for stepping or dragging your feet.

Keeping your feet under control is quite a challenge in netball. The rules of the game are quite specific. Once you have the ball, you cannot reground the grounded foot. To keep your feet under control, you will need to work within this rule.

The fast-moving nature of the game means that you have to develop a powerful take-off whether you are sprinting for the ball or flying high to take the catch. Keep your body well balanced and cushion your landing by using both feet as you move around the court. Remember, a well-balanced body is the basis of an accurate pass.

Running, landing, pivoting, stepping and elevating all assist you in your attacking play, while the recovery step and the side step make you a very valuable defender. Be patient with your footwork. Give your feet quality practice time. If you build very solid foundations, you will not have to return later to correct basic mistakes.

Before moving on to step 4, Attacking, evaluate how you did on the footwork drills in this step. Tally your scores to determine how well you have mastered the footwork needed to execute attacking and defensive skills. If you scored at least 85 points, you are ready to move on to step 4. If your score is 70 to 84 points, redo the drills to improve your score before you move on. If your score is less than 70 points, review step 3 and redo the drills before you move on to the next step.

Footwork Drills

1. Power Take-Off	___ out of 10
2. Leaping Around the Line	___ out of 20
3. Footwork Cone Circuit	___ out of 10
4. Ladder	___ out of 5
5. Agile Feet	___ out of 10
6. Balloon	___ out of 10
7. Two-Ball Drop	___ out of 10
8. Underarm Target	___ out of 10
9. Hand Tennis Off the Wall	___ out of 10
10. Recovery Step Practice	___ out of 5
Total	___ **out of 100**

Now that you have mastered the foundations of the game—catching, throwing and footwork—you are ready to begin to put these together to develop your attacking play. Having sound basics will help you meet the challenges of the next step, in which you will learn to move creatively on court.

Attacking

Whenever your team has possession of the ball, you are in attack. Each team member works hard to bring the ball down the court to the shooters so they can score. You need to see the space and quickly move into it. Your attacking skills can also open up space in a very crowded situation.

Attacking moves need an element of surprise to keep your opponents guessing, which calls for variety in your attacking play. You can achieve this in two ways: first by having a number of attacking moves that you can offer, and second by timing the use of these moves to increase their effectiveness. So attacking play has two important ingredients—the movement itself and the timing used to execute it. In this step, we look at both.

First we introduce you to the game's basic moves. The work you have done with footwork in step 3 forms an important basis for attacking moves. If you have been working hard at running, jumping and changing direction, and scored at least 85 points in step 3, you should handle this step with ease. If you are having difficulty with these movements, keep reworking them until you reach this score. Don't rush forward. If the foundation is not sound, you will

struggle to put things together. Take the time now to get it right.

Once you are moving confidently with your basic attacking play, we introduce timing. We look at some ways you can develop your sense of timing so that your attacking moves work for you on court.

The attacking moves covered in this step are basic to the game. Learn the basics and then combine and extend them to create your own moves. Individual flair is an important ingredient for winning attacking play.

To win a netball game, you must outscore the opposing team. You need to deliver the ball to your shooters frequently so they have more opportunities to score than your opponents do. Attacking moves are used to give your team the best chance of successfully bringing the ball down court.

Good attacking moves make it easier to pass the ball successfully. When moves are well executed, team members can read each other's play quite easily. There is no hesitation in releasing the ball, and players are confident. Attacking play like this makes it difficult for your opponents to counteract. On the other hand, attacking moves that are uncertain and hesitant cause the error rate to rise.

If your opponent is constantly beating you to the ball, you need to carefully examine your attacking skills. First check your starting position to ensure that you are generating a powerful take-off. Then look at the variety of moves that you offer. Is your repertoire too limited? If the problem is not in these two, then it must be related to your on-court execution of the moves, and this involves your timing. Poor timing makes a good move ineffective.

ATTACKING STRATEGIES

Five important terms are used in regard to attack play. You should understand them before we look at the most common moves netballers use.

- **Offer.** When you make an offer in netball, you simply execute an attacking move. You offer yourself to catch the ball. Use your speed and strength to produce a move that your teammates can read easily.

- **Re-offer.** If your first move is unsuccessful, make another. Remember, the player with the ball must pass or shoot within 3 seconds, so you should quickly offer another attacking move when your first move is beaten.

- **Preliminary move.** A move used before you offer the main attacking move. Your aim is to take the defender away from the area in which you actually want to receive the ball. Fakes and dodges are often used as preliminary moves. A well-executed preliminary move makes it difficult for the defender to read your offer.

- **Clearing move.** A clearing move is an advanced attacking move and is usually taught after players have mastered the preliminary move. It aims to create space for you to re-enter or to clear space for a teammate to use. It is a wide, arcing movement usually made towards the side of the court. From there you read the play to decide your next attacking move. A drive often follows a well-timed clearing run.

TIMING

Time your attacking move to give you the best chance of successfully taking the incoming ball. When you decide to offer is as important as your choice of attacking movement. If you go too early, you make it easy for your defender. If you go too late, you put pressure on your passing teammate. In a split second you must decide when to go. Learn to feel the pace of the movement on court. Do those around you operate at one pace, or are they able to mix things up? Use a variety of cues to time your move. The release of the ball, the pivot and the catch are common triggers.

Although leading players make it look as though it all just happens on court, don't be fooled. They have worked hard at their timing skills so that it now comes very naturally. Make sure you put in the work, too.

ATTACKING MOVEMENTS

There is a lot to understand in attack. The moves themselves—the drive, dodge, preliminary move, clear, fake, hold, roll-off and drop back—mixed with elevation will get you moving on the court. Just think of the havoc you can wreak on your opponent if you can combine these moves effectively and your timing is spot-on. When you see your opponent looking lost out there on court, you know that you have not only thought up a great move, but you have executed it to perfection.

Drive, or Lead

As the name suggests, this is a powerful run to the ball. It can involve a few steps, or it can contain many. It can also include a change of direction.

Starting from a balanced position with your weight down (figure 4.1*a*), assess the open court space you wish to move into and drive with your legs and arms while preparing to take the pass (figure 4.1*b*). As you land and rebalance with a wide stance, look for your passing options (figure 4.1*c*). The important part of any lead is that you hit top speed in a few strides and that you maintain it throughout the movement. If you have worked at your take-off in step 3, you have a powerful start to your drive.

Figure 4.1   Drive, or Lead

PREPARATION

1. Body balanced
2. Weight down
3. Head up
4. Aware of court space
5. Focus on player with ball

a

EXECUTION

1. Move into space
2. Drive with legs
3. Use arms
4. Hit top speed quickly
5. Prepare to take pass
6. Keep eyes on ball

b

56

FOLLOW-THROUGH

1. Land and balance
2. Look for passing options

c

Misstep
You are constantly beaten to the ball.

Correction
Increase the power of your movement. Lower your weight to start. Check your starting position. Change your timing by offering earlier or delaying your take-off.

The most common use of the lead is to drive hard away from an opponent, starting your move from your clear side, the side your defender is not completely covering.

The front cut (figure 4.2) is a very effective variation of this move. Rather than taking the first stride to the clear side, use a powerful step to cut across the path of your defender and

a   *b*   *c*

Figure 4.2 Front cut: *(a)* begin in balanced position; *(b)* cut across defender, making sure not to make contact; *(c)* continue to take pass.

continue on to take the pass. You must ensure that you do not contact your opponent when you execute this move. Keep your head up and your body well balanced at all times.

Dodge

This simple change of direction is a very effective attacking movement. Defenders find this move very difficult to respond to because it catches them off guard. They anticipate a single change of direction and are confused when the second change happens so quickly.

Starting from a low stance, transfer your body weight onto your outside foot; then explode back again (figure 4.3). A dodge can be executed from a stationary position or on the run. If you are doing it on the run, dig in quickly as you change direction.

For a double dodge simply repeat the movement. Make sure that you do not lose momentum on the second dodge. You must maintain your speed, agility and explosive power throughout for the movement to be effective.

Figure 4.3   Dodge

PREPARATION

1. Drop weight down quickly
2. Take weight on outside foot
3. Watch play

a

EXECUTION

1. Transfer weight to other foot quickly
2. Keep body well balanced
3. Keep weight down to generate powerful movement

b

FOLLOW-THROUGH

1. Weight transfers to other foot
2. Drive to take catch
3. Weight down
4. Strong movement

c

Fake

For a fake, you do not move your feet, only your upper body. The upper body creates an illusion that the whole body is about to move.

To execute the fake (figure 4.4), dip your shoulder, arms and waist to one side; then quickly recoil. It is amazing how often you can fool your opponent into following a well-executed fake.

Figure 4.4	Fake

PREPARATION

1. Body well balanced
2. Feet shoulder-width apart
3. Ball in both hands

a

(continued)

Figure 4.4 *(continued)*

b

c

EXECUTION

1. Hold ball firmly
2. Dip and recoil upper body quickly
3. Use a strong, convincing movement
4. Keep weight down and feet still

FOLLOW-THROUGH

1. Return to starting position quickly
2. Release ball safely

Misstep
Your opponent stays with you.

Correction
Learn to time your fake more effectively. Keep your movement sharp.

Hold

This is a stationary player-on-player move. It provides great contrast to the drive, in which you use your power to generate speed and cover distance. For the hold, you use your power to hold your opponent and protect the space that you wish to move into. As the ball is released, you step away from the hold and take the pass. The most common use of the hold is to set up in the goal circle for a high ball.

Timing is critical to the success of the hold. An effective hold is set as the play approaches and the attacker is looking for a quick, well-placed feed. You must also be sure that you do not cause contact that interferes with play when you use a hold.

To execute the hold (figure 4.5), begin with a wide base, knees slightly bent, to keep the defender out of your space. Tense your body and hold it strongly across the space you need. Your body should be upright and provide a physical barrier to your opponent. As you are setting up your hold, focus on the ball. Wait until the pass has been released before moving into your protected space to take the catch.

Figure 4.5   Hold With T Stance

1. Wide base
2. Body upright
3. Use shoulder, arm, and hip to hold off defender
4. Eyes on ball and opponent

Misstep
You do not hold your space strongly.

Correction
Widen your base and keep a strong holding position. Position your legs well to block your defender. Check your timing. You are either setting late or coming out early.

Misstep
You don't keep your eyes on the ball and fail to read when to set or release the hold.

Correction
Keep your eyes on the ball as you execute your move. When you have your back to the ball, turn your head and follow it with your eyes.

The four common applications are T position, back hold, front hold and side position.

- *T position* (see figure 4.5)—Turn your body side-on to your opponent. Your shoulder, arm, hip and leg should hold the defender's spine.
- *Back hold* (figure 4.6a)—Position immediately behind your opponent. Use a wide, strong base to keep her forward.

- *Front hold* (figure 4.6b)—The reverse of the back hold. This time take the front space and protect it.
- *Side position* (figure 4.6c)—Stand side-on to your opponent, placing your left foot on the outside of the defender's nearest foot. Hold strong with a wide base.

The hold is quite an advanced skill. If you are a young athlete, you should be moving well with free-flowing play before attempting this move.

a   b   c

Figure 4.6   Hold applications: *(a)* back hold; *(b)* front hold; *(c)* side position.

Roll-Off

The roll-off gives you a clever alternative when starting an attacking move. It is also used to counter a hold. There are two commonly used variations of the roll-off—full and half.

For the full roll-off, stand immediately behind the defender, facing the ball with head up and eyes on the ball. Transfer your weight through the leg on your turning side. Pivot on this leg, staying close to your defender to protect your space. Keeping your weight down, step onto the other leg, staying close to the defender to protect the space you are moving in; then open to the ball. As you roll, turn your head quickly to keep your eyes on the ball.

The half roll-off can be executed from in front of or behind the defender. When executing from behind your defender, stand immediately behind her, facing the ball. Transfer your weight through the leg on your turning side. Pivot 180 degrees. Stop and swing or step back onto your other foot, staying close to the defender to protect your space. Open to the ball. Keep your eyes on the ball throughout the movement.

Keep the body well balanced and controlled as you execute the roll-off to ensure that you do not cause contact.

Drop-Back

Not all attacking moves are made while leading towards the ball. Remember, you can use the space behind you too. Dropping back into this space will add another dimension to your attacking play.

The most common use of the drop-back is from a lead, drive or hold. Take a few quick steps into the space behind you and elevate to take the pass. Adding a preliminary move before dropping back will make the move even more difficult for your defender to read. A few quick steps forward towards the ball before you suddenly stop and drop back can be very effective. A fake before you drop back works well too.

Be bold. Try executing a few of your favourite moves by dropping back into the space behind you. It will remind you how important it is to use all of the space around you and not to become too predicable by always running forward to meet the ball.

ELEVATION

Elevation adds another dimension to your attacking skills. It provides an element of surprise and can test a defender's aerial ability. If you have exceptional leg power, you may find a straight standing jump effective to take a ball. Most players will combine elevation with a strong attacking movement. Practise taking off from both one foot and two feet. The two-footed take-off provides more power and control from the base, so use it when you can. (See figure 3.4 on page 39 for the two-footed take-off.) As you travel up from the take-off, make sure that you keep the body under control and take the pass at the height of your movement.

Successful attack play involves more than just working to the ball; off-ball movement counts as well. It is all part of winning attack play. When you begin to work seriously at developing attacking skills, you'll need to work with others in small groups or with your team members. You are getting ready for court play, and your practice sessions should reflect this.

DRILLS

Practise attacking moves on your own to start with, and then develop combinations. As you begin to master attacking moves, pay extra attention to when you make your offer. Timing is crucial to success when you are attacking. When you begin to play this game, you will find that a lot happens in a very small space and a short amount of time. As you watch good netballers play, you will notice that they just seem to know when to go. It looks so easy because their timing is so precise. To be effective, attacking moves require good timing. When you are comfortable with the attacking moves, use the drills to introduce the timing element to your attacking practice.

Attacking Drill 1. *Single Attack Moves*

These are best practised in small groups as part of a warm-up routine. Indicate the move to practise—for example, the drive (or lead). Select a partner to start the drill and stand about 5 to 6 metres apart. Your partner offers the attacking move—in this case a strong driving move—and you pass the ball. Place the pass so that your partner is fully extended to take the catch. Continually pass the ball as you offer your attacking moves. Once you and your partner have completed five successful catches with one attacking move, change to another.

To Increase Difficulty

- Introduce a creative challenge—for example, players cannot repeat an attacking move before they complete five successful catches.
- Every second move a player makes must use an offer and re-offer.

- Have three players work the drill. You'll need good timing to avoid working the same space as your partner
- Place a defending player between the attackers and allow them to apply token defensive pressure.

To Decrease Difficulty

- Have one player throwing and the other practising attacking moves. When the attacking player completes five catches, players change roles.

Success Check

- Speed off the mark.
- Strong lead.
- Eyes on the ball.
- Safe hands.
- Accurate feed.

5 attacking moves into space that are timed well and result in the catch taken at full stretch = 5 points

5 different attacking moves that are well timed and result in the catch being taken at full stretch = 5 points

Your score ___

Attacking Drill 2. *Front and Back*

Five attackers stand in a line behind one another. You are the feeder. Stand 4 to 5 metres in front, facing the attackers (figure 4.7). Call the moves to be practised—for example, dodge and drive. The first attacker offers the move. You pass. The attacker catches and pivots. The back player on the line now offers his move. The front attacker

passes to that player. He catches and throws a long ball back to you, the feeder. The first attacker moves to the back of the line, and the drill begins again. When you have passed to everyone, you join the line of attackers and another player becomes the feeder.

To Increase Difficulty

- Be creative—for example, use a different move from the player you follow.
- Elevate to every third ball.
- Use a preliminary move before you offer.
- Complete a full line without a drop. If you drop the ball, restart the line.

Success Check

- Confident, strong moves.
- Good timing.
- Pass ball to outstretched hands.

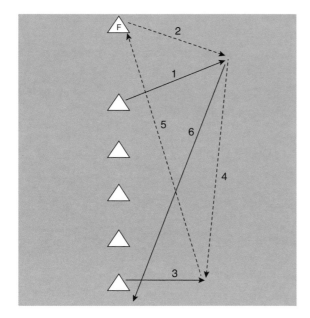

Figure 4.7 Front and Back drill.

Score Your Success

All 5 players execute successful attacking moves = 10 points

Your score ___

Attacking Drill 3. *Double Feed*

Two feeders stand in front of a line of four players (figure 4.8), about 5 metres away. Both feeders have a ball. To start the drill, the first player offers an attacking move to the nearest feeder, who passes the ball accurately. The attacking player returns this ball to the feeder and then offers a different attacking move to the second feeder.

The ball passes quickly between the feeders and attacker. As this attacker returns to the end of the line, the next attacker begins to make an offer to the first feeder. After each attacker completes two successful moves, the feeders join the attacking line, and two new feeders pass the ball.

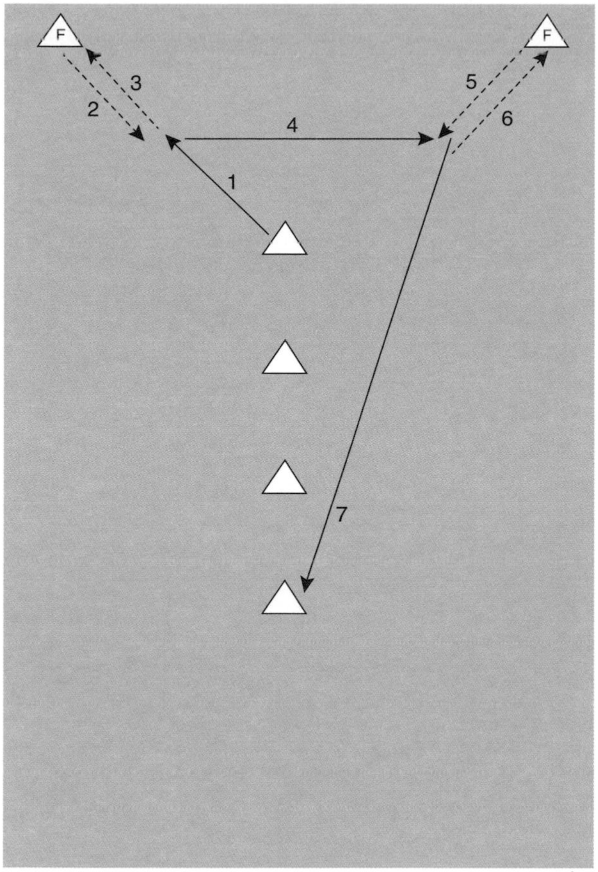

Figure 4.8 Double Feed drill.

To Increase Difficulty

- The second attacker starts to work when the first attacker returns the initial pass to the feeder. This means that the attackers follow each other through the drill.

- Attackers increase offers to three before the next player starts to work. Make sure that all three moves are quite different. You have to think and move quickly to master this drill.

- Place a defender between the feeder and the attacker to pressure the pass.

- Add another line of four players who stand alongside the original attacking line. On "Go", both attackers offer to one of the feeders and return the ball to the other feeder before offering to her. Make sure that you read each others' moves well and have good spatial awareness.

Success Check

- Strong offer.
- Offer easily read.
- Variations of attacking movement.
- Eyes on the ball.

Score Your Success

Complete 1 rotation in which all players offer successful attacking moves and feed the ball = 10 points

Your score ___

Attacking Drill 4. *Basic Timing*

Work in pairs. You are the feeder, so you have the ball. Stand 5 metres in front of your partner, the attacker. Both you and your partner face the same direction. Throw the ball to yourself by tossing it overhead and taking it at head height directly in front. As you take the catch, turn to face the attacker. The attacker watches the ball and reacts to the cue (the catch). As you take the catch, the attacker offers a move. Release the ball. The attacker takes the catch safely, then returns the pass to you so you can begin the drill again.

To Increase Difficulty

- As the feeder, begin to vary the height of the ball that you throw to start the drill. Use low and high balls.

- Vary the distance between yourself and the attacker for each pass.

- Change the cue. Use your pivot, and now try the pass.

- Once your partner has the ball, offer a well-timed move using the same cue. Keep the ball moving between you until you have made five well-timed moves; then start the drill again.

- Add a second attacker who stands close to the original attacker. Both players time from your identified cue. Pass to one. The other re-offers by timing off her attacking partner's cue. As you become proficient, add a floating defender.

To Decrease Difficulty

- As the feeder, call "Go" as you execute the cue to indicate to the attacker when the move should start.

Success Check

- Weight down, ready to offer.
- Body well balanced.
- Eyes on the ball.
- Strong offer on cue.

Score Your Success

Execute 5 well-timed attacking moves = 10 points

Your score ___

Attacking Drill 5. *One-Line Timing*

Five attackers are spread equally down two thirds of the court, facing the same direction. The timing cue is the catch. The first player throws the ball in the air, catches and turns. The second player offers a strong diagonal move to the ball. The first player quickly releases a pass to the second player, whose catch is the cue to trigger the next attacking move from the third player in the line. Continue this pattern up and down the line.

To Increase Difficulty

- Vary the distance between the players. Note how you need to adjust for short and long balls.
- Offer variations of attacking movements. You cannot repeat a move; each player must use a different attacking move.
- Use a high ball or a low ball on every second pass. Note the different speeds of the various passes.
- Change your timing cue. For example, instead of timing off the catch, use the pivot, the landing foot or the throw.
- Increase your line to 8 or 10 players spaced down the length of the court.
- Ignore the first offer from each player and wait for her to re-offer before passing.

- Use two cues—for example, use a preliminary move as the first cue and a drive as the second cue. If the first cue is the player's move, offer a dodge when she moves. If the second cue is the player's catch, re-offer with a drive as she pulls in the ball.
- Every second player uses a clearing move. The next player drives into her space and takes the ball. The player who made the clearing move then re-offers to take the next pass.

To Decrease Difficulty

- Start with a line of three or four players.

Success Check

- Watch the ball.
- Time the move from the cue.
- Attack strongly.
- Move the ball with speed into space.
- Use good footwork.

Score Your Success

Ball is passed up and down the line once without a drop, and all players offer well-timed moves = 10 points

Your score ___

Attacking Drill 6.   *Give and Go*

Half of the team goes to one end of the court and half to the other. Split into pairs and stand 12 metres apart, facing each other in lines. One player has a ball. The drill starts with the player who has the ball and his partner.

The player with the ball passes to his partner. The receiver makes an offer, then re-offers to take the ball. When both players have handled the ball, the pair at the opposite end makes its moves. Both players drive forward to offer. The ball is passed to either player. When the catch is taken, this is the cue for the partner to re-offer. When the ball is passed to this player, it provides the cue for the third pair to drive forward and offer. As each pair concludes its moves, the players continue through the working area to join the end of the opposite line.

To Increase Difficulty

- Each pair must make three successful passes before the next pair starts its moves.

- Place a floating defender in the middle of the working area to pressure the moves and passes.

To Decrease Difficulty

- Bring pairs in closer, about 6 metres. Reduce the handling so that each pair passes once before the next pair offers its attacking moves.

Success Check

- Watch the ball.
- Read the cue.
- Attack into open space.
- Move the ball accurately.
- Use good footwork.
- Vary the pace and movement.

Score Your Success

All players execute well-timed moves and handle the ball without a drop = 10 points

Your score ___

Attacking Drill 7.   *The Square*

This drill concentrates on attacking moves in a very confined space. Eight attackers in pairs form a square about 8 meters apart. Attackers must confine their offers to their corners of the square so they are working with three- or four-step moves.

One pair has the ball. One player throws the ball to herself to commence. As the catch is taken, the partner offers and the ball is thrown to her. Now that both players have handled the ball, they move it clockwise to the next pair. Both partners in the next pair offer, and the player who does not receive the ball re-offers. After both partners have handled the ball, the ball is passed to the third pair, who offers and re-offers. The ball continues to move around the square with each pair handling it before passing it on.

To Increase Difficulty

- Make three offers before passing the ball on.

- Rather than pass in sequence, pass randomly. When both partners have handled the ball, the last player with the ball uses eye contact to indicate which pair she will pass to. Once eye contact is made, that pair offers and re-offers before making eye contact with the next pair.

Success Check

- Good spatial awareness.
- Short, sharp movements.
- Well-timed moves.

Score Your Success

Complete 2 rotations around the square with good timing without a drop = 10 points

Your score ___

SUCCESS SUMMARY OF ATTACKING

Whether moving on the ground or elevating in the air, power and speed are keys to successful attacking movements. Choosing the appropriate attacking move for an on-court situation will be determined by your spatial awareness—can you see the space?—or your ability to create space—can you make it?

You will be most effective if you have a variety of moves so that you can keep the defender guessing. Develop the ability to move the ball quickly, and make sure you can also dig in and slow down the ball when necessary.

Time your moves well. Learn to feel the pace out on the court. Use a variety of cues to hone your timing skills. Remember that knowing when to go is as important as knowing which move to offer.

Before moving on to step 5, Defending, evaluate how you did on the attacking drills in this step. Tally your scores to determine how well you have mastered the attacking strategies and skills needed to move the ball. If you scored at least 50 points, you are ready to move on to step 5. If your score is 30 to 50 points, redo the drills to improve your score before you move on. If your score is less than 30 points, review step 4 and redo the drills before you move on to the next step.

Attacking Drills

1. Single Attack Moves		___ out of 10
2. Front and Back		___ out of 10
3. Double Feed		___ out of 10
4. Basic Timing		___ out of 10
5. One-Line Timing		___ out of 10
6. Give and Go		___ out of 10
7. The Square		___ out of 10
Total		___ **out of 70**

Now that you have mastered the basics of attacking play, we will move on to the role of defence. Some believe that defending is the less exciting role, but a winning team needs all players to be proficient in both attack and defence. Teams that rely purely on their back line players to turn over the ball have less chance of restricting their opponents from scoring. Winning teams know how to pressure every ball down the court.

Defending

Defending in netball is a challenge. The fast-flowing, high-scoring nature of the game means that the attacking skills receive a lot of attention. Moving the ball forward to the shooters in anticipation of a goal often appears more exciting than working the defence to deny your opponents possession.

Don't be fooled! Winning teams make sure they have a balance between defence and attack. Winning teams love to deny their opposition the ball, to force them into errors, to pressure them into making mistakes. The goal scored from a brilliant intercept brings the crowd to its feet. This is spectacular stuff, the plays people talk about long after the whistles have stopped and the game has ended.

Nobody said defence was easy. To make your mark, you need persistence, along with highly developed skills. And just for good measure, there are a few important rules that specifically relate to defending.

Netball rules state that you may not contact a player from the other team in a way that interferes with that player's actions. When the umpire calls contact against you, a penalty pass is awarded to the opposition. If you make contact in the goal circle, the shooter may take a penalty pass or shot. If you are penalised for contact, you must stand out of play, standing beside the thrower taking the penalty while it is taken. When you are out of play, you must wait until the ball is released before you move.

Misstep
You are penalised for contact when the attacker takes the ball.

Correction
Pull your upper body off the attacker. Use your outside arm to contest the ball.

Obstruction is the other rule that you must understand to become an effective defender. To defend an opposing player with the ball, your nearer foot must be 0.9 metres (3 ft) away from her landed foot. This is why you need the recovery step, which we looked at in step 3. The recovery step helps you to clear the distance between yourself and your opponent when you are beaten to the ball.

Misstep
You are penalised for obstruction.

Correction
Use the recovery step to clear the distance. Keep your arms down. Step back before raising your hands.

You obstruct when you defend within 0.9 metres (3 ft). If you obstruct, the umpire awards a penalty pass to the opposing team. If you obstruct in the goal circle, the shooter may take a penalty pass or shot. In either case you must stand beside the thrower taking the penalty, out of play, while the penalty is taken.

Defenders should train so they automatically recognise the legal distance from the attacker: 0.9 metres or 3 feet. Use a tape measure or ruler to measure this distance during practice, paint a line on the ground to work beside or use the diameter of the centre circle for recovery work.

When defending, you are trying to constantly pressure your opponent to cause him to make a mistake. Your team can then take possession of the ball and pass it down court for a shot at goal. Good defending allows your team to create more scoring opportunities by restricting your opponent's play. If the attacking team is allowed to move or pass the ball when and where they choose, very few mistakes occur. This team then completely dictates the terms of play.

When you defend a team and begin to restrict its options, its error rate escalates. Good defending creates turnovers. If you can capitalise on these opportunities, your team will be successful.

Defending is not simply about the skills of the three defence players. Each member of the team must be able to defend. The most effective defence comes when the whole team applies pressure. Remember, the greater the pressure, the greater the reward. This simply means that a team's ability to defend successfully relates to all team members' willingness to pressure their opponents' moves and throws. Defending wins games. The difference between two teams is often not their ability to attack, but their ability to do the unglamorous work in defence.

There are a number of ways to defend. In this step, we look at two key methods: playing one-on-one defence (shadowing) and defending off the player (anticipation). If you can master both of these techniques, you will have a very good foundation on which to build your defending skills.

PLAYING ONE-ON-ONE DEFENCE

The aim of defence is to dictate the terms of your opponent's attacking play and force a turnover of the ball. In one-on-one defence you aim to dictate the terms of attack before your opponent begins her move. This means that you try to force your opponent to move where you want her to, which of course will give you the best chance to intercept the pass.

For one-on-one defence, begin with a strong starting position: weight down, body well balanced, feet shoulder-width apart, hands held close to your body. You should begin halfway across the body on the ball side of your opponent, in front of your opponent, with your back turned to her, and have a view of the player and the ball. This is known as the front stance (figure 5.1). Being on the ball side means that the ball has to pass in front of you to reach your opponent. This gives you the best chance to intercept the pass.

The starting position reflects the intent of your defence. The front stance is most commonly used when you wish to intercept. If you have to protect space, use the back stance or a side stance. The back stance, in which you start immediately behind your attacker, acknowledges that you are prepared to sacrifice the front ball to protect the back space (figure 5.2). Goalkeepers often use this in their circle defence. They allow the long shot, but protect the area close to the goalpost.

Use the side stance (figure 5.3) to deny an attacker access to her strong move. For example, if your opponent likes to lead to the right, begin your defence on that side and try to force her to lead to the left.

Figure 5.1 The front stance places you in a good position to intercept.

Figure 5.3 Use the side stance to deny your opponent's strongest move.

Figure 5.2 Protect back space with the back stance.

No matter which stance you use, netball is a non-contact game. Your starting position should always be as close as you can get to make your presence felt without contacting.

Your starting position should give you the best chance for successful defending. This usually means that you should try to force your opponent wide, towards the side of the court. Carefully protect the busy central area of the court, the quickest route between both goals. If the attacking play flows quickly through here, it is very difficult to stop. Forcing the ball wide slows the attack and gives you a greater chance of success.

Watch the ball and your opponent. As your opponent moves, react and move in the same direction. As the pass is released, attack the ball and extend fully to intercept. If you are unsuccessful at gaining possession of the ball, recover quickly in front of your opponent and offer a defence of the pass or defend any down-court move (figure 5.4). Use the recovery step that we learnt in step 3 to quickly clear the legal distance from the landed foot of your attacker. Raise your arms to pressure the pass or anticipate the throw. Both of these skills are discussed in this step. The more advanced skills of blocking your opponent's down-court move or dropping back to double-defend are covered in step 8.

Misstep
The attacker loses you in the first few steps.

Correction
Adjust your starting position.

Figure 5.4 **Defending One-on-One**

PREPARATION

1. Weight down
2. Body well balanced, halfway across attacker's body
3. Head up; eyes on opponent and ball
4. Arms and hands close to body

a

b

c

EXECUTION

1. Follow opponent's move
2. Maintain view of player and ball
3. Extend to intercept pass

FOLLOW-THROUGH

1. Use recovery step and keep arms down
2. Reposition in front of player
3. Raise arms up and over ball
4. Pressure the pass

Misstep

The attacker beats you in the last few strides.

Correction

Focus on the ball when it is released. Keep attacking the ball. Don't stop.

Misstep

You lose sight of the ball when you start to defend.

Correction

Keep your head up. Open your starting position slightly so you can see the player and the ball. This will give you a broader view of the court.

Pressuring the Pass

To pressure the pass, use the recovery step to reposition yourself in front of your opponent, keeping your arms down by your side. Make sure you are the legal distance from your opponent's landed foot (0.9 m or 3 ft). Move your weight down so that you are well balanced. Extend both arms over the ball (figure 5.5). Pressure the point of release of your opponent's pass—watch the throwing hand to anticipate the pass. Remember, you can reposition your hands, but not in an intimidating manner. For example, you cannot wave your hands around to try to put your opponent off. If your pressure is effective, your opponent will focus on you rather than on the team member who will be receiving the pass, and that is when an opponent can make mistakes.

Figure 5.5 Pressuring the pass.

Misstep

You are penalised for contact when you start to defend.

Correction

Adjust your starting position so there is more space between you and your opponent. Keep your arms down.

Anticipating the Pass

Recover in front of your opponent. Keep your weight down and your body low, and watch the ball intently. As your opponent prepares to pass the ball, push your weight down strongly and bend your knees so that you feel like a tightly coiled spring (figure 5.6a). As your opponent releases the pass, spring upward at full stretch and try to intercept the ball (figure 5.6b).

a

b

Figure 5.6 Anticipating the pass: (a) weight down and knees bent; (b) as your opponent releases the ball, spring upward at full stretch.

DEFENDING OFF THE PLAYER

The aim of defending off the player is to gain possession of the ball from the attacking team through an interception. While defending off a player, you are aware of your opponent's movements, but the ball is the focus of your attention. Position yourself so you can drive hard to cut off an incoming pass. The element of surprise that such defence brings is a strength. Attackers become uncertain, which can increase their error rate.

Watch the player and the ball closely as they travel down court. Judge the speed of the ball and the distance it is travelling. Remember that the long high ball gives you the best chance to cover ground. Decide which ball to intercept. Attack the ball and take the pass at full extension (figure 5.7).

Figure 5.7 **Defending Off the Player**

PREPARATION

1. Body well balanced
2. Eyes on player and ball

a

b

c

EXECUTION

1. Decide when to go
2. Explode out
3. Fully extend to ball
4. Pull ball in

FOLLOW-THROUGH

1. Bend knees to land
2. Balance
3. Scan for attacking cue
4. Look to pass

Misstep
You miss the ball.

Correction
Time your attack to the ball. Make sure you can see both the player and the ball at the same time.

Misstep
You drop the ball.

Correction
Focus on the ball as you drive to intercept. Pull the ball in strongly.

DEFENCE DRILLS

Defending requires you to make decisions about your move, your opponent's move and the pass that is coming in. Drills need to focus on these aspects. You will notice that the drills in this section are done in small groups; it is very difficult to practise defending by yourself.

Defence Drill 1. *Shadowing*

You are the defender, and your partner is the attacker. Take a starting position for one-on-one defence. Call "Go". When the attacker moves, you must stay close for 3 seconds. Work hard to shadow every move.

To Increase Difficulty

• Change your starting position to the opposite side, to the back and finally to the front. Have a player stand out in front of you with the ball. Now keep both your partner and the ball in view while you work. Work all positions.

• When you can stay close for 3 seconds from these positions, have the player with the ball pass to your partner. Try to deflect or intercept the pass. If you are beaten, quickly recover and pressure the pass.

• The thrower now gives your partner three consecutive passes. Stick tight to your partner and see how many times you can take the ball or cause the attackers to make an error.

Success Check

• Body well balanced.
• Weight down.
• Eyes on the opponent and the ball.
• Feet shoulder-width apart.
• Arms close to the body.
• Quick feet and recovery.

Score Your Success

Stay close to the attacker for 3 seconds by using good one-on-one defence = 10 points

Your score ___

Defence Drill 2. *Line Defence*

Three attackers and three defenders stand in a line facing the feeder, who has the ball. The defenders wear bibs to distinguish them from the attackers. The first attacker prepares to offer. The first defender takes up a good starting position to

force the attacker wide. The attacker offers and the defender reacts to the move. The defender tries to intercept the pass from the feeder.

The successful player returns the ball to the feeder. As the ball is returning to the feeder, the next attacker and defender start the drill. After the defenders are able to successfully take three balls from the attackers, attackers and defenders change roles.

To Increase Difficulty

- Change the starting position of the defenders. Be sure you can keep the pressure on.
- Have each attacker try to take two consecutive passes. The defender must recover if beaten on the first ball and pressure the second move.
- Add three more pairs who stand beside the original players so there are two attacking lines about 3 metres apart. Both attackers offer, and both defenders work hard to push their attackers wide to cause an error or take an interception. Begin with each pair passing twice and build to five times. Vary the distance to the thrower and vary the distance between the attacking lines.

- Introduce a competitive element between attackers and defenders by allocating points for a successful pass for attackers and tips or intercepts by defenders. Challenge yourselves with drill variations.

Success Check

- Position well at the start.
- Force the attacker wide.
- Watch the player and the ball.
- Use quick feet.
- Attack the ball.
- Recover quickly.

Score Your Success

Defenders take 3 balls from the attackers = 10 points

Your score ___

Defence Drill 3. *Anticipation*

Two throwers stand about 4 metres apart and send shoulder passes back and forth. Four defenders stand between them but about 5 metres to one side. The first defender watches the first pass, judging its flight. As the thrower releases the second pass, the first defender runs at full speed to intercept the pass. If you have watched the first ball well, you should be able to guess the best chance to intercept it. The next defender repeats the process.

To Increase Difficulty

- Intercept the first ball.
- Throwers vary passes, using high balls and flat balls and including some bounce passes.
- Throwers and defenders vary the distance of their starting positions.
- The defender starts about halfway between the throwers. The throwers pass the ball back and forth as they move. The defender tries to intercept two passes to begin with,

building up to five passes. The throwers use the high ball until the defender's anticipation improves; then they put some speed and variety on the pass.

To Decrease Difficulty

- Coach calls "Go" to help the defender time his move.
- Defenders start the drill closer to the throwers.

Success Check

- Judge the flight and speed of the ball.
- Keep weight down.
- Attack the ball.
- Pull the ball in quickly.

Score Your Success

All 4 defenders complete 1 interception of the pass = 10 points

Your score ____

Defence Drill 4. *Defending the Pass*

The thrower has the ball. Stand next to your opponent about 5 metres away from the thrower. When your opponent offers to take a pass, the thrower releases the ball (figure 5.8). Contest the pass, but allow your opponent to take the pass. As soon as your opponent takes the pass, drop your weight and execute the recovery step you learnt in step 3. Use both legs to jump back and clear the legal space, keeping your arms down. Quickly raise your hands and pressure your opponent's throwing action. Reach out with both arms and hands, but be careful not to overbalance or you will obstruct.

Your opponent passes to the thrower, who drives behind you to take the pass. You are successful if your opponent delivers a poor pass or is called for a held ball. When the thrower has possession of the ball, restart the drill.

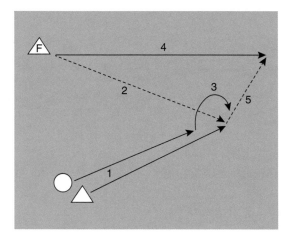

Figure 5.8   Defending the Pass drill.

To Increase Difficulty

- Vary your defence of the pass. Once you have cleared the distance, keep your arms down and wait to try to intercept the pass. Attackers can be lulled into thinking that you are not going to intercept if you keep your hands down. They may even step forward and shorten the distance because they do not see the physical barrier that raised arms present.
- Have your opponent offer and re-offer before taking the pass. You must defend well enough to be able to contest the pass as it comes in and then recover to pressure the pass as it is released.

Success Check

- Recover quickly.
- Clear the legal distance while keeping your arms down.
- Hold your arms and hands up once you are the legal distance away.
- Apply pressure to the throwing arm of the attacker with the ball.

Score Your Success

Successful defensive pressure results in your opponent's delivering a poor pass or being called for a held ball. Earn 10 points if you complete 5 successful executions of defensive pressure on the pass.

Your score ___

Defence Drill 5. *Diamond Defence*

Six players start the drill. Four players (the posts) stand in a diamond formation; the two on the sides are slightly offset. The attacker and defender stand about 2 metres from the player with the ball at the top of the diamond. The attacker must work a ball off each post while the defender maintains pressure on each ball, trying to tip or intercept the pass or force an error.

To Increase Difficulty

- Vary the size of the diamond by closing it down or opening it up.
- The defender must complete three clean interceptions.
- Add another attacker and defender.

Success Check

- Eyes on the player and the ball.
- Weight down.
- Strong positioning.
- Good anticipation.
- Attack the ball.
- Quick recovery.

Defence Drill 6. *Square Defence*

Mark an 8-metre square with four cones. One feeder stands on each side of the square, four feeders in all, one with a ball. Two defenders and an attacker are inside the square. To start the drill, the feeders and attacker work together to keep the ball moving (figure 5.9). The only rule is that the passer cannot pass the ball back to the player she received the ball from. Defenders can attempt to intercept any pass.

The defenders have to work every ball—driving hard, trying for the intercept, recovering and pressuring the ball if the first attempt is unsuccessful. When the defenders complete three successful defensive touches or interceptions, they and the attacker change places with three throwers and start the drill again.

To Increase Difficulty

- Work until the defenders have five successful defensive touches.
- Move the markers out 2 metres. Have another attacker and defender in the square.
- Add another attacker to the square.

Success Check

- See players and the ball
- Anticipate the pass.
- Attack the ball.
- Recover quickly.
- Keep defence tight.

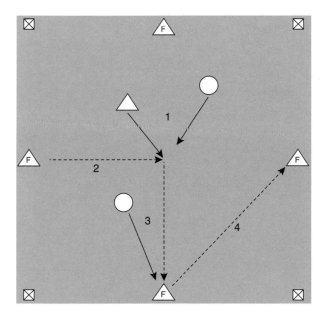

Figure 5.9 Square Defence drill.

Defence Drill 7. *Defender in the Middle*

For these drills, you do not shadow your partner and chase him across the court. Instead you will learn to sit back and focus on both ball and player movements, waiting for your chance to intercept the right pass. If you can learn to anticipate well on court, you will cause many problems for your opponents.

1. Five players stand in a circle about 5 metres apart from each other. A defender is in the middle (figure 5.10a). Players pass the ball around the circle, varying the types of passes they use, however they cannot pass to the players on either side of them. The defender has to anticipate the pass to intercept. If the defender is close to the ball, he puts his arms up over the ball to try to direct the pass, then recovers again to another defending position. Work eight balls.

2. Two throwers stand facing each other 3 metres apart. One has the ball. The defender stands behind the thrower without the ball (figure 5.10b). The throwers use two-handed straight passes to pass to each other and attempt to keep the ball moving between them. The defender uses a figure-eight movement to move between and around the throwers, trying to intercept each pass. When

the defender has attempted to intercept eight passes, he changes places with one of the throwers and the drill starts again.

To Increase Difficulty

• In the first part of the drill, increase to 10 or 12 balls.

• Increase the number of players. Up to eight players form the circle. Two defenders are in the middle, and they must work as a unit. One defender works the ball closest to him with his arms over, trying to force a high pass, while the other defender tries to intercept the pass.

• In the second part of the drill, take 6 balls from 10 attempts.

• Vary the passes to include high and low balls.

• The defender begins in reverse position so he is not facing the ball at the start of the drill or when moving behind a feeder, however the head is turned to see the ball.

• Vary the distance between the throwers by closing space down or opening it up.

To Decrease Difficulty

• Feeders use very slow passes until the defender gains confidence.

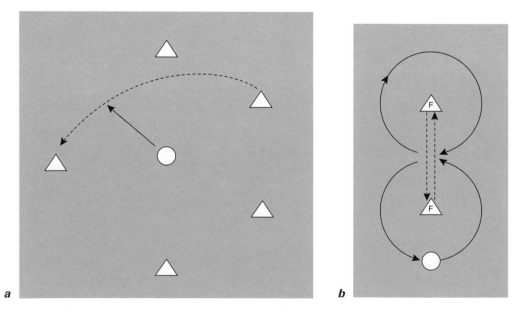

a   b

Figure 5.10   Defender in the Middle drill: *(a)* circle variation; *(b)* figure-eight variation.

Success Check

- Keep your eyes on the ball.
- Keep your weight down.
- Anticipate when to intercept.
- Attack the ball strongly.
- Recover quickly.
- No contact.

For the first part of the drill, complete 2 touches or interceptions = 5 points

For the second part of the drill, take 4 balls = 5 points

Your score ___

SUCCESS SUMMARY OF DEFENDING

Strong defence can win matches. Your ability to keep your opponents under constant pressure for four quarters will force them to make mistakes and create more opportunities for your team to score.

Use a variety of defending positions to unsettle your opponent. Make sure that you can chase your opponent around the court and that you can also anticipate when to run out for that spectacular interception. Finally, know the rules of obstruction and contact and play within them.

Before moving on to step 6, Combining Attack and Defence, evaluate how you did on the defensive drills in this step. Tally your scores to determine how well you have mastered the defending strategies and skills needed to thwart the attack. If you scored at least 50 points, you are ready to move on to step 6. If your score is 30 to 50 points, redo the drills to improve your score before you move on. If your score is less than 30 points, review step 5 and redo the drills before you move on to the next step.

Defence Drills

1. Shadowing	___ out of 10
2. Line Defence	___ out of 10
3. Anticipation	___ out of 10
4. Defending the Pass	___ out of 10
5. Diamond Defence	___ out of 10
6. Square Defence	___ out of 10
7. Defender in the Middle	___ out of 10
Total	___ *out of 70*

Now that you have learnt the skills of attack and defence, you are ready to combine them in step 6. This step will have you moving quickly from attack to defence, which takes you closer to real match conditions.

Combining Attack and Defence

So far we have looked at all of the game's basic skills: catching, passing, body movements, footwork, attacking and defending. Now it is time to put these basics together, to combine skills. In this step, we describe a number of ways to achieve this: drills, minor games and modified games.

The drills we have used to date have been designed to practise the specific skill covered in the step. This step is designed to get you to use two or three skills at once or in very quick succession. When you go on court to play netball, you need to be able to do two or three things almost simultaneously.

Minor games are great for practising individual skills. The competitiveness of the game situation allows you to build patterns of play that become the basis of team play. Minor games also provide an opportunity for the coach and the athletes to develop their sense of teamwork, to support and encourage each other's efforts and to advise in a constructive manner. In addition, they are fun.

Modifying the rules of netball brings us closer to match conditions. Modified games allow you to gain confidence on the court before you play that all-important first game.

Don't forget that the skills and practices we have introduced so far are the basic skills you need to play the game. In this fast-moving game you need to think quickly and look for new ways of doing things. Be creative—the new and the original add another dimension to your play.

On the netball court, skills are not used in isolation. When you handle the ball, you have to catch, land, pivot, read the attacking and the timing cue and then pass the ball—all within 3 seconds. That is busy! Also, your opponent will probably be defending you all this time.

When you are in defence, you have to try to dictate the space, pressure the move, intercept, recover and then go again. You really have to keep your focus to succeed defensively.

You also need to be able to swing quickly from attack to defence and vice versa to capitalise on the mistakes you force your opponents to make.

Combining skills enables you to practise in match-like conditions. It challenges you to do two or three things simultaneously or in sequence. It also helps you to understand the significance of the skills you have learnt so far.

COMBINING MOVES

You already have some experience joining movements together. Remember in step 4 when you had to offer and then re-offer your attacking moves? Success depends on your ability to read the play and react to the opportunities. Timing is crucial. Arriving too soon or too late can nullify all your hard work.

In defence you also began to combine moves using the recovery step (step 5). After working hard to dictate the space an attacker uses, you chased hard. When you were unsuccessful, you quickly dug in and recovered from the attacker.

However, combining movements does not relate to simply attacking and defending in isolation. It includes changing from one role to the other quickly to ensure that you capitalise on each possession. This is called *transition*.

Turnovers

When a turnover happens—for example, you intercept the pass—pull the ball in quickly and treat it like gold; it is. Be sure that you use it wisely and well; otherwise, all that great effort is lost.

Spatial awareness is the key. Look down court—way down court—quickly. Can you see a target for a safe, long pass? If so, go for it. A well-delivered long pass quickly shifts the momentum to the attacking team. However a poorly delivered ball sets up the defender to take a great interception and quickly swings the momentum back to your opponents. Use the long ball only if you believe it is on.

Don't be afraid to take the safe option. Watch the rush of excitement that sometimes comes with a turnover from a spectacular interception. Be disciplined and remember that the aim is to get the ball safely down court to your shooters. If it takes 10 passes to get there, so be it. The critical point is that your shooters get that all-important shot.

If you can capitalise on turnovers, you will be a very formidable team.

Misstep
You take the interception but throw away the pass.

Correction
On intercepting make sure you have good balance and control before you release the ball. Remember, you have to change quickly from defence to attack.

Double Play

Successful execution of the double play (figure 6.1) leaves you feeling good. It also helps move the ball very rapidly in attack. The centre and wing attack frequently use double play at the centre pass. Defenders use it to bring the ball out of the back third, whereas shooters love to use it when they have a clear run into the goal circle.

To execute the double play well, you have to combine two attacking moves with a quick hand-off to your nearest team member. It requires good judgment of court space and well-timed moves. To execute a double play, the attacker takes possession of the ball. She makes a quick pass off to a teammate nearby and then re-offers, using a strong down-court drive to take the next pass.

Figure 6.1   Double Play

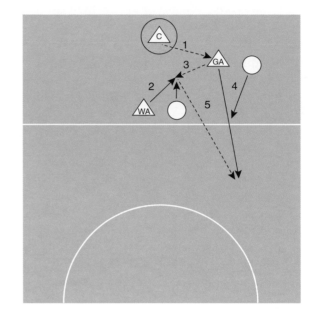

PREPARATION

1. Take possession of ball
2. Move weight down
3. Keep body balanced
4. Look down court

EXECUTION

1. Pass off (3)
2. Re-offer down court
3. Keep eyes on ball
4. Extend to take pass (5)

FOLLOW-THROUGH

1. Land and balance
2. Look for passing options

Misstep
The ball is intercepted.

Correction
Check the selection and delivery of your pass.

Misstep
You drop the ball.

Correction
You are going too fast. Slow down. Ground your landed foot and maintain good balance. Keep your eyes on the ball.

COMBINATION DRILLS

In netball terms, when we talk of combining skills, we refer to combining the basic skills of attack and defence into short bursts of play. The explosive nature of netball requires players to switch from one role to the other and back again in a very short span of time. The drills and games in this step enable you to experience these on-court demands.

Combination Drill 1. *Passing Under Pressure*

You have worked at throwing techniques and developing an accurate pass. Now it is time to put your knowledge and skills to the test by placing them under some strong defending. To be successful in this drill, you need to work on the third aspect of passing—making good decisions when selecting the right pass. In this drill, you will work the throw the same way you will on court during a game.

Mark the right half of a third with cones. Three attackers and one defender stand in this area (figure 6.2). Nominate each attacker to be either first, second or third. Attackers move freely in this court space, passing the ball between them. Each time the first attacker catches the ball, the defender quickly puts a strong defence on the

pass. When the first attacker is able to complete three successful passes while being pressured from the defender, replace the defender with a new player who pressures the second attacker's pass. Rotate so you all get a chance at being both an attacker and a defender.

To Increase Difficulty

- Add a second defender who applies some defence to either of the two attackers who are not under defensive pressure on the pass.
- Add a third defender. Each attacker is now under full defensive pressure on moves and passes.
- Finally, add a fourth defender to allow a double defence on an attacking player's passes. Each time a player releases the ball, two defenders have their arms outstretched to pressure the pass. This amount of pressure tests the attacker's ability to accurately select and execute the appropriate pass.

Success Check

- Attackers assess the defence.
- Attackers select and execute passes accurately.
- Defender focuses on the player and the ball.
- All players display good decision making.

Score Your Success

Attacking player being pressured completes 3 passes = 10 points

Defending player forces 3 bad passes or held ball calls = 10 points

Your score ___

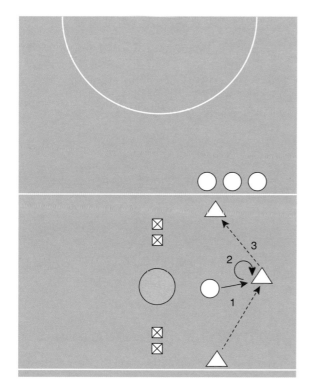

Figure 6.2   Passing Under Pressure drill.

Combination Drill 2.   *Across the Third*

You can work this drill across any third of the court. It begins simply with two attackers and one defender, but when you increase the difficulty by using three attackers and four defenders, it develops into a challenging drill.

To start play, two attackers stand on the sideline outside the court area; one has the ball. The defender is on the court. The attacker without the ball enters the playing area. The other attacker passes the ball to the on-court attacker and then enters the playing area; the attackers work the ball across the third (figure 6.3). The defender applies pressure to either player as they move across the third.

The attackers keep passing to each other, trying to reach the other side of the court without losing possession of the ball. The defender tries

to force an error. When the attackers are able to cross the court without losing possession of the ball, the players rotate to take the ball back across the third. When the defender causes an attacking error, substitute another defender so the first defender can have a rest. Make the changes quickly so players have to adjust immediately. If they lose possession of the ball, the attackers return to their starting positions and restart their run across the third.

To Increase Difficulty

- Add another attacker and defender so three attackers and two defenders are participating.
- Even up the ratio by adding a third defender so it is three attackers on three defenders.
- Overload the defenders by adding another defender. This makes it three attackers and four defenders. The additional defender really tests the skills of the attackers.

Success Check

- Attackers offer strongly and vary movement.
- Attackers make good decisions and pass accurately to the space.
- Attackers make strong re-offers.
- Defenders focus on the player and the ball.
- Defenders recover quickly to defend the pass.
- Go again. Persist.

Score Your Success

Attackers keep possession of the ball until they reach the far sideline = 5 points

Defender tips or intercepts the ball = 5 points

Your score ____

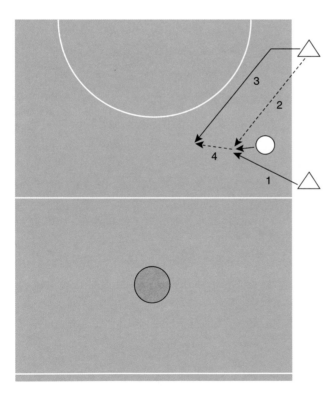

Figure 6.3   Across the Third drill.

Combination Drill 3. *Square Ball*

Create two teams of four players each. Each team wears a different coloured bib. Use cones to mark a 12-metre square on the playing court. Three members of each team stand inside the square. The fourth member, the substitute player, stands outside the square. The attacking team must work within the square.

Start the drill with team A in possession of the ball and team B in defence. Team A passes the ball among themselves until they make an error (figure 6.4). The coach umpires the rules of play within the square and calls an error when the attacking team loses possession of the ball or when a member of either team commits a rule violation.

Team B takes possession of the ball when team A makes an error and attempts to complete more passes than team A. When a team concludes its attacking attempt by making an error, the substitute player enters the square and rotates to a position within the team. Players must adjust roles quickly or be penalised. Both teams have three attempts to score the highest number of passes while in attack.

To Increase Difficulty

- Vary the size of the square.
- Overload the defending team. Allow the substitute player to enter the square as an extra player when his team is on defence. This means that there are three attacking players and four defending players in the square. The substitute on the attacking team remains outside the square.

To Decrease Difficulty

- Remove a defender from the play.

Success Check

- Maintain defensive pressure.
- Attack and execute confidently.
- Change roles quickly and smoothly.

Score Your Success

Team that completes the most attacking passes from 3 attempts = 10 points

Your score ____

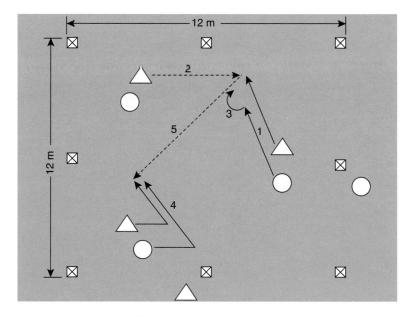

Figure 6.4   Square Ball drill.

Combination Drill 4.   *Down-Court Attack*

The Down-Court Attack drill and the Two in Each Third drill are designed to help you get the ball moving between thirds.

For the Down-Court Attack drill, divide the court in half longways, from goal line to goal line. Organise two teams of six players; both teams wear coloured bibs. Team A is in attack. Its members are in two groups of three behind the goal line. Team B is in defence with two members on the court in each third (figure 6.5). Team A tries to

bring the ball down court. The first three attacking players work together to keep possession of the ball as they take it from one goal line down the court to the other. As the attackers enter each third, the two defenders of team B try to force an error. If they achieve this, the attackers run to the end of the court. When both groups from team A have attempted their down-court attacks, change the roles of the teams. Make this a very quick changeover so players have to adjust to their new roles instantly.

To Increase Difficulty

- Reduce the number of players in the attacking group to two. (The attacking team lines up in pairs behind the goal line.) All three pairs attempt to bring the ball down court before the teams change over.
- Close down the working area to two thirds. Players must adjust to the reduced court space.

Success Check

- Look down court first, then narrow your focus.
- Use good spatial awareness.
- Maintain pressure on defence.

Score Your Success

First team to complete 3 down-court attacks = 10 points

Your score ___

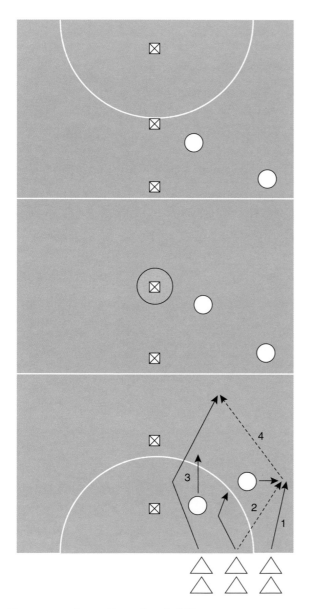

Figure 6.5   Down-Court Attack drill.

Combination Drill 5.   *Two in Each Third*

This is a more court-related version of combination drill 4. The attacking team is on court in the same way as the defenders: two in each third (figure 6.6). The attackers start with the ball at one end and must bring it safely down court. All players are restricted to the third of the court in which they start. Each player on the attacking team must handle the ball. The coach blows the whistle to start play. Each time the attacking team reaches the other end of the court, it scores 1 point. The ball remains with the attackers until they make an error. When the attacking team makes an error, it becomes the defending team. The winning team is the first one to score 3 points. Make sure you quickly transition from attack to defence. The coach or umpire should apply the 3-second rule quite vigorously.

Success Check

- Look down court first, then narrow your focus.
- Use good spatial awareness.
- Make good decisions.
- Complete accurate passes.
- Maintain pressure on defence.

Score Your Success

First team to score 3 points = 10 points

Your score ___

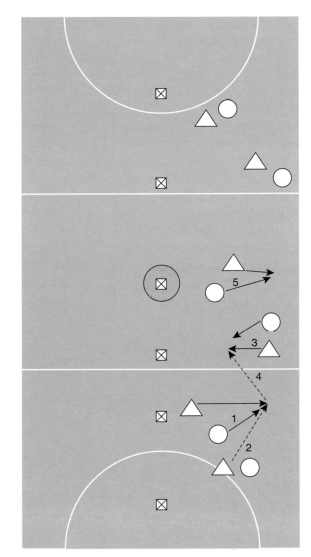

Figure 6.6   Two in Each Third drill.

Combination Drill 6. *Turnover*

This drill aims to simulate the options that are available when a turnover occurs. Team A has six players on court in the centre third and its attacking third. They are lined up as shown in figure 6.7. Their opponents are in the defensive role. Goalkeeper (GK), goal defence (GD) and wing defence (WD) closely mark their partners. Centre (C), wing attack (WA) and goal attack (GA) stand beside each other at the top of the goal circle about 1 metre apart. The drill starts with these three players executing a fast, three-man weave while travelling down the centre of the court towards the centre circle. All players closely watch the ball movement. Once the trio has passed the centre circle, it releases the ball directly to one of the midcourt players (GD, WD or C). This player reacts to take the intercept or loose ball. As this player controls the ball, the trio who had been weaving with the ball quickly runs to defend their opponents.

The attackers react to the turnover by quickly putting out strong offers. The player with the ball immediately scans down court to see if a long ball, preferably to a shooter, is on. Spatial awareness is critical. The long ball is the best option, but it requires good judgment to succeed. If the long ball is not on, the attacker selects a safe option and works hard to get the ball safely down court for a shot. When the attacking team loses possesion, both teams quickly change roles and restart the drill. The winning team is the first team to make three shots at goal from three turnovers. An alternative approach is to give each team 5 attempts. The winner is the team with the highest score.

To Increase Difficulty

- The ball can be released any time after the trio doing the three-man weave enters the centre third.
- Raise the goal to five shots at goal. Make it so the winning team has to get five consecutive shots at goal.

Success Check

- Focus on the ball.
- React quickly to the turnover.
- Look down court first.
- Keep possession and get the ball into the goal circle.
- Have spatial awareness.

Score Your Success

First team to take 3 shots at goal from 3 turnovers = 10 points

Your score ____

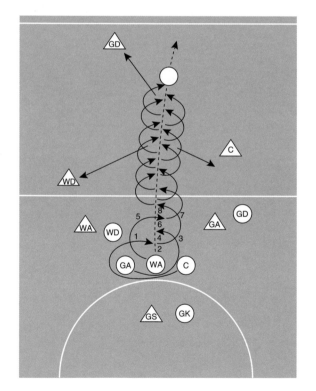

Figure 6.7   Turnover drill.

Combination Drill 7. *Minor Game: End Ball*

In this game, the ball travels up and down the court. Players attack and defend the ball as they do in a game of netball. Use either the full length of the court or one of the end thirds. Organise two teams of equal numbers and designate one player from each team as the end player (figure 6.8). If you are using the full court, the end player stands in the goal circle. If you are using one third of the court, the end player stands in a hoop beyond the sideline. Evenly space out the rest of the team, each with an opponent in a one-on-one style. Start the game at the centre of the area with a toss-up between different pairs each time.

When a team passes the ball successfully down court to its end player, it scores 1 point. If you are using goalposts, a team can score an extra point if it can convert the pass into a goal. The team must make at least three throws before the end player can catch the ball. If a player drops the ball, the game restarts with the opposing team throwing into play from the end player's area. After a score, change the end player and start the drill again with another pair taking the toss-up in the centre.

Very young players are allowed 6 seconds to handle the ball and also are allowed to shuffle their feet. Older players should use the netball rules of 3-second possession and no contact or obstruction; they should also adhere to the footwork rule.

End player

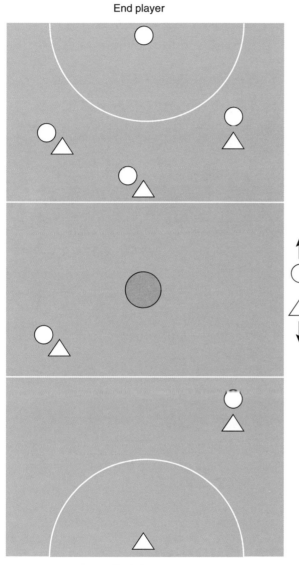

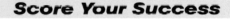

End player

Figure 6.8 Minor Game: End Ball.

Success Check

- Attackers find open space.
- Players control the ball.
- Bodies are well balanced.
- Defenders apply pressure.

Score Your Success

First team to score 5 points = 10 points

Your score ___

Combination Drill 8.   *Minor Game: Island Ball*

In this game, the defenders have to back their judgment to intercept, while the attackers require accurate, quick passing. Use cones to mark an area 8 by 16 metres, and divide this area into two side-by-side courts (figure 6.9). Organise two teams of six players. Four members of team A stand in the corners of their court, and four members of team B stand in the corners of their court. These players are the islanders. The remaining two players are the defenders, and they stand in the middle of their opponents' courts.

Start the game with a toss-up between a pair of defenders on the centre line. The winner passes the ball to his team's court. The islanders pass the ball among themselves while the defenders try to intercept and pass the ball across to their side. A team scores 1 point when its islanders complete four consecutive passes. When a point is scored, change one defender with an islander.

Success Check

- Watch the ball.
- Pass accurately.
- Decide which ball to intercept.
- Drive hard and extend toward the ball.

Score Your Success

First team to score 10 points = 10 points

Your score ____

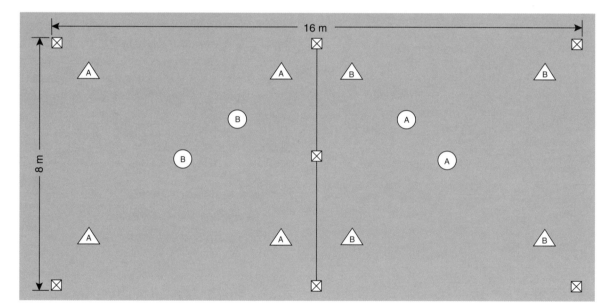

Figure 6.9   Minor Game: Island Ball.

Combination Drill 9.   *Minor Game: Numbers*

This game helps you to improve your passing in attack and your anticipation skills in defence. Mark off the centre half of one third of the court with cones. Number the attackers 1, 2, 3 and 4. Play a game of Keeping Off among the four attackers with the ball and two defenders wearing coloured bibs. The attackers must call a number as they throw. Six successful passes score 1 point for the attackers. The defenders score by touching the ball or by forcing the catching attackers outside the marked area. When a team reaches 5 points, two defenders and attackers change places.

Success Check

- Accurate passes.
- Strong moves in attack.
- Defensive pressure to cause attacking errors.

First team to score 5 points = 10 points

Your score ___

Combination Drill 10. *Modified Games*

Modifying the rules brings you close to match play. Following are some ways to do this:

- Modify the court to use one or two thirds or half the court or eliminate the goal circles.
- Modify the rules to allow more time (4 seconds) or less time (2 seconds) to handle the ball.
- Modify the footwork rule to allow an extra step for young players or no step for seniors to make them dig in on every ball.
- Modify the number of players on a team— one shooter only, no wing attack or no wing defence.

Use your imagination to create drills that simulate the game and stimulate players. Here is one example to help you on your way. It is played across one third of the court.

This game uses two teams of five players. Use one third of the netball court with two portable goalposts in the middle of each sideline. For each team, designate two attackers, two defenders and a centre, and position them as shown in figure 6.10.

Rules

- Teams toss for ends and centre pass.
- The winning captain elects to take the pass or identify the team's goal end.
- Only the two attacking players on a team can shoot for goal.
- A team earns 1 point if a shot hits the goal ring and 2 points if it passes through.
- Play restarts with a centre pass after each score.
- Centre players take turns passing the ball.
- Players rotate positions after each score.
- Players are allowed 6 seconds to pass and may take two steps with the ball. As players become more adept, apply the normal rules of the game.

Success Check

- Move into open space.
- Choose the correct pace.
- Keep body well-balanced.
- Apply pressure on defence.

First team to score 10 points = 10 points

Your score ___

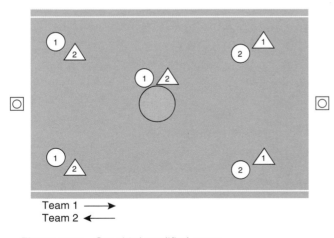

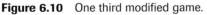

Team 1 ⟶
Team 2 ⟵

Figure 6.10   One third modified game.

SUCCESS SUMMARY FOR COMBINING SKILLS

A successful team must be able to combine attacking movements with good timing and accurate passing. The more variation in your movement and your passing, the harder you make it for your opponents.

When your opponents have the ball, it is all about your team working hard to defend every pass. Although defence may feel unglamorous, it will wear down the opposition and force mistakes.

Make sure that you capitalise on turnovers. Don't let all that hard work go unrewarded. Know when to use the long ball to send it way down court and when to slow it down and use a safe, close option.

Before moving on to step 7, The Front Third and Goal Shooting, evaluate how you did on the drills in this step. Tally your scores to determine how well you have mastered the skills to transition well from attack to defence and from defence to attack. If you scored at least 90 points, you are ready to move on to step 7. If your score is 60 to 89 points, redo the drills to improve your score before you move on. If your score is less than 60 points, review step 6 and redo the drills before you move on to the next step.

Combination Drills

1. Passing Under Pressure	___ out of 20
2. Across the Third	___ out of 10
3. Square Ball	___ out of 10
4. Down-Court Attack	___ out of 10
5. Two in Each Third	___ out of 10
6. Turnover	___ out of 10
7. Minor Game: End Ball	___ out of 10
8. Minor Game: Island Ball	___ out of 10
9. Minor Game: Numbers	___ out of 10
10. Modified Games	___ out of 10
Total	___ *out of 110*

We have now covered all the basics and learnt how to combine attack and defensive play. In step 7, we focus our attention on the specialist skills required to play in the front third. You will learn the important roles of the shooters and their feeders, the wing attack and centre.

The Front Third and Goal Shooting

The division of the netball court into thirds provides a unique characteristic of the game. Each third requires players to develop certain skills and tactics so they can play effectively within that court space. The next three steps look at each third and focus on the skills that will assist you to perform well in your chosen area of the court.

The back third is home to defensive specialists, who aim to restrict the opposition from scoring. The centre third is for athletic players who love to run. They link the defence and attack thirds, have the most court space to cover and need to run all game. The front third is where the attacking specialists work; they produce the team's score.

When you first play netball, make sure you have a run in each third. Then you can choose your preferred third from experience. Consider your strengths and the composition of your team before you nominate your position.

It is exciting to play in the front third. You have the chance to put the finishing touches on your team's down-court play, whether it's by placing one of those really delicate passes on the fingertips of your shooters or actually putting the ball through the ring and scoring a goal.

This step has two parts. We will begin by looking at the skills that the attacking unit needs to take the ball safely to the shooters. Then we will focus on the shooters, their techniques and ways to develop those crucial conversion rates. We aim for an 80 percent conversion rate or higher, which means that shooters must put in a lot of quality practice every day to ensure that they can finish off their team's good work.

SPECIALISING IN THE FRONT THIRD

The key function of the front third of the court is to attack—to deliver the ball safely to the team's shooters, who convert a high percentage of shots to goals. Scoring more goals than your opponent wins netball matches.

The hallmark of successful attack work is organisation. In a sport that requires you to make accurate split-second decisions, a basic plan is essential. A basic plan helps all athletes to understand their roles and enables them to more accurately time their movements. Of course, drilling until you are mechanical is not the answer either. The plan should provide the basic framework that is embellished by individual interpretation and ability. A healthy balance between order and flair creates an exciting, winning attack.

ORGANISING THE ATTACK THIRD

Given the importance of the shooters—they are the only people who can score—other team members should be responsible for bringing the ball down the court to them. The goal attack should not be the dominant centre-court player. Others can fulfil that role. The goal attack needs to be most effective in her area of specialisation: the attack third.

This thinking holds that one shooter should always be at home, in the goal circle, ready to take any ball that a team member decides is safe to pass in. It is interesting to note how often a surprise long ball from the centre third that is passed straight into the goal circle can find its mark.

In attack it is important to develop variety, which allows you to maintain possession. One way to do this is to organise the offers and to have a plan for the attack end that clearly identifies the role of the shooters during match play. There are many ways to achieve this. Here are a few examples.

Shooter Has the Circle

The team has a dominant goal shooter who is allowed to work the circle. The goal attack, wing attack and centre do all the attack work outside the circle. They combine well to deliver the ball to the goal shooter. The goal attack times her run into the goal circle, ready to offer if needed. The non-shooter takes a good position near the post for the rebound. When the team gives the goal shooter the circle, there is a high expectation that the goal shooter will offer strongly and shoot accurately.

Shooters Alternate the Lead

The shooter who has the lead takes the first ball that comes into the attack third. If needed, that player drives up hard to the transverse line to pull the ball into the front third. The other shooter works in the goal circle. One shooter calls for the lead to change. This usually occurs as the ball is returned to the centre after a goal has been scored. The shooters reverse roles until the lead changes again.

This tactic works well when both shooters are mobile players who can share the shooting and playing workload. Wing attack and centre play a secondary role, reading their moves from the shooters. They wait for a shooter to commit to a space before they offer. This avoids the problem of the outside feeder and a shooter heading for the same court space.

Shooters Are Playing Deep

The shooters are operating in the back half of the attacking third, towards the goal line. They wait for the wing attack and centre to work the ball into the front third before they begin to offer. The goal attack usually takes the first pass from the feeding players and then tries to pass it directly to the goal shooter (figure 7.1). This

96

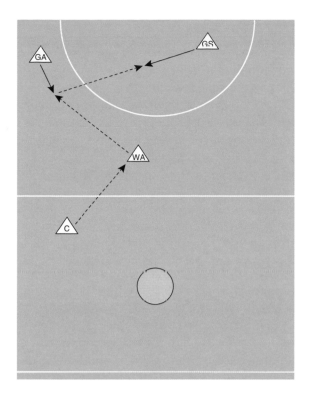

Figure 7.1 Shooters are playing deep.

play works well if shooters can work together as a unit; it does not demand the mobility needed to alternate the lead.

The Circle Is Closed

Both shooters operate in the circle; neither moves outside to take a pass. They wait patiently for the ball to be brought down court by other team members. Once the ball is on the edge of the circle, they offer strongly and try to take the ball in a good shooting position. This allows them to go straight to the goalpost to take a shot at the goal.

Closing the goal circle allows the shooters to concentrate on scoring, because they are working in a confined space. Both shooters need to be adept at working in the goal circle at the same time. When two defenders are also present, space is limited. For the goal shooter, holding her position becomes a key factor for success.

Other team members need to work harder on the down-court attack when the circle is closed. In particular the wing defence and goal defence must follow through the full centre third

and stay on the transverse line to back up the front-third attack.

The Lead Is Split

The goal shooter leads to balls that enter the front third from the left-hand side of the court as the goal attack leads to balls that come down the right-hand side. The shooter who does not lead is in the goal circle ready to take any ball that is passed in. When the leading shooter has taken the ball, he plays it on to the other shooter or to the feeders, and then drives hard into the goal circle. It is important to make sure the entry does not cut across another team member's path, particularly the shooting partner.

This is an easy way to sort the attack when you have two mobile shooters who are accurate and enjoy sharing the workload.

The Double Play

One of the shooters has the lead and drives out to take the ball as it enters the front third. The shooting partner prepares to offer in the circle. The leading shooter passes to one of the feeders, who attempts to take the ball close to the circle's edge. The feeder looks to the circle as if to pass to the shooter inside. This shooter uses a clearing run to exit the circle. The leading shooter enters the circle and drives hard to the goalpost to complete the double play (figure 7.2).

This is a good change of tactic best employed when the shooter on the lead has quite clearly lost her defender. This play allows her to drive home the momentum established outside the circle.

These are a few ideas for organising the attack; there are many more. You will enjoy planning your attacking moves and working out ways to communicate the play. Some teams use numbers; others use names.

Good attacking ends are organised and very skilful at changing their play at appropriate times. Don't wait until your moves have totally broken down before changing your pattern of play. Develop a feel for this. When you see the signs that your opponents have caught on to your strategy, change quickly to another pattern.

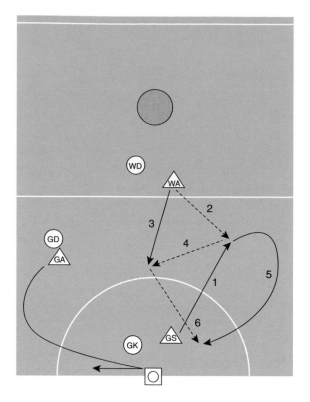

Figure 7.2 The double play.

Throw-Ins

The wing attack or centre should take throw-ins that are in the attacking third and outside of the goal circle. This allows the attack to operate with both shooters able to offer. Using a shooter to throw in outside the circle unnecessarily limits a team's options for attack. Because the on-court feeder is often under double defence, a clever tactic for this player is to use a clearing run to draw both the wing defence and centre away from the intended pass. This creates space for one of the shooters to work in.

Rebounds

Shooters should be able to contest the rebound successfully: It means goals. The shooter who is not taking aim should move quickly to the goalpost to cover the side of the ring opposite the shooting partner (figure 7.3, *a* and *b*). The ideal position is about half a step from the goalpost, feet at a wide stance, weight down, and eyes focused on the ball.

| Figure 7.3 | Rebounding |

PREPARATION

1. Get in position quickly
2. Hold position strongly
3. Keep eyes on the ball

a

b

c

EXECUTION

1. Shooter follows ball to post
2. Shooter not shooting elevates strongly
3. Good timing and body control required
4. Shooters contest ball strongly
5. Rebounding shooter pulls ball in quickly or taps ball safely

FOLLOW-THROUGH

1. Cushion landing
2. Control ball
3. Focus on ring
4. Remain steady then shoot

As the shot is released, turn to the post and watch the flight of the ball to the ring (figure 7.3c). If the shot is unsuccessful, jump strongly into the air to take possession or tap the ball to your shooting partner. The shooter who has executed the shot should follow the shot to the post and also contest the rebound. The rebound drills described in step 10 will provide good practice.

You are well equipped in the front third if you have three or four attacking plans that your team can execute with confidence. Once you have called for a particular play, use it whether you are operating from a centre pass, turnover or throw-in. Try to change your plan before the opposition has time to figure it out. Dictating the terms of play like this helps you win games.

FRONT-THIRD DRILLS

It is important that shooters work the circle together, have a feel for each other's movements and work in harmony. The feeders—the wing attack and centre—must be able to pass the ball to the shooters with pinpoint accuracy. The drills in this chapter are designed to assist you in developing these important skills. They start with simple tasks and limited defence. As your skill level and confidence rise, the defence increases to test you under match-like conditions.

Front-Third Drill 1. *Goal Circle Awareness*

Both shooters are in the circle. The feeders (the wing attack and centre) are on the outside with the ball. To start the drill, both shooters move freely within the circle. The feeders and shooters pass the ball from the outside to the inside of the goal circle and then back out again. After five passes, when the ball enters the circle for the third time, the shooter takes a shot.

To Increase Difficulty

- Add a defender inside the circle.
- Add two defenders and reduce the number of passes to three with one shot.
- Add the wing defence and centre outside the circle. Keep the number of passes to three with one shot.
- Split the circle in half, half on the left side of the post and half on the right side. Shooters must confine their movements to their halves.

- Split the circle in half, the top half of the circle and the back half. Shooters must confine their movements to their halves.

To Decrease Difficulty

- Reduce the number of successful passes to three and build up by two.

Success Check

- Move to space.
- Pass to space.
- Focus on the ball.
- Be aware of other players.

Score Your Success

Complete 5 successful passes and 1 shot = 5 points

Your score ___

Front-Third Drill 2. *Goal Circle Re-Entry*

A shooter and defender are inside the goal circle. The feeder (the wing attack or centre) is a few steps inside the transverse line of the attacking third. The shooter leads out to take a pass from the feeder, which the defender allows the shooter to take (figure 7.4). The defender then blocks the shooter's path to the circle. The feeder drives to the edge of the circle. The shooter passes to the feeder, then attempts to beat the defender, take the ball in the goal circle and score a goal.

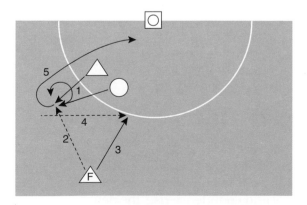

Figure 7.4 Goal Circle Re-Entry drill.

To Increase Difficulty

- The defender contests the first pass. If beaten, the defender adjusts and blocks the channel to delay entry to the goal circle.
- The shooter must work two balls in the goal circle before shooting.
- Add another defender who can double-defend the shooter or feeder.
- A second shooter and defender come on court. The shooter who is in the circle can offer alternative moves after the lead shooter has taken the first ball. The shooter outside the circle must be aware of all options available and re-enter the goal circle, aware of the positioning of the goal shooter and the space that is available.

To Decrease Difficulty

- Allow the defender to apply a token defence between the leading shooter and the feeder. Once the shooter begins to re-enter with confidence, work the drill as described.

Success Check

- Attack strongly.
- Watch the ball.
- Be aware of the defender.
- Create space and work in it.
- Learn to watch and operate off each other for successful attacking.

Front-Third Drill 3. *Taking the Lead*

This drill provides the opportunity for the goal shooter or goal attack to organise the lead. The goal shooter communicates the play to her attacking team members, who are on the court as shown in figure 7.5. Two defenders apply pressure in the attacking third; they are not marking specific players. They offer a floating defence and attempt to run and intercept loose balls. To start the drill, the centre, who is in the centre third, throws the ball into the air, then catches it. The attacking team brings the ball down court for a shot at goal.

To Increase Difficulty

- After scoring two goals, the goal attack calls for players to use a different lead. Continue in this manner until you have worked three or four lead changes.
- If your team really wants to use a certain play more frequently than the others, then allow the goal attack or goal shooter to call for this lead every other change.
- Add a third defender and allow the defending players to offer some one-on-one defence as well as some floating defence.
- Add a fourth defender to create full-pressure defence on the attackers.
- If you need extra pressure, introduce a fifth defender to really target a specific attacker or to float between players. In this case, the attack team's goal is to score one goal.

Success Check

- Good communication.
- Variation of movement.
- Well-timed moves.

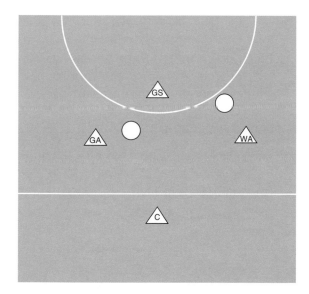

Figure 7.5 Taking the Lead drill.

Front-Third Drill 4. *Making Ground*

This drill assists the shooter who takes the ball on the outer perimeter of the goal circle to gain a closer shot.

The shooter has a ball and is in the shooting position facing the goalpost, a step or two inside the circle. A feeder (the wing attack or centre) is on the circle edge behind the shooter, just to the side of her shooting arm. The shooter takes aim, then quickly pulls the ball down, turns toward the feeder and flicks a quick pass. At the same time, the shooter quickly moves her back foot closer to the post. The feeder flicks the ball quickly back to the shooter, who quickly turns and faces the goalpost, then shoots. To be effective, the ball and players must move with speed.

Add a defender to the drill to defend the shot. The shooter must make sure she does not contact the defender with her foot when she steps closer to the goalpost. It is best for the shooter to slide her foot quickly towards the goalpost and then transfer her weight to both feet as she regains her stance.

Success Check

- Move with speed.
- Pass quickly.
- Slide the foot low and quickly.
- Recover, regain balance and shoot.

Score Your Success

Score 3 goals after gaining ground closer to the goalpost = 5 points

Your score ____

Front-Third Drill 5. *Using the Backup*

Although we are always keen to take the ball on the quickest route to the circle in match play, sometimes the players ahead are not timing well or their defenders are playing really well and you just can't take the ball forward. In this situation, you need to use the backup. When the ball goes back out of the attack third, it gives you time to re-set and re-offer.

Wing defence and goal defence are positioned near the attack transverse line. The shooters, wing attack and centre are in the attack third.

The ball is thrown on court in the attack third outside the goal circle. The nearest attacker retrieves the ball and looks into the goal circle to pass. She ignores the offer, then turns and passes the ball back to the centre third. The attack third players then have to re-set and re-offer to take the ball into the goal circle.

To Increase Difficulty

- Put defence on the backup players.
- Float two defenders in the attack third.

- Increase the number of defenders to three, then four.
- The first pass goes to the attack third and then to the backup players.
- Close down the court space by attacking only into the right side of the court, then the left side and then the centre corridor.

Success Check

- Wing defence and goal defence backup at all times.
- Good timing on attack.
- Good spatial awareness.
- Strong re-offers.

Score Your Success

Complete 4 successful attacking plays into the goal circle using the backup = 5 points

Your score ____

Front-Third Drill 6. *Back Line Throw-In*

In this drill, players practise the throw-in from the back of the goal circle (the goal line). Because either shooter can take the pass during a game, both should do so in practice. Both defenders defend the shooter in the circle. The wing attack and centre are well balanced on the edge of the circle. They are strategically placed on either side of the goal circle, about midway between the goal line and the centre of the circle. They are not defended.

As the shooter takes the throw-in, she should have three passing options available. The shooter in the circle offers first, and the wing attack and centre provide alternative moves if the shooter is well defended. The shooter passes the ball to the most appropriate offer, then quickly enters the goal circle and offers strongly in the direction opposite the other shooter.

To Increase Difficulty

- Add players to defend the outside feeders.
- Add defenders to the goal circle.

- The goal attack draws the defenders high in the circle. The shooter quickly passes a high ball, then steps onto the court to receive a strong flick or tap pass under the post. Now reverse roles.
- Use a fake or baulk pass from the throw-in.
- For a real challenge, the player taking the throw-in plays the ball off the goalpost and quickly steps onto the court before taking the ball. Remember, you will be penalised if you take the ball before you make contact with the court.

Success Check

- Options are easy to read.
- Offers are well timed.
- Pass is accurate.

Score Your Success

Score 5 goals from throw-ins taken near the post = 10 points

Your score ___

Front-Third Drill 7. *Sideline*

To begin the drill, the centre takes the sideline throw-in. Each throw-in is to be taken from a new position on the sideline. One defender is outside the circle and one is inside, and they float rather than pressure specific players. As the centre steps up behind the line, the goal attack and wing attack communicate who has the lead. The centre starts the drill by using the first offer. The ball is worked quickly onto the court and then into the circle, where the goal shooter takes a shot.

To Increase Difficulty

- Add a third defender to pressure the throw-in.
- Add a fourth defender and try to make three consecutive goals against a full defence.

- After two passes in the attack third, the ball must be played back into the centre third, using the backup players, forcing the attack end to re-offer to bring the ball into the goal circle.

Success Check

- See all available options.
- Vary movement.
- Use space wisely.
- Offer strongly.
- Pass accurately.

Score Your Success

Score 3 consecutive goals from sideline throw-ins = 10 points

Your score ___

GOAL SHOOTING

Netball has a unique shooting style. The ball is released high and usually while the shooter is stationary. In netball today, variations of the basic shot are used. The most common are derived from the high-release Australian style and the basketball-influenced Caribbean style.

The Australian style uses a high release with variation on the starting position. The Caribbean style commences in front of the body with a bent arm, but climbs to a point of release a little shorter than the Australian shot with a longer follow-through. Foot placement can vary—feet parallel, forward step onto non-grounded foot, or front and back stance.

Successful shooters aim for a minimum of 80 percent accuracy every time they take to the court. To achieve this accuracy, you need to be consistent in daily practice. If you choose to take on the responsibility of a shooting role, you must be prepared to commit to this regime.

Only two players on a netball team, the goal shooter and the goal attack, are allowed to shoot goals. All of the team's scoring comes from these two players, so you can see how important it is that they are accurate shooters. When the ball goes into the shooting position, the entire court and the audience focus on the outcome. A shooter needs to be cool, calm and collected under pressure.

Remember, netball matches are won by the team with the highest number of shots and the highest conversion rate (shooting percentage).

This is the responsibility that the shooters carry. You will know as soon as the ball leaves your hand whether your shot at the goal is successful or not. Developing good technique helps you to achieve a high conversion rate.

High Release

To execute the high release, begin by facing the goal ring with your feet shoulder-width apart, body upright and weight evenly distributed. Focus your eyes on the front middle section of the ring closest to you as you take your arm directly above your head until it is almost at full stretch. Always feel as if you can stretch a little bit farther. Rest the ball on the fingers of your shooting hand (figure 7.6a). Make sure your elbow and wrist are pointing towards the goal ring.

Place your non-shooting hand close to the ball but not on it in readiness for the release. Drop the wrist of your shooting hand backwards a few centimetres behind your head (figure 7.6b). As you drop the ball backwards, slowly bend your knees and gently put the non-shooting hand on the ball to steady it.

Move your wrist and fingers towards the ring, flicking the ball in a high arc (figure 7.6c). At the same time, take your non-shooting hand slightly off the ball and bring your body weight up to follow through on the shot. Your index finger is the last to follow through. This allows a slight backspin on the ball, which travels in a high arc to the post.

Misstep
The shot veers right or left.

Correction
Check that your fingers, wrist and elbow are lined up straight to the post. Use a straight follow-through to the ring.

Figure 7.6   High Release

PREPARATION

1. Facing goal ring
2. Feet shoulder-width apart
3. Body balanced
4. Eyes on front of ring
5. Arm almost fully extended with ball resting on fingertips
6. Wrist under ball
7. Wrist and elbow pointing to goalpost

a

EXECUTION

1. Drop wrist backwards a few centimetres behind head
2. Bend knees slowly
3. Place non-shooting hand gently on ball

b

(continued)

Figure 7.6 *(continued)*

FOLLOW-THROUGH

1. Flick ball with fingers and wrist
2. Slightly take non-shooting hand off ball
3. Aim to give ball high arc to ring
4. Index finger guides the release and imparts slight backspin
5. Bring body weight up
6. Follow through with fingers and wrists
7. Bring arms down

c

 Misstep
The shot is flat.

Correction
Check the starting position of your arm. Execute more drop at the top of the shot to ensure the ball travels in a high arc to the ring.

Misstep
You do not feel in control of the shot.

Correction
Go back to good basics. Check your balance. Focus on the ring. Run through a checklist of good shooting technique. Be confident.

For shots taken in close proximity to the goalpost, less leg bend is required. To generate more power to the shot as the length of the shot increases, you'll need to bend your knees further. For shots near the edge of the goal circle, you can also use a small jump to create extra power and lift on the ball.

Remember, the execution of the shot remains the same. Only the leg bend changes in relation to where you are in the goal circle to adjust the power of the shot.

STEPPING BEFORE A SHOT

Shooters should use the footwork rule to their advantage when a defender exerts strong pressure on the shot. A small sideways or backwards step creates more distance between the ball and the defender's arm. Shooters should also use the step to move closer to the goalpost when an appropriate opportunity arises. For example, when taking a penalty shot, step across in front of the defender to stop her coming in for the rebound. You need to have sound basic shooting technique before you begin to move.

Misstep
The defender is still able to pressure the release.

Correction
Lengthen your step. You are not gaining sufficient distance from your defender.

Misstep
You are off-balance when you shoot.

Correction
Shorten the step. It is too long and you are overbalancing.

As you take the catch, line up your shot and focus on the goal ring, ready to shoot (figure 7.8a). Quickly step onto the non-grounded foot to move away from the defender (figure 7.8b) or closer to the goalpost. Transfer your weight onto this foot, which initially was flat. Now transfer the weight up onto the ball of your foot. Staying well balanced, release the ball; then bring down the grounded foot and follow the shot into the post (figure 7.8c). Remember, if you reground your landed foot, you will be penalised for stepping.

Figure 7.8   Step Before a Shot

PREPARATION
1. Facing goal ring
2. Focused on front of ring
3. Body balanced
4. Arm almost fully extended and level with ear
5. Elbow and wrist pointing to goalpost

a

(continued)

Figure 7.8 *(continued)*

b

c

EXECUTION

1. Step away from defender
2. Transfer weight onto flat foot
3. Hold grounded foot just off surface
4. On release of the shot, come up onto the ball of the non-grounded foot
5. Remember footwork rule
6. Release ball

FOLLOW-THROUGH

1. Bring down grounded foot
2. Move to post for rebound

Misstep
The shot is too long.

Correction
Take your step and then pause momentarily. Focus on the goal ring before you release the shot.

A fair amount of experience is required to apply the step successfully. You need to know which foot you have landed on and be aware of the direction you need to step to gain an advantage for yourself. This is one of the game's advanced skills because you are shooting while balancing on one foot. Challenge yourself to attempt it when you are shooting consistently in match play.

SHOOTING DRILLS

To become a very good shooter, you need to practise daily. For beginners, a practice session should take about 10 minutes. Young athletes, up to 10 years of age, should work on a modified goalpost 2.43 metres (8 ft) high. As you begin to master the technique, increase the session to

15 minutes. Senior athletes should begin with a 20-minute session, building up to 30 minutes. All shooting sessions require total concentration because the aim is to be as accurate as possible.

The emphasis in preseason is on good shooting technique, which requires a daily shooting program. When the season commences, you maintain a daily program but include more variation of drills with some movement. During training, team opportunities will arise that will allow you to practise in match-type conditions with strong defence.

Shooting Drill 1. *Mirror Practice*

Stand in front of a mirror and line up your arms to shoot. Begin without a ball. As your technique improves, add a ball. Practise the movement as you watch yourself in the mirror.

Success Check

- Centre of the elbow points to the mirror.
- Centre of the wrist points to the mirror.
- Fingers of the shooting hand spread around the ball.

- Arm is above the head.
- Elbow and wrist point to the mirror as the hand drops slightly back behind the head.

Score Your Success

Shoot 5 imaginary goals using good form = 5 points

Your score ___

Shooting Drill 2. *Shooting With and Without the Goalpost*

Stationary shooting allows you to concentrate on technique, line-up, release and follow-through.

Place the ball on your shooting hand. Drop your hand backwards a few centimetres and flick the ball a metre or two directly above your head. The ball should arc straight up from your release.

Stand a step away from the goalpost. Prepare to shoot. Aim and release the ball so that it falls cleanly through the centre of the ring. Shoot until you hit five goals.

To Increase Difficulty

- Make the goals consecutive.
- Make the consecutive goals fall cleanly without touching the ring.
- Increase your starting distance from the goalpost.
- Gradually increase the number of consecutive successful shots to eight.
- Place the ball on the ground at your shooting spot. Sprint forwards four or five paces, turn and sprint back. Pick up the ball and shoot. Make three successful shots, sprinting between each one.

Success Check

- Keep the body balanced.
- Steady the ball with the non-shooting hand.
- Focus on the target.
- Position the arm and wrist in line.
- Bend the knee slightly.
- Follow through with the fingers and wrist.
- Impart a slight backspin on the ball.
- Ball arcs high on release.

Score Your Success

Ball arcs straight up from release 10 consecutive times = 5 points

Score 5 successful goals = 10 points

Your score ___

Shooting Drill 3. *Concentration*

Working with small back steps and small side steps allows you to develop concentration and refine your judgment. For each small step you take, you will need to adjust the pressure you put on the shot.

Start close to the goalpost. Begin with a successful shot. Take a small step backwards. From this position, make another successful shot. Step back again. Move only when your shot is successful.

Begin on the back line about 2 metres from the goalpost. Begin with a successful shot. Take a small step sideways. From that position, make another successful shot. Take another small side step, moving in an arc around the goalpost.

Use this drill to develop your ability to use the small side step to go around the circle as well as the small back step to go forwards and backwards to the goalpost.

To Increase Difficulty

- Score 10 goals from 10 attempts.

- Increase the number of steps to 8, then 10. Remember, do not take a step until you score a goal.

- Try for six consecutive goals from six consecutive steps. Can you increase this to eight?

- Reverse the steps. Start at the edge of the goal circle and take a step forwards when you score. Aim for six successful shots to start; then challenge yourself by increasing the number to 10 or 12.

- Score two goals from each point before you take a step.

- Gradually increase the length of your steps as your concentration and accuracy improve. The world's best shooters can start at the goalpost and step to the circle's edge before working in the reverse.

Success Check

- Keep the body balanced.
- Focus on the target.
- Elbow, wrist and fingers point to the post.
- Ball rests on the fingertips.
- Ball drops backwards as the knees bend.
- Follow through with the wrist and fingers.
- Ball has a high arc.

Score Your Success

Score 6 goals from 6 short backward steps = 5 points

Score 6 goals from 6 short side steps = 5 points

Your score ___

Shooting Drill 4. *Shaded Area*

This drill enables you to concentrate on your technique and to make judgments on the distance of the shot. Identify a specific area within the goal circle, for example, within 0.9 metres (3 ft) of the post, centre corridor or top half of the circle.

To begin, choose an area of the circle from which you are capable of making shots while maintaining good technique. When you have made five successful shots, choose another area that will challenge you a little more. (Advanced players should start with 10 successful shots.)

Once you are in match play, you should not only record the rate of success of your shooting (your shooting percentage) but also note the spot from which you take the shots. This will show the areas of the circle where you are struggling to convert. Use this drill to work on them.

To Increase Difficulty

- Score the goals consecutively.
- Juniors increase goals to 10.
- Seniors increase to 20.

- Introduce a feeder. Take a stationary ball, facing out of the circle. Turn to face the post, balance then shoot. Make one offer, take the pass, turn, balance and shoot. Remember to stay in the designated area at all times. Add a defender who defends the shot.

Success Check

- Focus on the ring.
- Judge the distance to the goalpost.

- Keep the body balanced.
- Keep the wrist and elbow pointed to the goalpost.
- Aim for a high arc to the ring.

Score Your Success

Score 5 goals (juniors) or 10 goals (seniors) from the shaded area = 10 points

Your score ____

Shooting Drill 5. *Shooting With Eyes Closed*

This is an excellent drill to develop a good feel for the post and to sharpen your concentration.

Stand close to the post, sight your target then close your eyes and shoot. As you release, learn to feel the distance you are shooting to the post. If you are really struggling, shoot a successful goal from the spot with your eyes open before you repeat the action with your eyes closed. Junior players try to score three successful goals with their eyes closed; senior players try to score five.

To Increase Difficulty

- Juniors build to five successful goals; seniors, to 10.
- Score the shots consecutively. Now move to another spot and repeat. Work only halfway out from the post.

- Have a feeder pass you the ball. Turn to the post, close your eyes and shoot. Start with the goal of three (juniors) or five (seniors) successful goals and then challenge yourself to increase this.

Success Check

- Body well balanced.
- Good technique.
- Good rhythm.
- Good timing.

Score Your Success

Score 3 goals (juniors) or 5 successful goals (seniors) with eyes closed = 10 points

Your score ____

Shooting Drill 6. *Square*

Identify a small square area (2 m) within the goal circle. Place the ball on the ground outside the square. Use short, sharp, high-intensity movements within the square until you are fatigued. Quickly pick up the ball and shoot five goals.

To Increase Difficulty

- Make the goals consecutive.
- If you miss, start that five again.
- As your work rate and accuracy improve, challenge yourself by gradually increasing the number of repetitions that you can do from the same spot. Do two sets of five then

increase the number of sets to three and then four.

Success Check

- High-intensity work rate.
- Variation of movement.
- Good technique.
- Accuracy at goal.

Score Your Success

Score 5 goals = 10 points

Your score ____

Shooting Drill 7.   *Shooting With Defence*

Working with a defender brings you closer to match-like conditions. Stand with a defender in the middle of the goal circle with the ball on the ground. Pick up the ball and assume a shooting position. The defender jumps back to the legal distance and raises his hands to pressure the shot. Take the shot. Once you have made five successful goals (10 for seniors), use a step to clear the defender's arms and repeat the drill until you have made five more. Step either backwards or sideways. Both of you should follow the shot to contest the rebound.

To Increase Difficulty

- Score the goals consecutively.
- Drive into the circle to take a pass from a feeder. Turn, balance and shoot. The defender waits in the circle and puts pressure on the shot.

- Start inside the circle and drive out to take a pass, and then drive in to take another. The defender is pressuring every move. Put the shot up and work to make five shots.

Success Check

- Maintain body balance.
- Focus on the ring.
- Be aware of the defender's pressure.
- Maintain technique.
- Use good footwork.

Score Your Success

Score 5 (juniors) or 10 (seniors) goals with a defender pressuring the shot = 10 points

Your score ___

Shooting Drill 8.   *Two-on-Two*

This drill allows you to practise some basic footwork skills in the goal circle, combined with passing under light pressure. The two goal shooters stand inside the goal circle, and two defenders stand next to them. The feeder is outside the circle with the ball. The feeder calls "Go" and passes to one of the shooters. The shooters must make three safe passes to each other before taking a shot for goal. Defenders must use the recovery step to gain legal distance and then raise their arms to pressure the shot.

To Increase Difficulty

- Increase to two feeders outside the goal circle.
- Have one shooter work against two defenders.
- Add a defender to the feeder outside the circle.
- Defend both feeders outside the goal circle.

- Pass three times outside the goal circle before the ball goes into goal circle, attacking passes in or out of the circle before the shot can be taken.

To Decrease Difficulty

- Use one defending player rather than two.

Success Check

- Create space with variation of movement.
- See the player and the ball.
- Pass accurately.
- Balance before shooting.
- Follow through for the rebound.

Score Your Success

Score 2 goals from 2 attempts = 10 points

Your score ___

Shooting Drill 9.   *Off-Balance*

You will no doubt have noted how we have stressed the need for good balance when shooting. However, occasions will arise when you may not have time to recover and you may have to shoot off-balance. This drill is designed to cover those situations.

Falling out of the court usually happens when rebounds close to the goalpost on the back line are strongly contested. You take the ball but over-balance and have to react quickly, deciding if you are going to shoot or pass. If you choose to take the shot, focus on the ring, making sure that your shot has a high arc as you move away from the post. To practise, have a feeder put a high ball out over the back line. Elevate and reach to retrieve the ball and shoot before you topple over.

The need to turn and shoot occurs when time has almost run out at the end of a quarter and you simply must get that shot up. Take the pass, turn instantly and release your shot even if you are off-balance. To practise, have a feeder place a variety of balls into the goal circle so you must turn and shoot immediately. Practise without defence. When you are confident, add a defender.

To Increase Difficulty

- Juniors attempt six shots from either side of the post.
- Seniors attempt 10 shots from either side of the post.

Success Check

- Focus on the ring.
- Maintain good body control.
- Release the ball quickly.
- Flick strongly with the fingers and wrist.
- Give the shot height and direction.

Score Your Success

Score 3 goals while off-balance = 5 points

Score 3 goals when turning and shooting immediately — 5 points

Your score ___

SUCCESS SUMMARY OF THE FRONT THIRD AND SHOOTING

The attack end needs to combine well to produce winning netball. Plan your attacking moves so you have a strong foundation on which to build a successful unit. Once all the players on the team understand their specific roles, you should try to be creative. The team that can add individual flair to a sound basic plan is difficult to beat.

Shooting accuracy is critical to a team's success. Shooters should aim for 80 percent accuracy or more. Daily practice is essential for developing good technique and accuracy. Once you are shooting consistently and the ball has a high arc, learn how to apply your technique when pressured by defenders.

If you feel under pressure and your shot is off, revert to the basics of good technique—good balance, wrist and fingers to the post, high release and a slower shot. Remember, you have up to 3 seconds to release the ball. When you are really competent, try the off-balance shot with movement.

Be confident at all times.

Before moving on to step 8, The Centre Third, evaluate how you did on the drills in this step. Tally your scores to determine how well you have mastered the skills of playing in the front third and shooting goals. If you scored at least 110 points, you are ready to move on to step 8. If your score is 70 to 109 points, redo the drills to improve your score before you move on. If your score is less than 70 points, review step 7 and redo the drills before you move on to the next step.

Front-Third Drills

1. Goal Circle Awareness   ___ out of 5
2. Goal Circle Re-Entry   ___ out of 10
3. Taking the Lead   ___ out of 5
4. Making Ground   ___ out of 5
5. Using the Backup   ___ out of 5
6. Back Line Throw-In   ___ out of 10
7. Sideline   ___ out of 10

Shooting Drills

1. Mirror Practice   ___ out of 5
2. Shooting With and Without the Goalpost   ___ out of 15
3. Concentration   ___ out of 10
4. Shaded Area   ___ out of 10
5. Shooting With Eyes Closed   ___ out of 10
6. Square   ___ out of 10
7. Shooting With Defence   ___ out of 10
8. Two-on-Two   ___ out of 10
9. Off-Balance   ___ out of 10

Total   **___ out of 140**

Now that you are familiar with the skills that you will need to play in the front third, let's look at the centre third. Midcourt players need a high level of fitness to be able to cover the court effectively. They constantly take the ball down court to feed the shooters while also working hard in defence to minimise the opposition's attack.

The Centre Third

Netball starts in the centre third. The centre pass starts each quarter of a match and restarts the game when a goal has been scored. The other major role of the centre third is to link the team's attacking and defending ends. Midcourt players should have a heightened awareness of these roles and develop skills that enable them to perform effectively on court.

When you look at midcourt play, you must remember the goal attack and goal defence, who both play an important role through the centre third. Although essentially these positions specialise in the front or back thirds, they still need to participate in some parts of training for midcourt specialisation.

SPECIALISING IN THE CENTRE THIRD

Winning your centre pass gives you a great advantage in attack. Sending the ball confidently and quickly out of the centre and into your attacking third towards your goal pressures your opponents. Defenders have difficulty containing free-flowing attacks.

To win the centre pass, your team needs to have well-laid plans that you can execute efficiently. Your team is given every second centre pass, and you need to use it well. When the ball comes out of the centre third with planned precision, it creates a confident and positive environment for your team. The shooters waiting behind to execute their moves can feel the confidence.

The reverse is also true. When a team struggles to take the ball out of the centre third,

the attack end struggles to create a flow. It is therefore important that your team can also defend the centre pass and try to slow the pace of the opposition's attack. Forcing the error and gaining a turnover is an example of a great play.

The other important role of the midcourt is to link the back and front thirds—in other words, the defending specialists with the shooters. When the ball comes out of the back third, your opponents have lost their opportunity to score—your team is now in a position to gain an advantage. The midcourt players must work the ball safely through their area so your team has a chance to score and capitalise on the good work of the back line.

WINNING THE CENTRE PASS

The captain's toss decides who takes the first centre pass. The winner has the choice of taking the centre pass or selecting the team's shooting end. It is quite rare for the winner to give away possession of the ball. It is a definite advantage to win the toss and get the first score on the board.

Consistently winning your centre pass—passing it successfully into your attacking third—is what good netball teams train to do. Your team's aim should be to win all of its centre passes and then to capture a few from the opposition each quarter—a very simple and effective strategy. Your team is given every other centre pass, which gives you as many opportunities for success as your opponents. The trick is to tip the advantage your way by intercepting some of their passes.

All of this reinforces the importance of the centre pass and the need to have specialised sessions on which to work during your training time. You and your teammates need a number of well-understood options to ensure that you can consistently win the centre pass.

As with other netball strategies, to win the centre pass your team must be organised. Four team members can offer moves. Usually two offers are given as the whistle blows, with the others ready to back up if needed. If all four offer simultaneously, then two or three moves will probably be wasted. Also because court space is limited, staggering the offers is much more effective.

The offers should come strongly as the whistle blows. The player offering should drive hard and fast to an open space. The centre concentrates on these offers and determines which one to use. The other two players prepare or begin to execute their offers by reading from the two moves. If the move is successful, then they do not need to offer any backup. If this is not the case, then they must quickly offer alternative moves. Remember, you have only 3 seconds from the whistle to get the ball away.

The following plays illustrate some options for winning the centre pass.

Wing Attack Has the Line

The wing attack takes the pivotal role on the centre pass so it is important that she prepare early.

Move quickly to the centre of the transverse line. As your centre prepares to enter the centre circle, offer a strong preliminary move. This draws the defence prior to the whistle. Remember, a well-executed preliminary move sends the defender in one direction while you make your offer in the other. You may recall that this move was covered in step 5. As the centre enters the centre circle, the whistle blows. This is the cue for you to put a strong offer out, to drive hard over the line and take the ball (figure 8.1).

The wing defence and goal defence are the backup players. If your initial moves from the wing attack are not strong, these players will

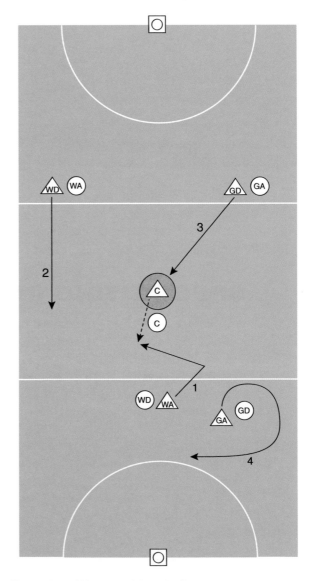

Figure 8.1   Wing attack has the line.

attack from the back transverse line. One drives close to the centre to take a straight pass, while the other stays wide to take a high ball. The goal attack produces a clearing move to the side of the court if her initial offer is not used. As soon as the centre pass is taken, the goal attack provides the first offer to pull the ball into the attacking third.

> **Misstep**
> The wing attack fails to take the pass.
>
> **Correction**
> Work harder on your preliminary moves so that you open the space before the pass.

Split

The wing attack and goal attack start from the middle of their transverse line (figure 8.2). The wing attack has the front position with the goal attack behind and on the move before the whistle as the centre prepares to pass. As the whistle sounds, both players offer, driving strongly in opposite directions. The centre passes to the best lead. The wing defence and goal defence offer backup leads after 1 second if it appears neither of the first leads will be used.

Wide Start

The wing attack and goal attack are on their transverse line, well apart from each other. They hold their positions on the line so one can cut to the centre and one can offer wide on the opposite side (figure 8 3) As the whistle sounds, the short offer comes first over the line, quickly followed by the other offer. Again, the goal defence and wing defence act as backup players if they feel the two attackers are struggling to pull the ball through.

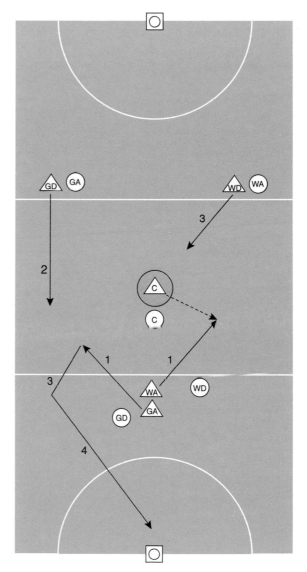

Figure 8.2 Using the split.

Misstep
Both players offer to the same side.

Correction
The player in the back should keep her eyes on the player in the front and offer to the opposite side.

Misstep
Both moves are covered.

Correction
Check your starting position. Work hard to get the inside position. If the defender gets the inside position, keep re-positioning.

Back Door

All four players are at their transverse lines. The attackers move behind their lines, looking as though they will offer. The opposition cannot read that the first move is about to come from the wing defence (figure 8.4). The wing defence drives to the open space and calls to the centre. The goal defence offers the second move, while the wing attack and goal attack provide the backup if necessary.

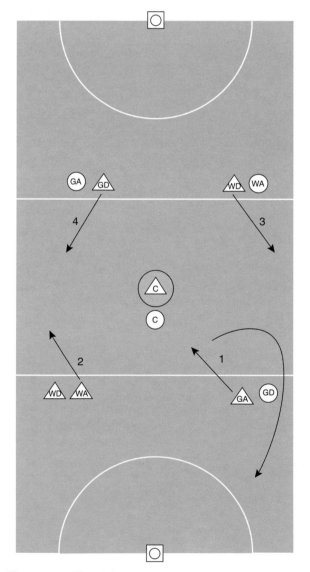

Figure 8.3 The wide start.

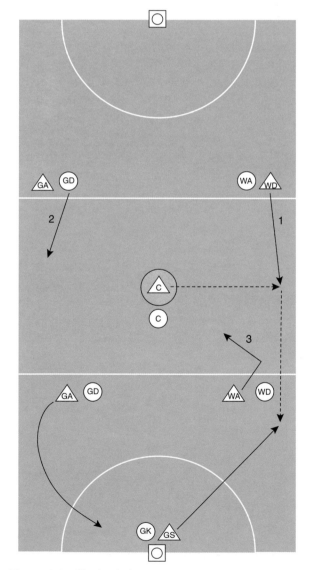

Figure 8.4 The back door.

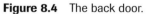

Misstep

Players on the back line can't break free.

Correction

You need to be quick off the mark and focused at all times. Be prepared to offer a variation of movements—for example, breaking back instead of always going forwards.

Centre pass play calls for you to be creative and explore your many options. The important point is to ensure that you have variety and understanding; you must know the order of the offers. It is fun to develop code words that signal to your team members just what the play will be. This is very helpful for young players. One of the easiest ways is to use numbers: 1 means wing attack, 2 means back door, which means either the wing defence or the goal defence. Another approach is to use key words: *drive* means wing attack, *sprint* means split. Of course it does not take your opposition long to figure out just what you are calling, so it's good when you can just read off one another.

Some teams use their centre player to signal the order of play. If the ball is on the right side, it means wing attack will offer first. If the ball is on the left, the back door, the wing defence or goal defence will offer first. More experienced players use their eyes to read the moves and use their voices only when needed. For the young or inexperienced, it is both fun and useful to signal or call centre pass moves.

DEFENDING THE CENTRE PASS

Although your team has the opportunity to attack from every second centre pass, it also has to defend every other centre pass. Remember this equation when you are organising your training time. Ensure that you spend equal amounts of time defending and attacking the centre pass. Some teams enjoy the attacking play and practise this almost to the exclusion of defence. Do not make this mistake. Keep good balance in your work.

Use the Double Defence

Use your numbers to your advantage. This form of defence works well when your opponents are obviously sending their centre passes through one player. Use your centre to double up your defence on that player, usually the wing attack, to try to cause an error (figure 8.5). You should have good decision-making skills if you are applying the double defence. At times you will need to take the double off, such as when applying it may disadvantage your team's next attacking move (e.g., when your opposing centre is allowed to drive to her goal circle undefended). Work to find the balance here and seek input from your coach and teammates.

Figure 8.5 Double defence on key players to help you win the centre pass.

Misstep
The wing attack easily beats the double defence.

Correction
Work together as a unit to close off the middle opening and force the attacker wide.

Dictate the Line of Attack

Work hard before the whistle blows to hold a strong starting position on the line. You should try to limit the attacker's options. Force the at-

tacker wide to the side of the court. Make sure you are on the inside so the ball has to pass you to reach your opponent (figure 8.6). If the centre does not throw with great accuracy, you have a good chance to force mistakes.

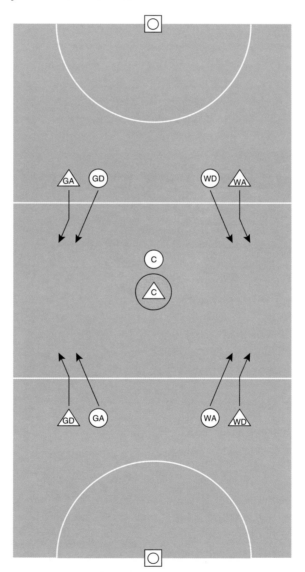

Figure 8.6 Force the opposition wide. Force the ball to pass you to get to your opponent.

Misstep
The defence allows the attacking player to get the inside position.

Correction
Keep re-positioning to hold the inside position strongly.

Pressure the Pass

No matter how well you defend the passing options, if the straight line between your opponents is not pressured, then you will have difficulty intercepting the ball or causing an attacking error. The centre concentrates on her opponent.

Stand the legal distance from the centre circle, drop your weight, and adopt a strong and imposing stance that protects the centre passing lane. Spread your arms wide to pressure the release. Once the pass has gone, quickly close the space and try to block your opponent's down-court movement.

Misstep
The defending player is called for obstruction.

Correction
Adjust to the legal distance—0.9 metres or 3 feet. Make sure you clear the distance before you raise your hands.

LINKING ATTACK AND DEFENCE

The other major role of the midcourt is to link the team's attacking and defending play. In attack you aim to create a smooth transition from the back third to the front third. If the ball travels quickly down court, the attackers find it easy to keep the flow going. Shooters can have difficulty timing their moves if the ball is stopping and starting on its way through the midcourt.

In defence it is important to maintain pressure on your opponents. It is very difficult for the defenders to operate successfully if their midcourt players allow the ball to travel rapidly down court. Remember, a turnover in your team's midcourt is that much closer to your own goal than one obtained in the back third.

Try to offer a range of defensive moves. Zone and press defences can be very effective when used smartly. These are discussed in detail in step 10.

OPERATING EFFECTIVELY AROUND THE GOAL CIRCLE

The centre, wing attack and wing defence are restricted from entering the goal circle during match play. They need to develop an awareness of the circle and be adept at working effectively around it. Remember, players who go offside (i.e., enter the goal circle) are penalised.

Although the goal circle is not a part of the playing area of the midcourt, it is a common playing area for the centre, wing attack and wing defence. For this reason, drills covering these skills are included in this step rather than in the front or back third steps. In a specialist session, take time to develop awareness and balance around the goal circle. It is best to do this work in 2- or 3-minute slots between very demanding work.

Many netballers feel they are best balanced on the goal circle when they are at full stretch on one leg, like a lunge. In fact, your body is better balanced on a wide base, with both feet on the ground. Use this stance as your starting point around the circle. Remember, a strong base not only keeps you well balanced, but also enables you to generate a powerful take-off if you need to quickly move away from the circle or contest the high ball.

CENTRE-THIRD DRILLS

A midcourt specialist needs good balance between attacking and defending skills because his role alternates at each centre pass. In general court play you must also react quickly to a turn-over by changing from attack to defence or vice versa. The drills in this section are designed to develop this ability and help to create winning moves for your centre pass.

Centre-Third Drill 1. *Centre Pass*

The ability of the centre to release the pass accurately is very important for success at the centre pass. This drill overloads the centre line to really challenge the centre's ability to release the ball accurately under pressure.

Three attackers are on the transverse line in the front third, and one defender is in the centre third. The centre is outside the centre circle with the ball, and the coach stands behind her. The centre steps into the centre circle. When the coach blows the whistle, all three attackers offer. The centre selects the most appropriate option and passes accurately. The coach assesses and discusses the choice with the centre.

To Increase Difficulty

- Add a second defender to the centre third.
- Add a third defender to the centre third.
- Repeat the drill with the offers coming from behind the centre circle. That means that all three offers start in the back third.

- Have all six offers coming out together, three from the back third and three from the front third.

To Decrease Difficulty

- Begin with only two attackers. After completing three consecutive successful centre passes, increase the number of attackers to three.

Success Check

- See all the options.
- Select the best option.
- Narrow your focus.
- Release the pass quickly.

Score Your Success

Complete 3 consecutive centre passes = 5 points

Your score ___

Centre-Third Drill 2. *Holding on the Line*

In match play, you will find that you frequently need to reposition at the centre pass. As discussed in step 4, the hold is a very useful move to protect space. This drill works on holding the line during a centre pass play.

As the defending player, position yourself on the transverse line to force your opponent wide for the centre pass. Your attacking opponent has 2 seconds to try to reposition on your inside. Neither player can enter the centre third or cause contact.

To Increase Difficulty

- After 2 seconds, the coach blows the whistle for a centre pass. The defender now contests the ball. Did she manage to channel her opponent wide?
- Now repeat the drill reversing the roles. Apply the hold from an attacking perspective. Hold your position strongly to protect the most direct line between you and your team's centre.

Success Check

- Keep your weight down; have a strong starting position.
- Constantly reposition feet and legs to hold your space.
- Keep your eyes on the player and the ball.

Hold the line position consecutively 3 times = 10 points

Your score ___

Centre-Third Drill 3. *Beating the Double*

As the name implies, this drill looks at how to create winning attacking moves to beat a double defence at the centre pass. Stand 1 metre back from the transverse line. One defender is with you; the other is immediately in front over the transverse line. Your centre stands outside the circle with the ball. As the centre steps forward into the circle to start the drill, offer a strong preliminary move to split the defenders and create space in which to work. As the whistle blows to start play, drive hard over the line to take the centre pass.

All players who contest the centre pass should practise against the double defence—it can be applied to any of them. In reality, the wing attack probably contests the double defence more than the other players, so give the wing attack every second or third set of centre passes.

To Increase Difficulty

- Try to beat the double defence without the preliminary move. Outrun or outjump your opponents.

Success Check

- Keep weight down to generate power.
- Work effectively before the whistle.
- See the players and the ball.
- React to cues.
- Fully extend to take the ball.

Beat the double defence on 2 consecutive centre passes = 10 points

Your score ___

Centre-Third Drill 4. *Applying the Double Defence*

This drill will help you develop skills you can use to apply a successful double defence at the centre pass.

The two defending players work together. As one of the defenders, you are behind the transverse line. Position yourself to direct the attacker wide. Your centre covers your opponent as he crosses the line. Use your voice to guide him. Keep the pressure on so you can both contest the ball.

Introduce the other centre-third players, but maintain the double defence on the wing attack. Allow any other attacker to take the centre pass. The attackers will then pass the ball down court towards their goal until they have made two passes in this attacking third. This requires the wing defence and centre to have a quick recovery to cover their players after applying the double defence. It is important that the opposition's centre is not given free rein to enter the attacking third from the centre pass. This can happen when a double defence is used.

Success Check

- Position early.
- Work together.
- Communicate your movements.
- Watch the player and the ball.

Intercept or force an error on 2 centre passes = 5 points

Intercept or force an error on 2 passes in the back third = 5 points

Your score ___

Centre-Third Drill 5. *Linking Attack*

The five attacking midcourt players are on court as shown in figure 8.7. The thrower stands in the back third with the ball. To start the drill, the feeder passes the ball into the back third. The player nearest to the ball drives hard to gain possession, then passes the ball to the next player who offers a strong move. This player then passes to the next, and so on. Players look for space to of-fer their moves and time their moves well so their leads can be used. All attackers work at these skills to enable the ball to travel quickly through the centre third. After the ball has crossed into the front third, the feeder releases the next ball and the drill begins again.

To Increase Difficulty

- Begin with a sideline throw-in.
- Close down the working area. You must all work on the right-hand side of the court or the left-hand side, and all moves must be made in the centre corridor (i.e., 5 meters either side of the circle). Can you adjust your timing and movement?
- A thrower begins play with a sideline throw-in from the back third.
- Place two defenders in the midcourt to pressure the attackers as the ball comes through.
- Each time you are able to quickly move the ball from the back third to the front third on three consecutive plays, add a defender until all players have an opponent; then overload with another defender.

Success Check

- React quickly.
- Read moves from each other.
- Offer strongly to open space.
- Watch the ball.
- Pass accurately.
- Vary your movement.

Score Your Success

Quickly and smoothly move the ball to link the back third and front third on 3 consecutive plays = 10 points

Your score ___

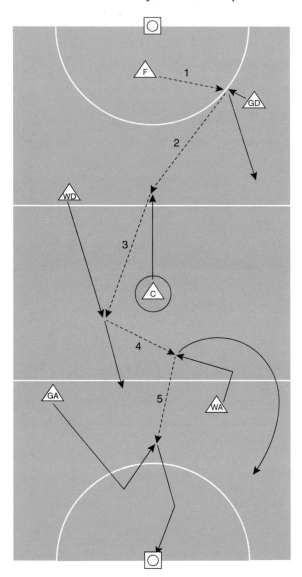

Figure 8.7 Linking Attack drill.

Centre-Third Drill 6. *Linking Defence*

This drill really works the first linking drill in reverse. The five midcourt players assume a defending role, and the three attackers are on court opposing them. The feeder is in the front third with the ball. To start the drill, the feeder passes to the nearest attacker (figure 8.8). This pass is the cue for the defenders closest to the ball to apply pressure. Defenders should cover offers, contest the pass and recover to defend the pass if they cannot intercept the first ball.

The defenders apply full pressure to each pass as the attackers try to work the ball through the midcourt. After the defenders are successful (i.e., they intercept, cause a deflection or cause a poor attacking pass), return the ball to the feeder who restarts the drill.

To Increase Difficulty

- Apply a centre-court zone or press.
- The feeder starts the play from a sideline throw-in from the attacking third.
- When the defenders are able to cause three breakdowns, add another attacker until all players have an opponent. Now overload with an extra attacker.

Success Check

- Work together.
- Stay confident.
- Communicate.
- Maintain pressure.
- Attack the ball.

Score Your Success

Defenders cause 3 breakdowns of the attacking play = 10 points

Your score ___

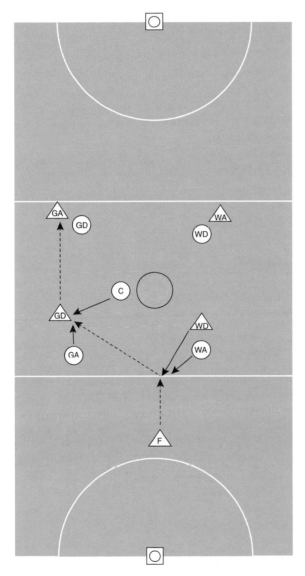

Figure 8.8 Linking Defence drill.

Centre-Third Drill 7. *Out of Play*

This drill makes you adjust quickly to a change of possession. Two teams are on court without their goalkeepers. The shooters at either end of the court are the only players allowed in the goal circle and the only ones who can score. They must confine their movement to 3 metres from the goalpost. Use cones or draw a line to mark their area. If a shooter comes out of the marked area, her team loses possession. The coach walks on the court to begin the drill and awards any penalty that must be called against a midcourt member of team A. Team B has possession and must work the ball to its shooter. The only condition is that all on-court members of team B must handle the ball before the shooter can take the pass and shoot for goal.

To Increase Difficulty

- Once both teams are able to move the ball well and score goals, your coach can introduce some random penalty calls. Make sure you are adjusting quickly when possession changes.

Success Check

- Midcourt players react quickly.
- See spaces.
- Make accurate passes.
- Quickly move the ball out but keep it well controlled.

Score Your Success

First team to score 5 goals = 10 points

Your score ___

Centre-Third Drill 8. *Shooters Out*

Two teams line up on court without their shooters. In this drill the goalkeepers simply start or end the passage of play and are stationary at the top of their goal circles. In this drill, you practise linking in very match-like conditions, which requires you to rapidly switch from attack to defence. The team with possession of the ball is in attack.

The team that wins the toss gets possession first. The goalkeeper on the winning team has the ball, and his team is in attack. Try to pass the ball down court to the opposition's goalkeeper. Your team must handle the ball in each third before passing it to the goalkeeper. If you achieve this, you score 1 point. Your opponent's goalkeeper then sends the ball into attack for his team. You are now in defence.

If your team loses possession as the ball comes down court, simply play on. You must quickly change to defence and try to win it back. Each time you pass the ball to the opposition's goalkeeper, your team scores 1 point. Normal match play rules apply.

To Increase Difficulty

- The attacking team must pass back at least twice before passing to its opponent's goalkeeper.
- Overload the midcourt by adding another attacker and a defender to the drill.
- Open the space by removing one pair.
- Close down the court space. Mark off the right side, centre corridor, and so forth, and make sure that you can adjust your play to the crowded space.

Success Check

- Quick decision making.
- Good teamwork and communication.
- Early pickup of cues.
- Accurate passing.
- Quick adjustment from attack to defence.

Score Your Success

First team to score 5 points = 10 points

Your score ___

Centre-Third Drill 9. *Balance Catches*

These practices will assist the centre, wing attack and wing defence in moving confidently around the edge of the goal circle.

Stand on the circle's edge with a wide base, facing the goalpost. The feeder stands two steps in front of you. The feeder releases 10 quick passes at varying heights. You must quickly retrieve each ball and return it to the feeder without leaving the circle's edge and without overbalancing into the goal circle. The feeder should pass the ball so you can extend forwards to take the ball and confine sideways movement to one step. It is important to have quick, accurate reactions.

Once you can take 10 consecutive balls without leaving the edge of the circle or falling into the circle, introduce a partner to contest the balls. A wide base is even more important now to help you hold your position on the edge of the circle. Make sure the feeder places the ball so both players can contest it fairly.

Once you can take five consecutive balls without leaving the edge of the circle or falling into the circle, combine this work with some fast movements. At the beginning it is good to maintain your balance while you are stationary, but in match play you need to do this with movement. Work through the drill sequence using a mobile start. Move three or four strides away from the circle. Drive hard onto the edge of the circle, and then quickly work the drill as before.

To Increase Difficulty

- Vary your starting position. Work with your back, right or left side to the circle.
- The defender pushes your body as you take the ball. Can you maintain your balance?
- Stand 1 meter off the goal circle. Hold a strong position on the defender. The feeder passes the ball to the edge of the goal circle. Pull off the defender with good timing to take the pass.

Success Check

- Have a strong body.
- Have a wide base.
- Pull the ball in quickly.
- Protect the ball with your body.
- Keep your weight low.

Score Your Success

Take 10 consecutive balls without leaving the edge of the circle or falling into the circle = 5 points

Take 5 consecutive balls without leaving the edge of the circle or falling into the circle with a defender = 5 points

Take 5 consecutive balls without leaving the edge of the circle or falling into the circle with a defender and with movement = 10 points

Your score ____

Centre-Third Drill 10. *Find the Edge*

This drill helps with your goal circle awareness. Stand two steps away from the circle and focus on the line that marks the circle. Close your eyes. Move forward quickly to the line. Open your eyes. Are you at the line?

To Increase Difficulty

- Stand on the edge of the circle facing the goalpost. Quickly shuffle three steps to the right with your eyes closed. Are you still on the circle?

- Shuffle three steps to the left. Are you still on the circle?
- Reverse your starting position and repeat the drill.

Success Check

- Judge distance.
- Visualise distance.
- Move confidently.
- Move on the edge.

SUCCESS SUMMARY OF THE CENTRE THIRD

A centre-court player needs to be fit and have speed and agility. Be creative and learn to read the game well. To succeed, you will need a good balance between your attacking and defending skills. Know when to attack and when to clear or hold before you re-offer as you take the ball forwards to the front third. Pressure every pass through the midcourt when your opponents are heading for their goal third. Forcing a turnover in the centre third is crucial to overall team performance.

Before moving on to step 9, The Back Third, evaluate how you did on the drills in this step. Tally your scores to determine how well you have mastered the skills needed to play in the centre third of the court. If you scored at least 80 points, you are ready to move on to step 9. If your score is 60 to 79 points, redo the drills to improve your score before you move on. If your score is less than 60 points, review step 8 and redo the drills before you move on to the next step.

Centre-Third Drills

1. Centre Pass	___ out of 5
2. Holding on the Line	___ out of 10
3. Beating the Double	___ out of 10
4. Applying the Double Defence	___ out of 10
5. Linking Attack	___ out of 10
6. Linking Defence	___ out of 10
7. Out of Play	___ out of 10
8. Shooters Out	___ out of 10
9. Balance Catches	___ out of 20
10. Find the Edge	___ out of 5
Total	**___ out of 100**

The final step that deals with an area of specialisation is step 9, which focuses on defending in the back third. A strong defensive unit that intercepts and forces errors will give its team more scoring opportunities. Winning teams have a back line that works hard as a unit to pressure and contest every ball in that third.

The Back Third

The two key players in the back third are the goalkeeper and the goal defence. The main objective of these players is to restrict the opposition's shooting opportunities. The wing defence and the centre also play within the back third, but their court space is restricted to the outside of the goal circle. They cannot defend within the circle.

When the ball enters the goal circle, the centre and the wing defence players should reposition themselves on the circle's edge so that they can provide support for their defenders. This might involve retrieving loose balls that have been deflected or tapped to them, or defending their opponent so that shooters have difficulty passing the ball out to their teammates. Once a defender gains possession, the wing defence and the centre should offer strong attacking moves to drive the ball down court towards their own goal.

SPECIALISING IN THE BACK THIRD

The defence unit—the goalkeeper and goal defence within the goal circle and the wing defence and centre outside—are the team's last line of resistance. Playing in these positions, it is your job to restrict the number of shots your opponents take. As the team's last line of defence, your defending skills need to be more fully developed than those of your teammates.

Although all team members offer defence, players in the back third must be able to exert constant pressure to wear down the opposition. When your opponents have to work hard for every ball in their attacking end, they drop balls, pass inaccurately and miss goals. On the other hand, the shooting percentages rise when the ball flows easily into the goal circle.

Defenders need to develop a good understanding both of each other and of their outside players (the wing defence and the centre), so they can work together as a unit.

DEFENDING IN THE CIRCLE

Because defenders need to put in extra work to defend the circle, the goal circle is an appropriate place to focus on as we look at the back third. There are a number of ways to defend in the goal circle. Each relies on the ability of the two defenders to coordinate their movements and work in tandem. You can tell a good back line—its members work together to constantly pressure the shooters. Defenders who work in isolation make it easy for shooters to succeed.

Defending One-on-One

As discussed in step 5, one-on-one defence simply means taking responsibility for one player. In most instances it is a case of defending your opponent; however, it is not limited to this. One-on-one defence can also include a deliberate switch of opponent, a tactic usually used within the goal circle, or a switch that occurs in the course of play. Each defender should be able to switch to defend the other shooter when necessary.

One-on-one defence means that a shooter is never left unattended in the goal circle. It is most effective against a balanced attack, when both shooters share the responsibilities for their team's score.

Misstep
The shooter easily gets free.

Correction
Adjust your starting position. Make sure that you can see the player and the ball at the same time.

Playing Double Defence

As discussed in step 8, in this play both defenders combine to pressure one shooter. The pressure from a double defence should be strongest when the ball is passed into the goal circle so the shooter has to contest the catch against both defenders. The defenders should position themselves so they restrict the shooter's catching, passing and shooting options. One defender should be able to cut off the front ball, which is usually a flat or low ball, and the other should restrict the back ball, which is usually a high ball. Double-defence combinations can take a front and back starting position as close as possible to the shooter (figure 9.1a) or offset a metre or so to either side of the shooter while maintaining a front and back split (figure 9.1b). The most common application of a double defence in the circle is on a goal shooter, who is obviously the opposition's key scorer.

a   b

Figure 9.1 Double defence: *(a)* in front and back positions; *(b)* in the offset position.

Misstep

The shooter easily beats the double defence.

Correction

Look to change your starting positions. Come off the player. This often causes the feeders to be hesitant on the release of the pass. It is vital that you communicate well with your teammate.

Splitting the Circle

In this approach to defending the circle, defenders have clearly identified areas of responsibility. Although defenders are aware of their opponents' moves, they do not chase the shooters within the goal circle. Instead they focus on the ball, which they attempt to intercept in their area.

The defenders offset each other; one is responsible for the front ball at the top of the goal circle while the other is responsible for the back ball along the goal line (figure 9.2). The defenders constantly reposition as the ball comes down court, ensuring that they are well placed to intercept the pass in. They rely on the players outside the circle to pressure the ball, because they have a better chance of intercepting if the long, high ball is used. Balls fed from the edge of the circle are hard to intercept.

The circle also can be split using the right- or left-hand side of the circle. When this split is operating, you watch the ball as it travels down court. Taking your cue from where each pass is taken, constantly reposition so the defender who is ball side covers the front ball while the other takes the back of the circle. This means that when a midcourt player is releasing the pass on the right-hand side of the court, the defender who has the right-hand split will be forwards. If the ball swings across court, the defenders reposition.

Outside the split circle the wing defence and centre vary their defence. Chase with a hard man-to-man defence then offer a similar split across the crucial centre corridor. Working as a unit, try to prevent low, quick balls from entering. If you can force the ball wide and long, the back defender will have a good chance to intercept.

Use this type of defence as a primary defence if both defenders have strong anticipation skills. It can, however, develop lazy defenders who are not prepared to do the hard chasing when needed. It is best to use the splitting the circle defence intermittently as a strategy for unsettling an attacking rhythm.

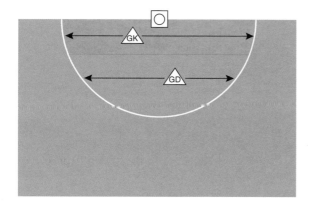

Figure 9.2 Splitting the goal circle.

Misstep

The circle is open. Shooters feel no pressure on the ball as it comes into the circle.

Correction

Focus on the ball as it comes down court. When it enters the attack third, make sure you constantly re-position to close down the circle.

DEFENDING THE SHOT

Even after your best efforts, defenders are often beaten within the circle. Make sure you do not give up when the shooter takes aim. Remember, the harder you make life for shooters, the more likely you are to be successful, particularly in those all-important final minutes of a close contest. When you are beaten for the ball in the goal circle, recover quickly to defend the shot and then prepare to rebound.

When defenders were first allowed to defend the shot at goal, most shooters used a low release; as a result, defenders with a strong jump were very successful. Today shooters have a high release, and defenders have to play smart to extract a return from the defence of the shot. A varied defence is important because it can unsettle the shooter. Your presence and pressure can distract her so that she focuses on what you are doing rather than looking at the target, the goalpost. Let us look at the two main ways of defending a shot: the lean and the jump.

The Lean

When the shooter takes possession of the ball, use the recovery step to move to the legal defending distance from the shooter's grounded foot. Balance on either one foot or both and stretch forward to pressure the shot as close to the point of release as you can (figure 9.3). Balancing on one foot allows greater extension to the ball, whereas two feet gives you better body control. Using the arm opposite the leg you are standing on will maintain good extension and body control when executing the lean on one leg. Allow your body to hang in the space between you and your opponent. Be sure you don't lean over too far and overbalance because you may make contact.

Most times you execute the lean in front of your opponent, but don't hesitate to try the side and back as starting positions for the lean. If the shot is close in, the back position can be a real nuisance to a shooter. Remember, variety is important.

Figure 9.3 Using the lean to pressure the shot.

Misstep
You overbalance and are penalised for obstruction.

Correction
Practise holding the lean for the full 3 seconds. Check that you are the legal distance from the shooter.

The Jump

When you jump, you are trying to deflect the shot. Recover to the legal distance as for the lean, but rather than stretching out, take a strong starting position. Crouch low beneath the shooter's immediate focus (figure 9.4a). Watch the shooter's hand. As the shooting action begins, uncoil like a tight spring. As the shooter releases the ball, propel yourself up and forwards (figure 9.4b). Aim to cut off the shot close to the point of release. Make sure you do not contact your opponent, or you will incur a penalty. After you have defended the shot, prepare to rebound. Don't assume that the shot will score. Of course, many do, but what you are waiting for are the missed goals. They are the ones that you can rebound and send down court to give your team a chance to score.

a   *b*

Figure 9.4 The jump: *(a)* set up for the jump to deflect a shot; *(b)* upon release, propel yourself towards the ball, avoiding contact.

Misstep
You are called for obstruction.

Correction
Adjust to the shooter's timing. Some shooters shoot more quickly than others.

Misstep
You are called for contact.

Correction
As you reach to intercept the shot, make sure you do not contact the shooter's arm.

BACK-THIRD DRILLS

The drills presented here are structured to enable you to build a repertoire of specialised defending skills through well-planned challenges. Begin with the basics, and as you are able to handle them confidently, progress to the more challenging drills. Remember that it is better to develop one skill really well in a session than to lightly touch three or four.

Back-Third Drill 1. *Circle Practice*

Begin with one defender and one shooter in the circle. The second shooter and defender work outside the circle. Shooters pass three times to each other before putting up a shot. Defenders work to cause a breakdown of the attacking play, to tip or to intercept the ball. When this occurs, the two groups switch roles. The two working outside the circle move to work the inside of the circle and vice versa.

To Increase Difficulty

- Use only the right side of the court. When the defenders are able to cause an attack breakdown, switch to the left side.
- Both shooters and defenders work within the circle. The wing attack and wing defence operate outside.
- Add the centre players to the outside team.

Success Check

- Focus on the ball and the players.
- Control your body.
- Stay balanced.
- Attack the ball.
- Apply pressure.

Score Your Success

Each defender causes a breakdown before the shooter takes a shot = 5 points

Your score ___

Back-Third Drill 2. *Double Defence*

One shooter and two defenders are in the circle. The defenders position for a double defence of the shooter. Two undefended attackers (centre and wing attack) are outside the circle with the ball. Starting from the transverse line, they pass the ball back and forth for up to five passes, watching for the best pass into the circle. Defenders constantly reposition to ensure that both can contest the ball when it comes in.

To Increase Difficulty

- Allow the second shooter to enter the circle.
- Add the centre to the attacking team.
- Add the defence on the wing attack and centre.
- Add the midcourt backup players, the wing defence and goal defence. The ball starts with these players in the midcourt. Any of the four attacking players can try to pass the ball

into the shooter as they move the ball down court. Players using the double defence need to constantly reposition to keep the pressure on the goal shooter.

Success Check

- Defenders constantly reposition to cut off the pass.
- One defender is in front of the attacker on the ball side.
- Both defenders contest the pass.
- Defenders work together to deny the shooter possession.

Score Your Success

A defender takes possession of the ball passed in to the goal shooter = 5 points

Your score ___

Back-Third Drill 3. *Splitting the Goal Circle*

Defenders use an offset defence in the circle. One takes the front half of the circle, and the other covers the back. They position on either side of the goalpost, one forward for the front ball and one deeper to cover the long pass. One shooter is in the circle. The other is working the outside. Defenders constantly reposition using quick footwork to cover balls that may move into their split of the goal circle. The shooters pass freely to each other as they move around the area. The defenders concentrate on cutting off the pass by intercepting, tapping or flicking the ball away from the shooters. Only one shooter is in the circle at any time.

To Increase Difficulty

- The second shooter enters the circle. Add a wing attack and wing defence outside the circle and commence the drill near the transverse line in the goal third. The wing defence varies from playing one-on-one to sitting at the top of the circle and looking for the intercept.

- Add the two centres and begin the drill in the midcourt. When the defenders can successfully disrupt three passes, the wing defence and the centre change their defending pattern.

- Start the drill again, this time using a right and left split of the circle.

Success Check

- Constantly reposition.
- See the player and the ball.
- Keep the passing options covered.
- Watch for the intercept.
- Attack the ball to intercept.

Score Your Success

Defenders disrupt 3 passes between shooters = 5 points

Your score ____

Back-Third Drill 4. *Two-on-One*

Two shooters are in the circle with the ball. They move freely about the circle, passing the ball back and forth. The shooter who receives the fifth pass takes the shot. One defender works in the circle, trying to take the ball from the shooters before the shot goes up. When a defender is successful, she earns a rest and is replaced by a partner.

To Increase Difficulty

- Add the wing attack to the outside of the circle. The shooters may now pass to each other or to the wing attack, who moves around the edge of the circle to support them.

- The defender must defend the shot and then follow in for the rebound.

Success Check

- Know where both shooters are.
- Focus on the ball.
- Apply pressure selectively.
- Work to cause an attacking error.

Score Your Success

Intercept the ball before the shot goes up = 5 points

Your score ____

Back-Third Drill 5. *Out of Play*

Both shooters and defenders are in the goal circle. One shooter has the ball at his feet near the edge of the goal circle, ready to take a penalty shot or pass. His defender is standing beside him out of play.

The second shooter positions near the goalpost for a rebound or a pass. The second defender positions midway between the shooters. The shooter bends to pick up the ball to commence play. The defender must watch this shooter carefully and make a split-second decision whether to pressure the shot or defend the pass. The decision must be made very quickly, or the defender could find himself caught in the middle doing neither.

To Increase Difficulty

- Take the penalty at the midpoint and then in the front half of the goal circle.

- Shooters now work until the shot goes up. This means that the defender who is out of play must quickly offer a defence once the penalty has been released. Follow through with a rebound if the shot is unsuccessful.
- Add the wing attack to the edge of the circle. The pass can now go to the other shooter or outside the circle to the wing attack.

Success Check

- Use a strong starting position.
- Be ready to react; anticipate.
- Read the play and react instantly.

Score Your Success

Defender picks the right option and offers the appropriate defence for the situation 5 times = 10 points

Your score ___

Back-Third Drill 6. *Outside Defence*

The wing attack has the ball at the transverse line, and the wing defence is pressuring the pass. Both centres are in the centre third about 3 metres from the transverse line. The wing attack calls "Go". The attacking centre drives into the goal third to take the pass. The wing attack and centre must work the ball to the circle's edge. The centre and wing defence defend every move and try to stop their opponent from landing at the circle's edge with the ball.

Success Check

- Focus on the ball and the players.
- Use your voice to direct if necessary.

- Maintain pressure.
- Watch the ball closely and decide when you can intercept. Once you decide the intercept is on, commit yourself and go hard to take the ball.

Score Your Success

Stop the attackers from reaching the edge of the goal circle 3 times = 10 points

Your score ___

REBOUNDING

Defenders should work together to rebound successfully. They should dictate the terms of the defence by working hard to establish strong rebounding positions. One defender should control the air, going after the ball, while the other controls the ground. At times, however, both may need to contest in the air.

As the shooter begins the shooting motion, the defender who is not offering a defence of the shot establishes a strong rebounding position on the opposite side of the goalpost from the shooter. If you are this defensive player, take a position about half a step out from the goalpost. Widen your stance, weight down, to hold your space (figure 9.5a). Focus on the ball. Work to keep the shooter behind you. Use a rapid side step to protect your space, if necessary. A strong rebounding position allows you to recover balls that come over to your side of the ring or to simply let the ball go out of play so that your team has the throw-in.

As the shot at goal is released, the defender who has offered the defence on the shot quickly turns to the goalpost, blocking the shooter's path for the rebound (figure 9.5b). If you are this defender, work your legs hard across the direct route to the post. You want to be in a similar position to your defending partner but on the opposite side of the ring. Remember, space is at a premium, so you need to use your body well to protect your space. Keep watching the ball and your partner, and be aware of where your shooters are.

As the ball hits the ring, the defenders make a split-second decision whether one or both will contest the rebound. You dictate the terms of play most effectively when one defender contests and the other controls the ground. One defender should explode up to the ball and try to take it at full extension (figure 9.5c). Remember, a one-handed rebound allows you greater extension. If you can control the ball, pull it quickly into your body and use a deep knee bend to cushion your landing. If you are unable to control the ball in the air, tap it to yourself or to your partner. While you are working the air, your partner should continue to work the ground to ensure that you are still controlling the vital space close to the post.

If you and your defending partner are finding it difficult to control rebounds, both of you should contest the ball. Two defenders working the air sends a strong message to the shooters. It also gives you maximum firepower under the ring. Work together to use the space wisely. Remember to use the tap if you need to reach a bit farther.

Once you have control of the ball, move it forward safely. If the long pass to wing defence or centre is on, use it. Otherwise, take the safe option and pass between each other.

Figure 9.5 Defensive rebounding: *(a)* starting position; *(b)* blocking the shooter's route to the post; *(c)* contesting the rebound.

REBOUNDING DRILLS

Although defenders must work together to successfully secure rebounds, practise on your own at first to learn the proper footwork, timing and jumping skills.

Rebounding Drill 1. *From the Wall*

Place a cone next to the practice wall. Mark a cross on the wall at goalpost height (3.05 m or 10 ft) directly above the cone. Stand facing the wall and throw the ball to the target on the wall. Jump strongly to pull in the ball. Make sure you do not contact the cone when landing. Absorb the impact of the landing by bending your knees when you contact the ground. Remember, a two-handed pull gives you the best control over the ball. A one-handed pull provides better extension. Practise both.

To Increase Difficulty

- Turn sideways to start the drill.
- Try the drill on the opposite side.
- Contest the rebound with your defending partner.

- Move to the wall quickly to take the rebound. Start 1 metre away from the wall. Time your run in so you elevate and pull the ball in as it hits the target.
- Both defenders contest the rebound. The player who does not control the rebound drives down court to take a pass.

Success Check

- Achieve powerful elevation.
- Take the ball at full stretch.
- Pull the ball in strongly.
- Land on a stable, wide base.

Score Your Success

Collect 5 consecutive rebounds = 10 points

Your score ____

Rebounding Drill 2. *Goalpost Rebounding*

When you practise rebounding at the goalpost, you work in match-like conditions. Begin the work alone. As your confidence and skill level increase, introduce an opponent and then your defending partner and her opponent. This drill will develop good body control when you try those strong jumps. It will also help you time your move precisely.

The feeder stands behind the goalpost. The rebounder is on court, half a stride out from the post, with her eyes on the goal ring. The feeder throws the ball onto the goal ring. As it hits the ring, the rebounder elevates strongly to take the ball as close to the ring as possible.

Stretch elastic straps across the top of the goal ring so the ball rebounds from every shot. Begin with one defender and one shooter in the goal circle. The wing attack is on the edge of the circle with the ball. The wing attack calls "Go", and the shooter offers. The defender allows the shooter to take the pass. The defender then defends the shot and follows in for the rebound.

To Increase Difficulty

- Contest the rebound with a partner.
- Include two more rebounders (one defender and one shooter) in the drill. This allows the two defenders to work as a team.
- Add the outside players so that the ball can be passed out of the back third when the defenders win the rebound.

Success Check

- Establish a starting position.
- Lower your weight for a strong take-off.
- Take the ball at maximum extension.
- Protect the ball once you have it.
- Absorb the impact of landing.

Score Your Success

Collect 5 consecutive rebounds = 10 points

Your score ____

SUCCESS SUMMARY OF THE BACK THIRD

If you are playing in the back third of the netball court, your main role is to defend. In your specialist session you should hone these skills. This will enable you to increase your effectiveness on court.

To be successful, players in the back third need to work together to offer a strong, varied defence every time the opposition takes the ball towards its goal. Being able to play one-on-one, split the circle and double-defend in the circle makes it difficult for your opponents to score. You exert even more pressure if you defend the shot and develop a strong rebound.

The outside players must work hard to keep the pressure on the feed, forcing the opposition either to place a high ball into the goal circle (making it easier for the defenders to intercept) or to slow the pass down (allowing more time for the back line pair to reposition to the ball). Holding up the ball enhances the circle defenders' chance for success.

Before moving on to step 10, Developing Strategies and Using Space, evaluate how you did on the drills in this step. Tally your scores to determine how well you have mastered the skills needed to play in the back third of the court. If you scored at least 50 points, you are ready to move on to step 10. If your score is 35 to 49 points, redo the drills to improve your score before you move on. If your score is less than 35 points, review step 9 and redo the drills before you move on to the next step.

Back-Third Drills

1. Circle Practice — ___ out of 5

2. Double Defence — ___ out of 5

3. Splitting the Goal Circle — ___ out of 5

4. Two-on-One — ___ out of 5

5. Out of Play — ___ out of 10

6. Outside Defence — ___ out of 10

Rebounding Drills

1. From the Wall — ___ out of 10

2. Goalpost Rebounding — ___ out of 10

Total — ___ *out of 60*

You have covered all the basic and specialist skills for each third of the court, so you are very close to match play. It is time to put all this together and focus on the team. Step 10 covers the basic strategies behind team play and the importance of using court space effectively. As you work your way through this step, all you have learnt will begin to come together as you use your skills to develop your court craft.

Developing Strategies and Using Space

Being a member of a netball team provides many challenges. The best team members are those who make a positive contribution to the total team effort. Make sure you work at this. You will not maximise your talents unless you learn to work with others. Assess the strengths and weaknesses of yourself and your teammates.

Play to your strengths in competition and work to perfect your strengths and to improve your weaknesses in training. Try to develop two or three plays that are yours, moves that you enjoy and that always work for you. Let them be your trademark, the moves that other netballers respect you for. Then build a strong repertoire of other moves around your strengths. In tough times, having strong basics to pull on will serve you well.

Remember that the effective combination of the skills of seven athletes makes a much more formidable team than the efforts of a few individual stars. That does not imply that great teams do not have their stars—they do—but that is not all they have. The team members working with those really talented athletes also have important roles to fulfil. They do not sit back and let the stars do all the work. Make sure your team acknowledges each player's importance. When everyone feels part of the team, you are on your way to being successful.

TEAM PLAY

The netball court can become quite congested with 14 athletes working on a relatively small court space. Team skills allow you to organise the court space effectively, which lays a strong foundation for your team's success.

Early netball team strategies tended to adopt a very rigid approach in which set plays, called *systems*, were practised relentlessly. The modern approach is to have one or two basic strategies for attacking and defending from which the team builds its playing patterns. Creativity and individual flair are important to successful teams.

Make sure you spend as much time developing space awareness as you do developing strategies. Do not rigorously drill system play, which encourages you simply to follow instructions instead of developing creativity and learning to adapt to specific challenges. Team skills should challenge you to think on court. Thinking players make winning teams. Some simple strategies for attacking and defending will help you organise your team effectively.

THREE-OPTION ATTACK STRATEGY

One of the basic strategies on which teams build patterns revolves around a three-option attack. Whenever your team has possession, the player with the ball should have three passing options.

The first option is to pass to a player who leads strongly and is in front of her opponent. This lead, which should be offered quickly, is easily read and is initiated as soon as the catch is taken. Experienced players can even initiate the offer before the catch is taken.

The second option is to pass to an alternate front move. This player makes a judgment on the likely success of the first offer and moves when it becomes clear that the first offer has been too well defended and the player with the ball is in trouble.

The third option is a backup that is usually generated from behind the player with the ball. It is the safety valve and is offered quickly and surely. Sometimes this is just a simple back pass to allow the attack to re-offer. At other times the player uses a long, high ball to move the ball away from the congested area of play.

Often the second and third moves are not made, or if offered, are not needed or used. They should, however, be available in case they are needed. In a really close game, the team that has all three options operating puts itself in a strong position for success.

Applying the Strategy

We will now look at common scenarios and show basic strategies for moving the ball down court. These examples are not hard and fast rules; they are simply ways that you can apply the three-option strategy. The first, second and third options are represented by the numbers in the figures. Be creative and interpret the plan around the plays that work for your team. If your team can deliver the long ball accurately, your strategy should reflect that talent. Once the ball has passed the halfway line, the first attacking move should be offered in the circle. In this instance, looking in to the goal circle is the basis of your strategy. Rather than making a more conventional short pass, focus on the goal circle and look to send the long ball to the shooter as the first move, even from the centre third.

Misstep
You pass to a covered attacking player.

Correction
Make sure you can see all your options. Be patient with the ball and give the attacking players time to lose their defenders.

Misstep
Your pass selection is poor.

Correction
Make sure you recognise the type of pass required and execute it well.

In the Back Third

Rebound taken by goalkeeper (figure 10.1): The wing defence offers the first down-court move. The centre offers the second down-court move. The goal defence provides the backup.

Sideline throw-in from goal defence (figure 10.2): The wing defence offers the first down-court move. The centre provides the alternative option, and the goalkeeper is the backup.

Baseline throw-in from goalkeeper (figure 10.3): The goal defence offers first, the wing defence follows and the centre provides the backup. In this case, with the play starting on the goal line, the backup is provided by the centre, who drives into the back third to move a long ball through. This simply means that he takes a long ball just inside the transverse line, which allows the ball to travel quickly over the third. Obviously, the move cannot be generated from behind the player with the ball. However, there are still three options ready for the team member with the ball.

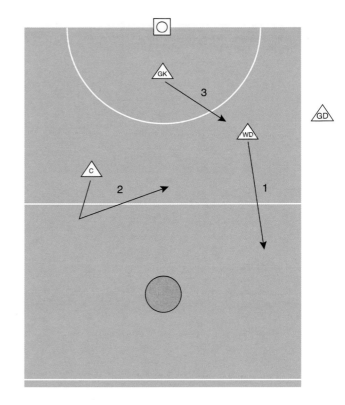

Figure 10.2 Sideline throw-in from goal defence.

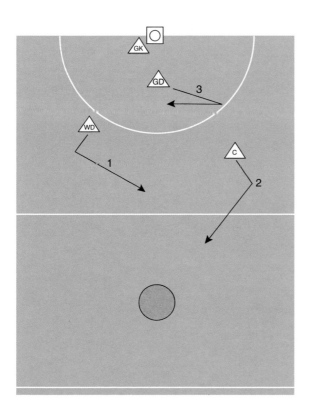

Figure 10.1 Rebound taken by goalkeeper.

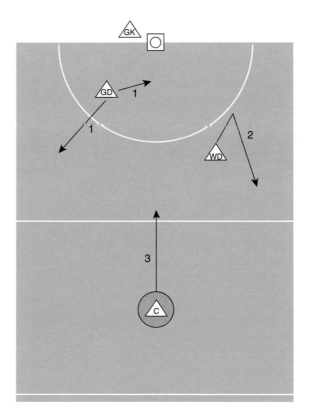

Figure 10.3 Baseline throw-in from goalkeeper.

In the Centre Third

Sideline throw-in from wing defence (figure 10.4): Use this when the wing defence has the ball close to the transverse line. The centre provides the first offer; the goal defence, the second; and the goal keeper is the safety valve.

Centre with ball in back third (figure 10.5): The wing defence drives hard down court to move the ball through midcourt. The wing attack is the second option, and the goal defence is the safety valve. Another approach is to use the wing attack and goal attack as the first and second options and the goal defence as the backup.

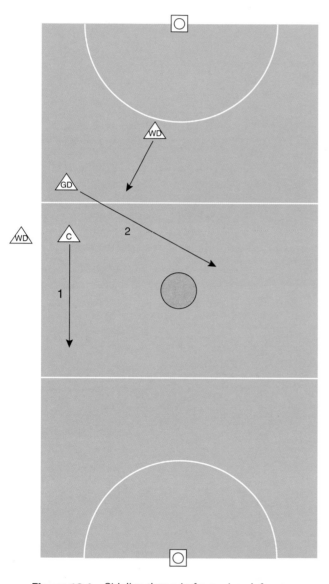

Figure 10.4 Sideline throw-in from wing defence.

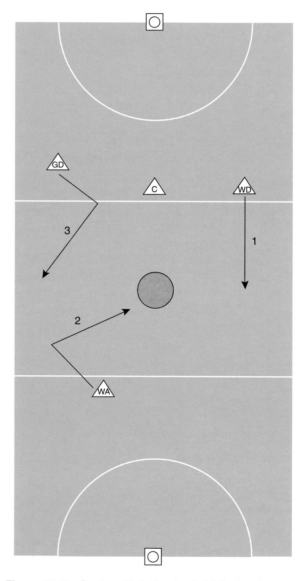

Figure 10.5 Centre with ball in back third.

Wing defence with ball in centre third (figure 10.6): The centre offers first, the wing attack offers second and the goal defence provides the safety valve. An alternative is to use the wing attack or goal attack as the first and second options and the goal defence for the backup.

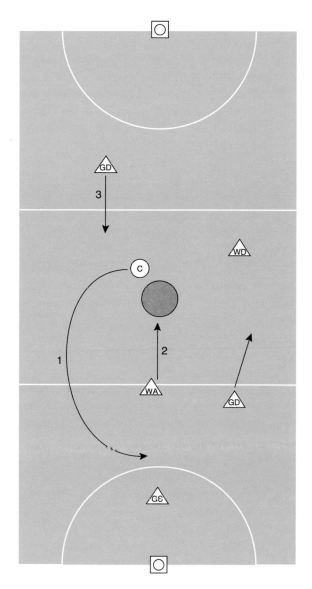

Figure 10.6 Wing defence with ball in centre third.

In the Front Third

Centre with ball in midcourt (figure 10.7): The attack uses the shooter on the lead. The goal shooter offers first, the wing attack provides the alternative and the wing defence is the backup.

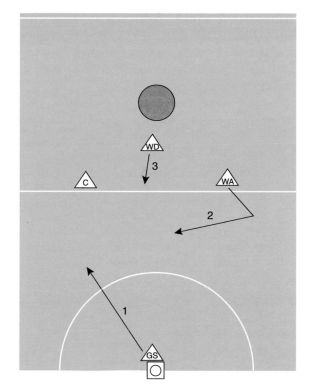

Figure 10.7 Centre with ball in midcourt.

Wing attack with ball near transverse line (figure 10.8): Look first into the circle as the goal shooter offers. The goal attack offers the second move, and the centre is the backup.

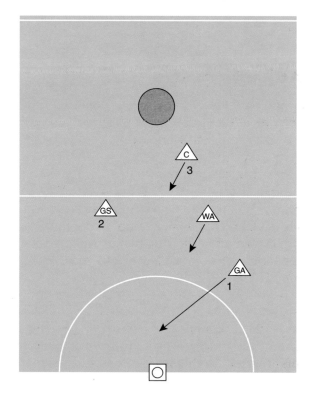

Figure 10.8 Wing attack with ball near transverse line.

Goal attack with ball outside the goal circle (figure 10.9): The goal attack looks into the goal circle first. The goal shooter offers first, the wing attack is ready with a second offer and the centre provides the backup.

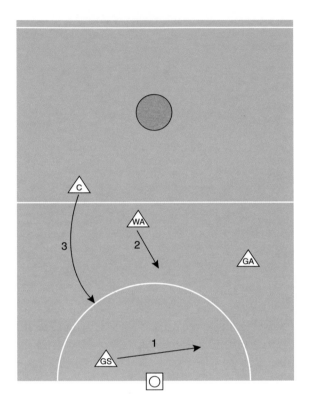

Figure 10.9 Goal attack with ball outside the goal circle.

Adjusting the Strategy

If you are a junior player, you might find it difficult to have three moves organised for each throw. When you are learning the game, you have so much to think about: getting your feet under control, passing the ball accurately, timing the offer and reading the move. The best approach is to start with the most basic form, one lead, and build the additions over time. This might take all season or two or three seasons depending on your skill level and your on-court application.

Begin by concentrating on the first move. Each time your team has possession, only one player takes responsibility for making a successful attacking move. The thrower waits only for this attacker, waiting for a successful break. The attacker keeps offering and re-offering for the full 3 seconds. This approach gives the attacker time to try two or three variations of his move. The weakness with this one-player approach is that there are no alternatives for passing.

Use team practice time to develop an understanding of, and confidence in, team strategy. Tell your coach how the strategy feels on court. Then begin to apply the strategy in match play, making sure you support each other. Acknowledge plays that work well.

When your team is able to use the first lead well, introduce a second option. Use the backup option (the safety valve) before you use the second forward offer. It is important not to be locked in to thinking that the ball must always travel forwards. Introducing the backup move as the second part of the strategy reinforces the fact that keeping possession is more important than passing forwards. Successful teams understand this principle.

If you find that your team is working well with just two options, don't force the issue. Polish what you do well, and keep it simple and working rather than complex and confusing. Finally, introduce the third part of the strategy when the team needs a new challenge. At this time use the second forward offer.

Once you have the three-player strategy working well, begin to extend yourselves by developing variations. For example, ignore the first offer and use the second one. This allows you to vary the timing of your team's movement and passing to unsettle the opposition.

Now your team must commence the first offer from behind the player with the ball, the second move from in front and the third a quick sideways hand-off. Again, that element of surprise can catch the defenders off guard.

When the centre has the ball midcourt (figure 10.10), the first move is from the goal defence, who starts behind the thrower. The second move is from goal attack in front, and the third is from the wing attack in front.

For variation, the first lead will use the touch space to offer even though they are facing the thrower. The second move will drive towards the thrower and the third move will originate from behind.

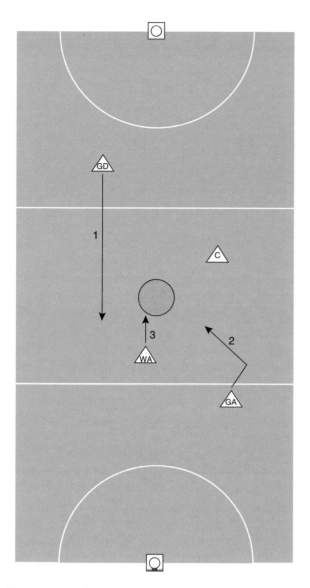

Figure 10.10 First move from behind the player with the ball.

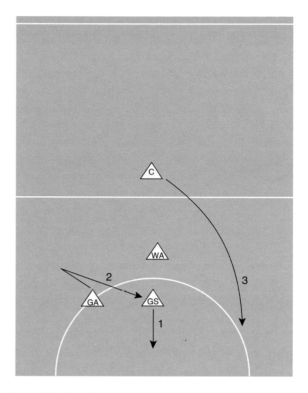

Figure 10.11 First move uses back space rather than the drive, or lead.

When the wing attack has the ball near the goal circle (figure 10.11), the goal shooter drops back for the high ball. The goal attack offers the second move, which originates in front of the thrower and the centre offers the safety move from behind.

Now try two simultaneous moves for the first offer. The player that is not used re-offers to provide the second move, and the backup uses back space. Two simultaneous first offers are followed by two simultaneous offers for the second move. This will involve four players before the backup is used.

You will discover numerous variations of this strategy. Learn the basics well, and then create your own patterns. Timing, spatial awareness and accurate passing are critical to the successful execution of this approach, so watch these elements closely as you work.

DEFENCE STRATEGY

Pressure, pressure, pressure and then a little surprise. After reading step 5, you know that defending is the non-glamorous part of court work. The rules often seem biased against the defending player. To be successful, the defence strategy must involve all seven players trying to restrict their opponents' opportunities. Leaving defending to the back line defenders is a recipe for disaster. The best defence strategy involves a commitment from all team members to apply defensive pressure.

Focus on the defensive pattern that works best for your team. We have always favoured one-on-one as the basic strategy. It enables team members to take responsibility for their own players. However, to be really effective, you will need to have other strategies that you can use. Zone, or press, defence, discussed later in this step, develops good anticipation skills and can certainly unsettle opponents. On the other hand, double defence creates more on-ground pressure on the attacker's movement. If you pressure well all match, you are likely to be rewarded for your efforts, particularly in the final minutes of each quarter and the last passages of the match. After setting the basic strategies, look for plays that add variety, and assist team members to keep the pressure on.

The key to success in defence is the amount of pressure you generate. Many players work diligently to cover the first move, but when they are unsuccessful, they simply drift out of play. To develop an effective defence strategy, team members must work before the ball comes in and continue to work long after the initial attacking lead. When you have unsuccessfully defended your opponent's initial move, regroup your efforts and apply pressure again. Teams that have the ability to do this can exert the type of pressure that wins matches.

Your defence strategy must have variety. Use one-on-one as your foundation. After making the initial move, you should recover and exert more pressure on the pass and the player. Develop your repertoire to include double defence, blocking, denying, channelling and the zone, or press, so you can introduce surprise elements that can unsettle the opposition. Remember to keep strategies alive and growing or they will become redundant and easy for the attacking team to beat. Introduce periods of play during which you come off the hard, chasing work and apply an anticipation-based approach to your defence. (Refer to Defending Off the Player in step 5, page 74.) Such tactics can help change the tempo of a game, a valuable ploy in tight encounters.

Using the Double Defence

Every time the ball goes out of court and has to be thrown in, the defending team has a player advantage on court. Use it well. The most common way to do this is to place a double defence on the player likely to receive the first pass on court. You can also use the double defence to nullify dominant players on the other team, particularly the wing attack at the centre pass or an outstanding goal shooter. In step 8 we looked at the double defence at the centre pass (page 121), and in step 9 in the goal circle (page 132).

The key to the successful use of a double defence is to position early and wisely. Both players need to be positioned before the attacker begins his move. Stand close, about a step away from the attacker. Offset so that one takes the front side, and the other has the back (figure 10.12a). The front player should be ball side. Now work those legs and keep the pressure on as the attacker begins to move.

You can also apply double defence as an alternative to pressuring the pass when your initial efforts to defend have been unsuccessful. As your opponent takes the pass, quickly size up just where you think she will throw the ball. Drop back into that passing lane and try to provide additional pressure on the attacking lead coming out to meet the ball. In this situation, you are watching the ball, with little view of the attacker behind you. Your teammates should talk to you to guide and encourage you. Work with your teammates to position yourself effectively. Listen for their calls and respond. If the attacker suddenly finds she has two defenders to contend with, she might react and make a mistake.

Although a double defence seems easy to apply, it is not. You and the other defender position yourselves so that both of you restrict the most beneficial options for the attacker. Work together to maintain this close pressure, and if the pass is made, both of you contest the catch (figure 10.12b). It is surprising how often two defenders will use the double defence quite strongly during the initial move and then only one of them will contest the pass. Reducing the pressure in this way means you do not maximise the benefit of the double defence. If the attacker receives the pass, one defender should use the recovery step and pressure the pass. The other should pick up the undefended player. Good communication is essential. When the double defence is successful (figure 10.12c), remain in control. Finish off your good work by delivering the ball safely down court.

Figure 10.12 | Double Defence

a

b

PREPARATION

1. Position to cover front ball halfway across or on the side
2. Position to cover high ball
3. Feet shoulder-width apart; weight down
4. Arms close to body
5. Eyes on player and ball

EXECUTION

1. Both maintain close position
2. Do not contact
3. Back defender uses voice to direct movement
4. Both contest pass

FOLLOW-THROUGH

1. Land and balance with bent knees
2. If successful, look for all options as shown
3. If unsuccessful, split with one recovering to pressure the pass and the other to pick up another player

c

Misstep
The double defence is ineffective.

Correction
The back defender must use her voice to direct movement.

Blocking, Denying and Channelling

Blocking, denying and channelling is another style of defence that can be effective. It can be worked from the first move or from the recovery step. Position yourself directly in the line of attack in which your opponent wants to move. Wait for your opponent to move. Keep your weight down and establish a wide base and a strong upright position. As soon as your opponent moves, begin to defend so that you block and deny the down-court route. Work hard to hold up the attacker by using rapid side steps from side to side to stay in front of her (figure 10.13). Make the attacker go very wide around you, channelling her to the side of the court so that you protect the centre corridor. As you face the attacker, concentrate primarily on her movement. Although you should be aware of the ball, do not focus on it. Holding up your opponent is of major importance. Remember, the rules do not allow you to contact the attacker. Have the attacker contact you—that is good defending.

Figure 10.13 Use rapid side steps to block off down-court moves.

Misstep
The attacking player easily gets past you.

Correction
Use small, quicker steps to continually reposition the attacking player.

Applying Zone, or Press, Defence

Zone, or press, defence takes the focus of your defence work from your individual opponent to the on-court space that the opposition team is trying to pass the ball through. The focus of the zone, or press, is to pressure the ball side of the court. Working as a unit, try to cut off the short pass and force a high, long ball for the back players to intercept.

Keeping your weight down so you are ready to pounce, focus on the ball. You should also be aware of player movement around the zone or press. Anticipate where your opponents are likely to pass. As soon as the ball is released, the nearest defender decides whether an interception is on or the zone, or press, defence unit drops back, anticipating the next passage of play. The long, high ball is the defender's delight; short, sharp passes present more of a challenge. Make sure you are confident defending both.

Go out hard to attack the ball. A strong running defender coming straight for the attacker can cause a handling error. Good communication among players in the defensive unit is critical. Remember, the interception or error comes

about because the unit worked together. Be sure that you acknowledge this.

Start with a three-player defensive triangle and build your numbers as your confidence grows. Be creative about when and how you apply this defensive strategy. It can be a powerful weapon in tight matches if you are courageous. The following paragraphs describe when to apply this strategy.

Misstep
You fail to intercept the ball.

Correction
Focus on the ball and continue to apply pressure on the ball side of the court. Keep your feet moving. Have the courage to attack the ball when it is in your area. Improve communication among those in the working unit.

Zone, or Press, at the Transverse Line

The zone, or press, at the transverse line can be used when the ball is coming out of the back third near the transverse line. Use this strategy after a penalty or throw-in because it gives players time to set up. Three players of the defending team quickly leave their opponents and form a triangle at the top of the centre third (figure 10.14). Their aim is to force the long, high ball over the zone, or press, for the back line players to intercept. The goal attack and the wing attack are about 1 metre behind the transverse line, and the centre is about 1 metre behind them. All players have their weight low and use rapid side shuffles across the area to cut off space. All players are ready to attack the ball as it comes into their areas.

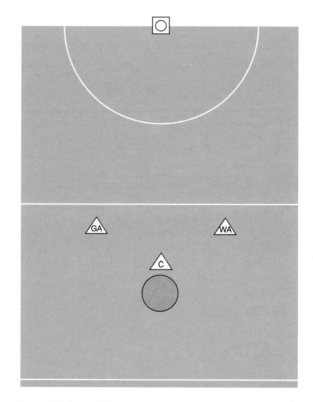

Figure 10.14 A three-player zone, or press, protects the centre corridor.

Zone, or Press, in the Attack Third

Move the zone forwards and increase the number of players to force the high ball as soon as your team swings into defence from a back line or sideline throw-in. The goal shooter positions just inside the top of the circle. The goal attack and wing attack position halfway down the third with the centre in the middle near the transverse line but within the centre third (figure 10.15). Players focus on the ball, ready to attack the pass once it enters their areas. If the ball penetrates the zone, or press, drop back as a unit to anticipate and contest the next pass.

Often the attacking team is thrown by this tactic and releases a wild pass. Another option attackers often use is to send a long, high ball down the side of the third. This should be easy for your centre, wing defence or goal defence to intercept.

Zone, or Press, Across the Centre Third

A zone or press defence can be used when the ball is coming down court to the opponent's goal end. All five players move quickly to the centre third when the call is given to set the press (figure 10.16). If it is set from a throw-in, players have adequate time to prepare and set up the zone, or press, on the ball side of the court. Defenders are mobile, watching the ball and moving to cut off space in their areas. They are ready to attack the ball or pressure the pass as it enters their area. The zone unit moves to pressure the side of the court that the ball is travelling down.

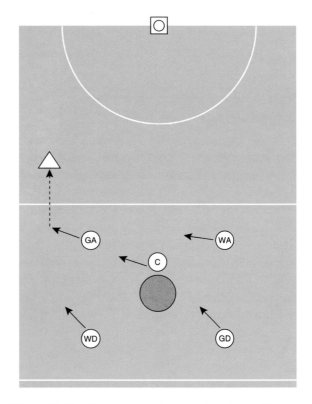

Figure 10.16   A centre-court press when the ball is coming down the right side of the court.

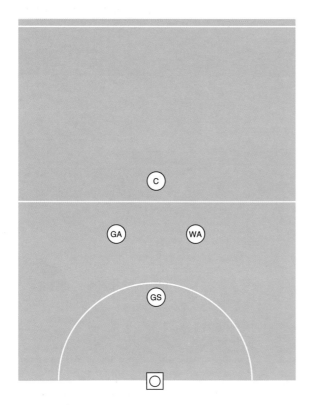

Figure 10.15   A zone, or press, set by attacking players when they are defending on a back line throw-in.

STRATEGY DRILLS

The following drills are designed to help you build team strategies in attack and defence and build your on-court awareness of space. They are designed to allow you to move freely within the court to open space and to teach you to use it well when working with other players. Of course, in defence you are trying to deny your opponent the use of this space. You are now very close to that all-important match play, so work hard on these final touches to give a very polished first performance.

Strategy Drill 1. *The First Move*

The three back line players—the goalkeeper, goal defence and wing defence—begin in the back third with the centre high in the centre third (figure 10.17). The goalkeeper has the ball on the goal line and is preparing to take a throw-in. As soon as the goalkeeper steps behind the back line, players offer their moves to bring the ball out of the back third and into the centre third. Goal defence offers first, and the wing defence and centre are ready with alternate moves. When the goal defence takes the pass, the wing defence offers her move. The goalkeeper enters the court ready to back up. The wing defence passes to the centre player offering in the centre third as the goal defence and wing defence back up. The ball has now travelled across the back third and entered the centre third.

To Increase Difficulty

- Ignore a first lead from one player and use a backup. Did you lose momentum before you were able to bring the ball across the back third and into the centre third?

- Have the wing defence and the goal defence change roles. This means that the goal-keeper passes to the wing defence, who then looks for the goal defence.

- Start the drill on the court. Have both defenders near the goalpost for a rebound. A player shoots and misses. The defenders rebound and play the ball to the wing defence, who plays on to the centre.

- Start the drill with the goal defence taking a sideline throw-in. The ball goes to the wing defence, who plays on to the centre with the goal defence and the goalkeeper giving backup.

- The coach throws the ball on the court. The nearest defender runs to pick it up, and the drill starts from this player. Are you able to adjust to an on-court turnover or loose ball?

- Repeat the drill but now introduce defending pressure by using your attackers to defend. Use two at first and allow them to float among players. Add a third and then a fourth as the attacking confidence of the team grows.

- Use the methods described in the section Three-Option Attack Strategy to work the midcourt and the front end.

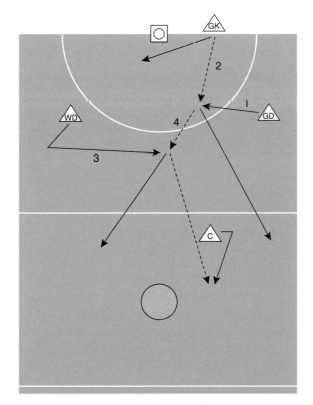

Figure 10.17 The First Move drill.

- Put all players on the court and link the play in all three sections so that the ball can travel the full length of the court.

Success Check

- Strong, definite attack moves.
- Variation.
- Well-timed moves.
- Good spatial awareness.

- Awareness of all options.
- Strong backup.
- Accurate passing.

Score Your Success

All 4 players combine to successfully bring the ball across the back third and into the centre third 3 times = 10 points

Your score ____

Strategy Drill 2.   *Blocking and Channelling*

Stand beside your opponent, ready to defend. The feeder is about 6 metres in front of you, and a receiver is a similar distance behind you. Your opponent moves to take the first pass. Go with your opponent, but allow him to take the catch. Use the recovery step to clear the legal distance, keeping your weight down, and focus on your opponent. As your opponent passes off to the receiver and then drives down court to make a double play, let the pass go. As soon as your opponent begins to drive down court, move up onto him quickly and shut down his space by stopping or slowing his forward movement without contacting.

To Increase Difficulty

- Contest the pass fully and then recover to block the down-court movement.
- Block the first move to the ball. Start in the reverse position (facing your opponent) as close as you can without causing contact.

Quickly work your feet across the path that your opponent wants to move into. Turn your head so that you can see the ball. Try to hold up the first move and then apply the block from the recovery position, if you are unsuccessful.

Success Check

- Move up quickly to shut down space.
- Use quick footwork.
- Be aware of where the ball is.
- Have a strong body without contact.

Score Your Success

Shut down or slow down the attacker's drive 3 times = 10 points

Your score ____

Strategy Drill 3.   *Double Defence*

This drill allows you to practise the double defence. Remember to work together and to avoid contact.

The feeder is immediately behind the sideline, ready to take a throw-in. The attacker is on the court, 5 or 6 metres in front of the feeder. Two defenders apply a double defence to the attacker. One defender positions between the attacker and the ball to cut off the front ball, working to force the attacker to the sideline to shut down the space she has to offer in. The other is behind the attacker to stop the high ball. The attacker offers, and the

defenders try to stay close to the attacker so that they can contest the pass.

For the second part of the drill, the feeder stands on the court with the ball beside a defender. Another defender and an attacker are 3 to 4 metres away. The feeder throws the ball into the air and jumps to take the catch. The defender jumps but does not contest the catch. They land, and immediately the defender drops back to form a double defence on the other attacker. The thrower attempts to pass successfully.

To Increase Difficulty

- For the first part of the drill, add another attacker and defender who can offer to the first ball. The double defence now has to split to pick up the original feeder when the new attacker has the ball.
- For the second part of the drill, divide one third of the court in half lengthways. Add another attacker and defender. This means that three attackers and three defenders are in the identified area. The attackers begin with the ball. They are trying to put 10 successful passes together. The defenders contest each throw. If they are beaten, they drop back and double-defend the next pass. They are trying to complete three successful double defences. See who wins.

Success Check

- Players use good communication.
- Defenders work together.
- Defenders deny space.

Score Your Success

Attackers beat the double defence and take the pass safely = 5 points

Defenders deny the attacker possession 3 times = 5 points

Your score ____

Strategy Drill 4. *Zone or Press*

The press operates on a triangle formation that reacts to the position of the ball. Begin with the simple formation, a three-player press on a transverse line, and then build the drill to add challenge.

Three players are in a triangle formation in the centre third, near the transverse line. Two players are at the front and are about 2 metres from the line and 6 metres apart. The third player is about 6 metres away in the middle behind them near the centre circle. The two throwers are in front of the triangle in the goal third with the ball. As they move freely about in front of the zone, they pass the ball to each other. The triangle reacts to the position of the ball by moving up to pressure the pass when it is on their side or dropping back slightly if it is on the opposite side.

To Increase Difficulty

- A receiver comes on court and works behind the defenders. The throwers now have the option to try to pass the ball to the receiver. When the ball is passed, the nearest player runs to intercept. The defenders try to intercept three passes.
- Add a second receiver to the back of the defenders and try to achieve three intercepts.

- Add a third player who works in the middle of the triangle. Make sure that short balls cannot get through. Force the ball out wide or up into the air to give the zone the best opportunity to intercept.
- Add the wing defence and the goal defence to the back of the centre third and repeat the drill until all five attackers and defenders are working a full centre-court zone.
- Put the goal shooter up front and repeat again with all six working together to channel the ball wide to force the intercept or cause a handling error.

Success Check

- React to the ball when it enters your area.
- Use good communication.
- Attack the ball.

Score Your Success

Press reacts successfully to 6 passes = 10 points

Your score ____

CREATING SPACE

Space is a precious commodity on the netball court; not a lot of it is available. The game revolves around the ability to create space, to occupy it and to defend it. Understanding the importance of space on the netball court helps you to become a thinking player. A player who is aware of the need to find open space and use it wisely can make a good contribution to team play.

Whether in attack or defence, you should think about space. In attack you are looking for ways to open the space so that you can take the pass. In defence you need to know where those openings are so that you can cut them off from your opponent. Your awareness of space should not be restricted to your own playing needs. Also consider what space the players around you are using or will use.

Using space is really the final ingredient of good play. We have looked at the moves, understood the terms and worked at timing. If you can do all this and use court space well, you will have much success on the netball court. The drills in this step will help you develop your awareness of space.

USING SPACE DRILLS

The final four drills in this step focus on the use of available court space. Make sure that you can make space and that you can see where the space is. Developing your spatial awareness is critical for on-court success.

In any one practice session, use a variation of these drills two or three times. When you can complete the drill and score the maximum points, add another challenge.

Using Space Drill 1. *Offset One Third of the Court*

Three attacking players are in one third of the court. One player throws and catches the ball to start play. The other two players offer simultaneously, using space well and with good timing. The player with the ball selects the offer and passes the ball. The new thrower now has two leads offered so selects a player and passes. The three players continue to move the ball among themselves like this as they work for good spatial awareness and variation of movement. If both players lead to the same space, stop the drill. Players should address their poor use of space and then restart the drill.

To Increase Difficulty

- Every third pass must be a high ball.
- Add a fourth attacker.
- There must be a bounce pass and a high ball in every five passes.
- On the whistle, the player with the ball must dig in (stop) while the others keep re-offering.

- Introduce defenders. Begin with two. When the attackers complete 10 consecutive passes while using the space well, add a third defender.

- To really close the space, add a fourth defender. In this case, attackers must complete six consecutive successful passes while using the space well.

- As you are working through the constantly changing space, close it down to, say, the goal circle, or take a midway approach and use half of the third. Remember, at times on court you will feel that you have loads of space in which to work, but at other times space will be very restricted and crowded. You need to learn to handle all of these situations, so adapt as the available space changes in practice.

Success Check

- Good spatial awareness.
- Eyes on the player and the ball.
- Voice used to call the play when needed.
- Strong, definite attacking moves.
- Variation of movement.

Attackers complete 10 consecutive passes while using their space well = 10 points

Your score ___

Using Space Drill 2.   *Offset Two Thirds of the Court*

Three players are in each of two adjoining thirds of the court. The drill starts in one third. Each player in that third handles the ball before it enters the adjoining third. Simply pass the ball back and forth from third to third. All three players offer and handle the ball before passing it across the transverse line. All players offer into space.

To Increase Difficulty

- Increase to four players in each third.
- Change the available space.
- The first player to handle the ball as it enters the third must rehandle it before passing it back into the other third.
- Take two passes before passing the ball back into the other third.
- Use a long throw to pass across the transverse line.
- Use only two-handed passes to deliver the ball.

- One player must use a preliminary move every time the ball enters your third.
- Add defenders, beginning with two and working up to three or four.
- Vary the working space.

Success Check

- Strong attacking moves.
- Variation of movement.
- Accurate passing.
- Good spatial awareness.
- Good timing.

Pass the ball up and back 3 times with good use of space = 5 points

Your score ___

Using Space Drill 3. *Offset Full Court*

Three players are in each third of the court. The ball starts at one end and travels up and down the court without a handling error or players using the same space.

The only limit to this drill is your imagination. After attempting the To Increase Difficulty variations, create your own related to the performance of your team; then add defence. This really challenges your ability to find space. Try to incorporate two or three short bursts of this work in each team session. You will notice that your ability to find space and use it wisely really starts to develop.

To Increase Difficulty

- Don't use the same move as the player before you.
- After the ball crosses the transverse line into the new third, pass it back to the third it came from before passing it forwards to the next third.
- If you drop the ball, start that passage again.
- You must use a high ball to cross the transverse line.

- All players must use one hand to catch and throw.
- Use only high balls.
- Add defence.

Success Check

- Good spatial awareness.
- Eyes on the player and the ball.
- Good timing.

- Strong attacking moves.
- Accurate passing.
- Variation of movement.

Score Your Success

All players use space well and pass the ball up and down the court with no handling errors = 10 points

Your score ___

Using Space Drill 4.   *From the Corner*

Working from awkward spaces will really challenge your spatial awareness. Four attackers and their defenders are on court in the goal third. The wing defence and goal defence from the attacking team are near the transverse line in the centre third.

The goal attack steps outside the court to take a throw-in from the corner of the court on the back line or sideline just before they intersect. The wing attack has a double defence on the goal attack and must work this crowded space to take the first pass. Once the wing attack has the ball, she back passes to the midcourt players, who then send the ball forward. The ball must reach the circle for a shot with a maximum of three passes or it is passed back to the midcourt to begin the attack again.

Defenders have many opportunities to force errors—a tight initial double defence, hard chasing as the ball comes back and good intercepting when a pass is released.

The attackers earn 1 point when they score a goal. The defenders earn 1 point when they intercept or cause an error. Whenever a point is scored, players rotate their starting positions so all attackers take the first ball and all defenders pressure the initial move.

To Increase Difficulty

- Defend the midcourt players.
- Close the playing area down to half of the third.

Success Check

- Good spatial awareness.
- Well-timed moves.
- Variation of movement.

Score Your Success

First team to score 5 points = 10 points

Your score ___

SUCCESS SUMMARY OF DEVELOPING STRATEGIES AND USING SPACE

The final part of your preparation for that all-important first game is to develop your awareness of space and to begin to build your team strategies.

Developing the ability to move the ball well as an attacking unit requires good spatial awareness, timing and variation of movement and passing that is controlled and delivered into the player's space.

Applying defensive pressure requires good spatial awareness and variation of approach. The pressure should be on whenever your opponents have the ball. Communicate well with each other. Acknowledge your successes. Denying your opponents the space they desire can be very tough work.

Successful teams know how to work together and have confidence that their teammates will always be there to provide that all-important back up.

Before moving on to step 11, The Winning Team, evaluate how you did on the drills in this step. Tally your scores to determine how well you have mastered strategy and the ability to create space. If you scored at least 60 points, you are ready to move on to step 11. If your score is 45 to 59 points, redo the drills to improve your score before you move on. If your score is less than 45 points, review step 10 and redo the drills before you move on to the next step.

Strategy Drills

1. The First Move — ___ out of 10
2. Blocking and Channelling — ___ out of 10
3. Double Defence — ___ out of 10
4. Zone or Press — ___ out of 10

Using Space Drills

1. Offset One Third of the Court — ___ out of 10
2. Offset Two Thirds of the Court — ___ out of 5
3. Offset Full Court — ___ out of 10
4. From the Corner — ___ out of 10

Total — ___ *out of 75*

You are almost ready to take your place in that all-important first match. Just before you do we want to introduce you to the elements of good teamwork in step 11. Successful teams don't just happen. All team members work hard to combine their talents effectively. Remember, it is not only your good basic skills that bring success. Learning to combine well with your teammates is critical for overall good team performance.

The Winning Team

Nothing feels quite as good as winning. Winning once is good. Doing it consistently is better; it is what you train for. A successful team not only has to work hard to develop skills and strategies and raise fitness levels; it also needs to develop strong teamwork.

If you evaluate successful teams in netball and other team sports, you will notice some common characteristics among the players. They enjoy playing together, they go out hard and try to win, but they also can handle losing graciously and are good sports. Players on such teams are confident and enjoy being challenged. They show huge respect for one another, their opponents and the rules of play.

Successful teams do not happen overnight. You need to constantly work at building skills both on and off the court. Start by making sure that you are using each practice session to be a better team member. Watch your teammates. Appreciate their court craft—the way they move, their favourite throws and their work rate. Then look a little deeper at yourselves as a team. Are you enjoying being out there? Do you try new things? Do you help those around you? And what happens when things go wrong?

Off the court, some teams like to spend a lot of time together, whereas others prefer to use this time to pursue other interests. Both approaches work because winning teams understand and respect not only their team members' skills and abilities, but also their interests and ambitions. Successful teams have a balance between the individual and the group.

This step will look at some of the key ingredients of winning teams to help you develop these all-important skills.

TEAMWORK

Netball is often referred to as the ultimate team sport. It has earned this reputation because of the crowded nature of the court and the fact that only two players—the shooters—can score.

With 14 players on court, space is at a premium. You have to be aware of the space you are using and the space that is available for your team members. You rely heavily on these judgments to pass the ball successfully up and down the court. Those who play sports on broad fields have a lot of space in which to move so a poor decision can be easily rectified. In netball, a poor choice is costly. Netballers need to read off each other constantly because each move they make affects their fellow team members directly. Working together as a unit is what successful netball is all about.

The rules of the game state that the ball must be handled in each third of the court. Netball teams have to link the thirds together. If the midcourt is struggling, you cannot simply bypass it. You must work with them to find a way through. This means that even when the ball is not in your third, you must be ever watchful, ready to offer a backup move or give moral support to your team members farther down court.

When the ball reaches the goal circle, either of the shooters may shoot for goal. These are the only two members of the team who can score. The rest of the team relies on the abilities of the shooters to put the ball through the ring to win games. A team can be passing well and moving the ball to their shooters quite regularly, but all this hard work will be negated if the shooters fail to convert. Successful teams understand the additional responsibility that the shooters have and work hard to support them. Well-placed passes into the circle make life so much easier for hard-working shooters. Acknowledging each goal scored shows the shooters that you appreciate their skill.

Teamwork is important to netballers because they rely on each other to be successful. Great shooters will not succeed if the team does not deliver the ball frequently, and the team that can deliver the ball regularly will not succeed if its shooters lack accuracy.

Misstep
An individual fails to combine with other team members.

Correction
Make sure team members' roles are clearly identified. All players should have input into the overall team performance and goals.

TRAINING

The tone of the team is set on the practice court. Here the base of your teamwork is established. Each training session should be enjoyable and challenging for the players and the coach.

Planning is essential, but it should be adapted as the session rolls out. Keep a watchful eye on each segment of the session, making sure you have mastered the skills and strategies of the session before moving on to something else. If you are really struggling, stop and revert to the basics, challenging yourself again when your confidence returns. If you struggle in training, you are likely to struggle on court.

To develop those winning ways, creativity should be alive and well on the training court. Take a step back and observe whether you are simply doing as you are told, or trying new and different ways to play. Do some experimenting, and encourage your teammates to do the same. It is better to find out what you can achieve and where your limitations might be before you are under the pressure of competition.

Another issue to examine is your attitude to training. Are you focused on the task, giving it your all, or do you have other things on your mind? If you drift in and out of a training session, you will do the same thing when the game starts. This is simply not good for the team. When you are in the heat of competition, nothing short of total concentration will do.

How do you relate to your teammates as you work? Are you inclusive, recognising and making allowances for each other's differences? Does your team include the supertalented as well as the limited player within the group? Players most often have trouble fitting in at the extremes of ability. Actively seek out and support anyone who is not included. Players who feel left out in training will find it difficult to function effectively when match play begins.

Finally, look closely at how you react when things go well and when they go badly. Do you have that touch of class that allows you to behave graciously when things get hard? Can you keep your cool and work to find a solution? Do you feel supported and reassured to try again? If your teammates (or you) exhibit undermining behaviour, address it as a group. Your team will fall apart under pressure if such behaviour takes hold.

Misstep

Some team members display a poor attitude to training.

Correction

Players with a poor attitude should work with a good role model within the team, one who has a good work ethic.

COMPETITION

Competition should first and foremost be fun. Netballers love to play, to compete and to pit their talents and strategies against their opponents. They also love devising game plans. Hours are spent developing tactics, and probably even more hours are whiled away on the post-mortem of a match. Enjoying the thrill of competing is where a winning team starts.

Once you step out onto the court and the umpire's whistle blows, the contest begins. It is different from training. In training, if you make a mistake, you can try again until you get it right. During a match you don't have that luxury. Mistakes are costly. What this means is that competition brings with it a level of pressure that is absent from training. Coping with this pressure will be important if you are to become a winning team.

The first thing to realise is that you are all in this together. Each player has an important role. To win, you will need to combine your individual skills with those of your teammates. Focus on this to begin so that you are quite clear about what you are trying to achieve. Having a clear game plan helps abate the panic that pressure can bring. Step out knowing what you want to do and how you will go about achieving this. Be confident. You have a plan; see if you can implement it. Keep it simple and flexible, and you will handle pressure well.

Once play is underway, be quick to work out your strengths, what is working well today. Play to your strengths, but have a little in reserve. Winning teams know how to use their strengths to dominate and then add variety. This really frustrates the opposition. Just as they begin to feel confident that they can match you, the game plan changes. Always try to dictate the terms of play so you are setting the pace, not trying to catch up to it.

As the match progresses, make sure that you stay positive and supportive. Acknowledge good play and do it twice as loud for those outstanding passages. Let each other know that you really appreciate the effort. Don't miss those unglamorous moves that make all the difference—the clearing run that opened space for someone else and the dogged defence that stopped the pass.

When mistakes happen, sort them quickly; then move on. When a player drops the ball, she does not need to be chastised. She needs some positive reinforcement and guidance to encourage her to attack the next ball with confidence. Be there for her.

Whenever you compete, you can win or lose. That's the exciting thing. Winning teams know how to win and how to lose. They thrive on the challenge, and when the game goes their way, they enjoy the spoils. It's great to share the victory with each other, the coaching staff and friends and supporters. A touch of humility and acknowledgment of your opponent's efforts should be in there, too. When the result goes against you, pay tribute to the victors and then quietly go about analysing the result. Finding the breakdowns in play and working to improve is what it is all about. Blaming and shaming other team members has no place in a successful team.

Misstep

Your team has a high rate of errors during games.

Correction

Go back to good basics. First look at your own game to see what you can do better before you look elsewhere within the team. Remain positive and supportive as a team.

PEOPLE

Good people are critical to the success of a netball team. The talent of the athletes, the expertise of the coach and their specialist staff and the support of parents, partners and club administration are key ingredients for success.

A positive can-do attitude inspires the group to reach that little bit further, particularly when things are not going according to plan. Enjoying a challenge allows you to adapt and try new ways. Simply doing what you have always done will not take you to the top of the ladder when the season ends. Now let us take a closer look at the people who make up the winning team.

The Coach

The coach's role is pivotal to the team's success. Coaches create the environment in which the team can flourish, setting the standards for players and support staff. Their leadership skills are critical. Convincing others to adopt their philosophy, getting them to commit to the bigger picture and not run private agendas, is essential as is fostering a belief and the confidence that winning is achievable. Above all else, the coach must have a passion for the game, thrive on the challenges and enjoy the athletes.

Initially, coaching was like a one-man band. Today, coaching is more akin to an orchestra. The head coach is the conductor over the support staff—assistant coaches, specialist coaches and the various sport science and sports medicine staff who are experts in their own right. Maintaining harmony takes great people skills. As in an orchestra, it takes only one member of the team to be off-key to ruin the performance. Winning teams are led by coaches who know how to get all sections of their orchestra playing the same tune.

Top coaches know when to hold the reins tight and when to let things flow. They can quite clearly identify what is not negotiable and where there is room to move. The ground rules are clearly understood by all, although they are never quite set in stone. Wise coaches allow themselves a little flexibility to cope with the unexpected. Experience teaches them that not everything that affects their team is under their control.

Successful coaches are students of the game from the day they first take on the role until they retire. They learn from their players, the opposition, the superstars, the experts, other coaches and other sports, by watching, reading and listening. Their thirst for knowledge is what sets them apart. Simply doing what they did last year is not good enough. They rethink, re-tack, review and renew.

The Players

Netballers have a highly developed sense of teamwork. They understand that to be successful they need to combine their talents with the talents of those around them. They need to make allowances for the strengths and weaknesses of others so that the skills of all are greater and more effective than the skills of one.

Successful players take calculated risks. They do the basics very well but can also add their own touch of magic. They are confident, not arrogant, and thrive on the challenges that training and competing offer. They have a desire to win, to succeed, and they are prepared to apply themselves to the task. They know that those who take shortcuts will be found out when the going gets tough, so they put in the hard work and do all that it takes to be the best they can be. They combine a great work ethic, a hunger for knowledge, a respect for the talents of others and an unwavering belief in their own ability.

Top netballers are adaptable. They are not fazed by sudden changes in their regime or on-court situations. Although they like to operate within a basic structure, they are not left floundering if this alters. Being flexible helps them to cope when others might fall apart. This is a very important characteristic for handling umpires. Many of the rules rely on the umpire's interpretation, which often means that variations exist from one end of the court to the other. Being adaptable helps netballers succeed.

Above all else successful netballers have a great passion for the game. They enjoy being out on court, respect the rules and can't wait to do it all again even better the next match.

The Captain

The captain is the on-court leader of the team. It is not uncommon for teams to have co-captains who share the role or to rotate the captaincy among a number of experienced players.

Once she takes the toss, the captain assumes responsibility for leading the team's on-court performance. It is a challenging role. Not only must the captain play well herself, but she must also reinforce the team's positive play and support those who are struggling. Smart captains recruit experienced players in each third to assist. This takes the pressure off and allows others to share the leadership responsibilities.

The coach relies on the captain for an accurate picture of on-court play. A good captain can feel the mood and pace of the game as well as read the play. Their accurate assessment of what is actually happening out there is invaluable to the coach.

Off-court the captain is the eyes and ears of the coach regarding team dynamics. It is important for the captain and coach to have an open and honest relationship in which things can be said in confidence. Successful captains can negotiate the delicate balance of being part of the playing group and part of the management team at the same time.

Team captains should also have good social skills. They are often called on to speak in public on the team's behalf. They must be competent to tackle this important role because what they say reflects on all team members. If you are a team captain, seek help if you are nervous. You will be surprised at how much you can improve if you find a good teacher.

The Bench

Everyone on the team wants to be on court right at the start of the match and stay there for the duration. Competitors love to compete. However, the reality is that only seven players of the team can take the court together, which leaves up to five players on the bench.

It is important for players to contribute to the team's efforts when on the bench. There is no place for self-pity or doubt. The team needs the bench players to be ready to hit the court running if the coach looks their way. When on the bench, be supportive, wish those who start on court well, watch the play closely and offer positive and constructive comments at the breaks.

Prepare your own plan from what you see unfolding on the court. What works and what does not should be quite clear from your court-side view. If the call comes, be confident, step up and deliver. If you don't make it, stay positive, put in some extra work to compensate for the lack of match play and try again next game.

Support Staff

The team behind the team is a good way to think of the support staff (e.g., a specialist coach who works with the defenders or a strength and conditioning coach who develops a fitness program). Their job is to support the coach and the players. Regardless of the speciality they bring to the team, support staff must work through the coach.

The coach ensures that all members of the support staff work to the one game plan and that no personal agendas come into play. The coach and the support staff need to be aware of the problems each will face. Each must become familiar with the body of knowledge of the others' specialities. In other words, they must educate each other so that their work can have a direct impact on the performance of the players.

Team Management

Winning teams need management that supports their endeavours. Management needs to keep arrangements running smoothly so the players and the coaching team know what is expected of them on and off the court. Doing the simple things well is their speciality. Life is so much easier for the players when management is efficient and supportive. The members of a team with good management support feel secure because they have confidence in the arrangements that are made for them.

Parents

Parents seem to come in one of two varieties—supportive and nightmare. The former can be a great asset; the latter are best kept well clear of the courts.

Parents should understand that the players and the coach work together to build their team; for this reason, they should address any issues that arise to the coach. They must always be conscious of the need to be tactful and succinct. The coach has many demands on his time and should not be distracted by petty concerns.

Parents who reinforce the coach's message at home make a valuable contribution to teamwork. The real gems are those who just quietly give their time to support the team in many helpful ways—by getting the courts ready, timekeeping, keeping score or umpiring and by preparing nutritious snacks for the team to enjoy at the end of training sessions or competitions.

TEAM DRILLS

Developing a successful team takes time. Work on it every session. Starting with a challenging, fun drill can set the tone for the session to follow.

Closing the session in a similar manner allows you to leave on a positive note, looking forward to the next time you train together.

Team Drill 1. *Tail Tag*

All members of the team are in the centre third. Each player has a tail, a coloured band tucked into the back of his shorts. On "Go", athletes move freely around the midcourt, trying to snatch the tail from another player. Players must use their speed and create space to stay away from their teammates. Once he has pulled a tail off, the victor tucks it into his shorts. The coach blows the whistle to stop the drill after 30 seconds. The winner is the one who has collected the most tails. Redistribute the tails and start the drill again. Repeat two to four times.

To Increase Difficulty

- Change the movement pattern—for example, everyone must run backwards; then everyone must use shuffle steps.

Success Check

- Read the movements of the other players.
- Vary your movement and speed.
- Use space wisely.

Score Your Success

Collect the most tails = 5 points

Your score ___

Team Drill 2. *Ball Tag*

Divide the squad into two equal teams. Each player wears a bib to identify her team. All players are in the centre third. One team has the ball. The team with the ball moves around, passing the ball to each other. Working within the footwork rule, players use the ball to tag or touch as many of their opponents as possible within 30 seconds. The team without the ball works to avoid being tagged. A player who is tagged is eliminated from the game and goes to stand on the sideline. The coach blows the whistle to stop the drill after 30 seconds. Teams change roles, and the drill restarts. Repeat two to four times. The winner is the team with the most tags or touches.

To Increase Difficulty

- Introduce a second ball. Players now must avoid both balls.

Success Check

- Communicate well with your team members.
- Apply the footwork rule when in possession.
- Pass the ball quickly and accurately.
- Vary your movement and use space well.

Score Your Success

Achieve the most tags or touches = 5 points

Your score ___

Team Drill 3. *Beat the Shooters*

Divide the squad into two teams of six players. One team (the runners) line up behind each other at the corner of the baseline. The other team (the shooters) line up behind each other at a cone placed midway in the goal circle (figure 11.1).

On "Go", the first runner sprints around the attack third sidelines, transverse line and back line and back to her line and tags the next runner, who repeats the sprint. The first runner returns to the back of the line and the process is repeated until the shooting team calls "Stop". The running team earns 1 point for every completed run. If "Stop" is called when the runner is only partway around, she does not score a point.

On "Go", the first shooter attempts to score a goal from the cone. If she scores a goal, she passes the ball to the next person in line. If she misses, she quickly retrieves the ball, returns to the cone and shoots again. The shooter must continue to shoot until she scores a goal. When all six players have scored a goal, they call "Stop" and the runners count how many runners completed a full run. The teams rotate, and the drill starts again. The team that scores the most runs wins.

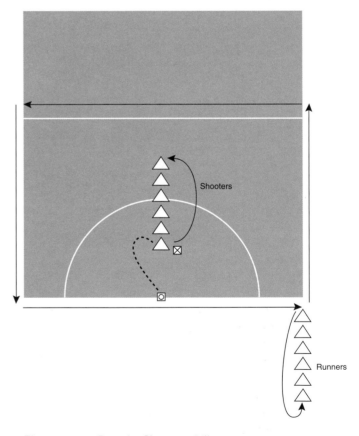

Figure 11.1 Beat the Shooters drill.

To Increase Difficulty

- Move the cone to the side of the goalpost or take it back another step.
- Each shooter must score two goals before passing the ball to the next shooter.
- Runners run backwards along the sidelines and sprint across the transverse line and the back line.

Success Check

- Shoot accurately.
- Maintain full speed throughout the sprint.
- Give strong support and encouragement to each other.

Score your Success

Complete the most runs = 10 points

Your score ____

Team Drill 4. *Pass and Shoot*

Two lines of six players stand 3 metres apart and evenly spread down the court between the two goal circles and about 2 meters in from the sideline. Both teams face the middle of the court and work to the goal circle on their right-hand side. In front of each line (about 2 metres) stands a worker with a ball (figure 11.2).

On the whistle the worker passes the ball quickly to the first person in his line. The first person in line quickly passes the ball back as the worker moves down court towards his team's goal circle. The worker must pass to each player on the line. If a ball is dropped, recommence the drill from where the mistake occurred. The last feeder passes a high ball into the goal circle, aiming to place the ball close to the post to give the worker an easy shot for goal.

The worker must score. If the shot is unsuccessful, the worker quickly retrieves the ball and tries again from the spot where he has the ball. If the ball goes out of the court, the worker comes back into the goal circle and retakes the shot opposite from where the ball went out.

On a successful shot the line moves one space to the left as the shooter retrieves the ball and passes to the player closest to him on the line. The team quickly passes the ball down the line back to the starting position while the worker sprints to join the space at the end of the line. As the ball is passed down the line, the new worker times an offer to take the ball where the drill began. He then moves down the line, passing to each member before reaching the goal circle and attempting to score a goal.

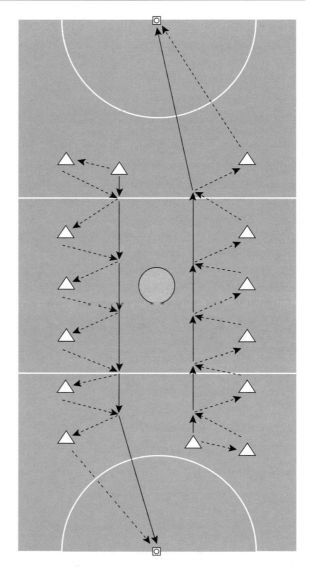

Figure 11.2 Pass and Shoot drill.

Repeat until all players have a chance as the worker. The winner is the first team to finish the drill by passing the ball back to the top of the line once all players have scored a goal.

To Increase Difficulty

- If the ball is dropped, it goes back to the top of the line to recommence the drill.
- Vary the passes. Each member must use a different pass to the worker as the ball travels down the line.

Success Check

- Worker times movements well.
- Players execute accurate passes.
- Players support and encourage their team members.

Score Your Success

First team to finish the drill = 10 points

Your score ____

Team Drill 5. *Channel Ball*

Divide into two teams of six. A good way is to have attackers against defenders. Each team has four foam netballs. One team is the throwing team, and the other is the running team.

Form a channel lengthwise on the court. Throwers spread out on the outside of the channel. The running team tries to get from one end of the court to the other and back (one run) without getting hit by the ball as the throwing team passes to each other (figure 11.3). A runner who is hit remains in the game, trying to score as many runs as possible. Only two players are allowed to run at one time. Work for a specified length of time such as 2 minutes, and then change roles.

To score the drill, count the number of runs minus the number of times a ball hit a runner. The winner is the team that scores the most runs after the hits are subtracted.

To Increase Difficulty

- Have teams complete a second or third change of roles before deciding the final score.

Success Check

- Work together as a team.
- Pass accurately.
- Vary your speed and movements.

Score Your Success

Complete the most runs after subtracting hits = 10 points

Your score ____

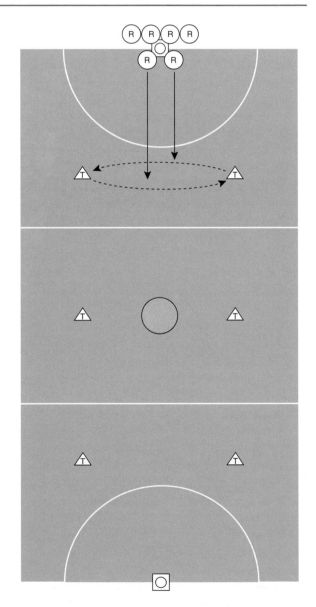

Figure 11.3 Channel Ball drill.

Team Drill 6.   *Netball Disc*

This game uses all netball rules, particularly footwork and contact rules. You also will need one flying disc and two teams of six or eight players (one team wears bibs). Toss for the first pass. The loser of the toss selects the end.

The aim of the game is to keep passing the flying disc until it passes on or over your attacking baseline. The team that wins the toss starts the game from its opponent's baseline. If the defending team intercepts the disc, it becomes the attackers and the other team becomes the defenders. The team scores a point each time the flying disc goes over the baseline. After a team has scored, its opponents take the pass from the baseline and the game restarts towards the opponent's baseline. The first team to score

3 points (juniors) or 5 to 8 points (seniors) wins the game.

Success Check

- Good team communication.
- Controlled footwork.
- Good use of space.
- Good body control.

Score Your Success

First team to score 3 points (juniors) or 5 to 8 points (seniors) = 10 points

Your score ____

SUMMARY OF WINNING TEAMS

Success begins on the training court, flows into competition and is driven by the talents and skill of the players and coaches.

Winning teams embrace success, enjoy the challenges and handle wins and losses with ease. They work together, acknowledge their individual talents and shortcomings and put these together in a winning formula.

Before moving on to step 12, The Fit Team, tally your scores to determine how well you have mastered teamwork. If you scored at least 35 points, you are ready to move on to step 12. If your score is 25 to 34 points, redo the drills to improve your score before you move on. If your score is less than 25 points, review step 11 and redo the drills before you move on to the next step.

Team Drills

1. Tail Tag	___ out of 5
2. Ball Tag	___ out of 5
3. Beat the Shooters	___ out of 10
4. Pass and Shoot	___ out of 10
5. Channel Ball	___ out of 10
6. Netball Disc	___ out of 10
Total	___ *out of 50*

You are now ready to tackle step 12. This last step focuses on the important area of fitness. You need to make sure you are able to maintain your competitiveness throughout the game. Winning teams can apply pressure in attack and defence for four quarters. To achieve this, you must have a sound overall level of fitness.

The Fit Team

Netball has changed enormously since the genteel days of Madam Osterberg's Physical Education College, when ladies walked sedately around the court in their long, flowing dresses, passing the ball. Today the international scene is dominated by finely tuned athletes moving with incredible speed and control. It's fast and furious and no place for the faint of heart. Today's players need to undertake fitness training to ensure that they are capable of absorbing the pressures that the muscles and the joints generate and to help prevent injuries.

A number of fitness components are important for on-court success. The game is often described as an interval team sport because it requires short, high-intensity efforts that are repeated frequently throughout the match. This means that you must have high levels of both aerobic and anaerobic fitness to ensure that you can maintain your speed and power for the duration of the game.

The rapid on-court changes of direction demand high levels of agility, acceleration, core stability and flexibility. This step looks at these important components of fitness and suggests ways you can develop them. We also consider the age of the athlete. The needs of young, active athletes are quite different from those of the more serious seniors or those at the elite level.

Both the athlete and the coach must understand their specific requirements and work together to achieve a high level of fitness. Although personal trainers and fitness specialists have an important role to play, they should work to the coach and athlete unit to ensure that the programme is written to address specific on-court requirements. The programme should be written around the position the netballer plays and her level of fitness. Abdicating the responsibility for writing the programme to others is not an option.

To be a successful netballer, you must be able to offer a variety of moves quickly. When the game begins, it is easy to offer powerful moves, but as the game progresses, the body tires and you begin to lose momentum. You may drop the ball or mistime your lead. Your opponent may sense that you are losing pace and apply the pressure. Suddenly you are struggling to be competitive.

Fitness helps you to maintain the power of those first few moves throughout the entire match. A high level of fitness allows you to make your on-court movements quite effortlessly.

Those silly little mistakes don't creep into your game because you are still feeling quite fresh and in control. You can focus on the ball because you are confident that you can maintain your pace and quality of movement right up to that final whistle.

Well-designed fitness programmes help prevent injuries. They ensure that the muscles and joints that absorb so much pressure during match play are able to cope with the stresses and strains of the game.

KEY COMPONENTS OF FITNESS

Energy systems: The body has two energy systems—aerobic and anaerobic. Short, sharp movements use the anaerobic system. The aerobic system allows you to maintain these movements over the period of the game by providing the oxygen your muscles need for energy. As you become more fit, your body is able to more readily transport and absorb this oxygen. As a result, you are able to play and train longer without tiring. It is therefore important that your programme train both energy systems.

Acceleration: Being able to produce a strong take-off is the key to success whether you are sprinting to the ball or elevating to take a high pass. Many moves you will offer during a game will involve acceleration from a jog, shuffle or stationary position. These moves average less than 2 seconds, but the acceleration involved in making a position, evading an opponent or intercepting a pass is critical for success. Acceleration for netball is best developed over short distances, one or two strides to 5 or 10 metres with 20 meters being the maximum distance.

Agility: The basic movement patterns of netball involve numerous sideways movements, sudden changes of direction and quick starts and stops. You will use shuffling or sideways movements at speed and full effort between 100 and 300 times in a game depending on the position you play. It is important that agility drills relate to these netball-specific movements. Aim to keep your body well balanced and apply power in your movements as you stop, start and weave your way around the court.

Aerobic endurance: A high level of aerobic endurance will enable you to play and practise longer at higher intensities. To develop aerobic endurance, you need to work very intensely running, swimming cycling or rowing very fast—possibly above race pace—before resting for a moderately long period. Repeat the exercise a number of times. For example, perform aerobic activity 10 times for 30 seconds each time with 90 seconds of rest between times. Be cautious in the use of steady-paced work. There is a limit to the level of fitness that can be achieved through masses of long runs.

Core stability: Core stability relates to your body's ability to provide support to the spine and pelvis as you move. Core stability is essential for maintaining an upright posture, especially for the explosive movements that netball requires. You are working the region bounded by the abdominal wall, the pelvis, the lower back and the diaphragm to stabilise the body during movement. Whenever a person, moves the core region is tensed. This tension is usually made unconsciously and in conjunction with a change in breathing pattern. As the load increases, the core muscles contract to form a stable ball-like core region against which the forces are balanced in coordination with posture.

Flexibility: Keeping your body supple allows you to achieve a full range of motion of all joints so you can turn, stretch, twist and bend without any stiffness or aching. Good flexibility allows you to scoop that low ball as easily as you can turn in the air. Exercise increases the amount of flexibility in a joint while decreasing the amount of resistance. A good stretching routine is invaluable for warming up, cooling down and home training.

Power and strength: Successful netballers are explosive. They can elevate, take off, change direction and stop with powerful movements. These explosive actions require high levels of force to be exerted over a relatively short period of time. Maximum force and rate of force have been shown to be important to the execution of these moves. Resistance and plyometric training develop the strength qualities of maximum force and rate of force.

FITNESS TRAINING

Your coach should be aware of both your chronological age and your training age. Young athletes who are playing a number of sports require only a very light touch, whereas serious athletes need periodised programmes to guide them throughout the year. Your programme should focus on the position or positions you will play. A fast-moving midcourt netballer and an aerial shooter have different needs. Your programme should recognise and accommodate your specific needs.

You need to be committed to your fitness training. Simply going through the motions is not good enough. Fitness training is often done alone away from the team's training session. Embrace the challenge, organise regular times to do the additional work and work at top pace. You will need a great deal of discipline to get the best out of yourself when no one else is around, but the reward will be an important life skill.

Remember that fitness programmes are really guides. They should be adapted as the season progresses to take into account your strengths, weaknesses and injuries. Netball-specific field tests that can be administered quite easily court side or at home have an important role to play. They will give you a good starting point from which to build your programme. They will also provide feedback throughout the season. You will be able to see whether you are actually improving your elevation, speed or other fitness component. Never work blindly in this area. Always know why you are doing specific work and whether you are actually benefiting from it.

Young Athletes

Young athletes should beware of rushing into a serious training regimen. It is more beneficial to long-term development for young athletes to compete in a wide range of sports and activities for as long as they can. Coaches and trainers should work with, not against, the other sporting and recreational interests of young athletes.

Coaches and trainers shouldn't assume that the younger generation has done all the basic movements that were part of the early years of past generations, such as climbing trees, throwing stones, chasing, dodging and playing on the swings. These daily activities enabled children to develop important physical skills such as balance, agility and speed besides ensuring that their core strength and joint strength were addressed.

What this means for today's young netballer is that an effective fitness programme should focus on cross training and developing core strength and joint strength through simple body weight activities. Young players should be actively encouraged to run, swim, cycle or play other team sports both in competition and for recreation.

Netball-specific fitness is best done half an hour before your training session commences. Make sure that you have plenty of variety in your activities so that you vary the stresses and strains your young body is handling. Be aggressive and really attack the task at hand. It lays a great foundations for an important life skill. Here are some ideas to help you on your way.

Junior Netball Strength and Conditioning Training Programme: Early Off-Season

Aerobic Endurance

Objective: Develop aerobic fitness

Frequency: Twice a week

Duration: 30 minutes of easy-to-moderate aerobic activity (75 to 80 percent maximal heart rate)

Notes

- Warm up with a 5-minute run (65 to 75 percent maximal heart rate). Follow with 5 minutes of lower-body stretches for the calves, hamstrings, quadriceps, iliotibial band, hip flexors and glutes, spending 1 minute on each area (3 reps of 10 seconds on each side).

- Team and court games can be substituted for these training sessions.

- Easy runs (you can talk while running) can be replaced with another aerobic activity such as swimming, using a stepper or rower or riding a bike.

- Cool down with a 5-minute run (65 to 75 percent maximal heart rate). Follow with 5 minutes of lower-body stretches for the calves, hamstrings, quadriceps, iliotibial band, hip flexors and glutes, spending 1 minute on each area (3 reps of 10 seconds on each side).

Stability and Flexibility Programme

Objective: Develop stability and flexibility in the shoulders, trunk and hips

Frequency: Three sessions per week, alternating between sessions A and B

Duration: 30 minutes, plus a 16-minute stretch to cool down

Notes

- Commence the workout with a proper warm-up. Spend 5 minutes jogging, skipping, rowing, riding a bike or using a stepper.

- Be sure to use the correct technique to maximise the benefit of the exercise. Do the exercises slowly and under control with good technique. See your coach for technical feedback and correct load.

- These sessions can be done as a circuit. Be sure to maintain good technique.

- If this workout does not precede court training, complete a 16-minute stretch on completion. Stretch for 3 reps of 10 seconds on each side, and try to increase the stretch on the second and third reps. You will spend 1 minute on each area. Complete a 10-minute lower-body stretch that stretches the calves (soleus and gastrocnemius), hamstrings, quads, groin, iliotibial band, hip flexors, glutes and lower back (flexion and rotation), doing two sets for each part. Complete a 6-minute upper-body stretch of the upper and lower trapezius, shoulders (rotator cuff), chest (pectorals), biceps and triceps.

Session A

1. **Side lunges.** From an upright position, turn your right foot out and take an exaggerated step sideways with your right leg (figure 12.1). Continue to lower your body by flexing your right knee and hip. Return to your original standing position by strongly extending your right hip and knee. Keep your head and shoulders upright during the lunge. Your lead knee should point in the same direction as your foot throughout the lunge. Perform the exercise on the right leg and then the left leg. Use dumbbells or a barbell for added resistance.

Figure 12.1 Side lunge.

2. **Opposite arm and leg extensions.** Lie facedown with your arms stretched overhead. Raise your head, one arm and the opposite leg (figure 12.2). If you do this properly, you should feel a stretch in your lower back. Lower your head, arm and leg to the starting position at the same time. To increase the intensity, raise both arms and legs simultaneously. Hold; then lower and repeat.

Figure 12.2 Opposite arm and leg extension.

3. Dips or bench dips. For dips, mount a shoulder-width dip bar or place your hands on the edge of a weight bench; keep your arms straight and your shoulders above your hands. Keep your hips and knees straight and your head and eyes facing straight ahead. Lower your body by bending your arms (figure 12.3). Push your body up until your arms are straight. Repeat. For bench dips, stand between two parallel benches that are slightly less than a leg's length away. Place your hands on the edge of one bench, arms straight with shoulders above hands. Rest your heels on the adjacent bench with your legs straight. Lower your body by bending your arms until your rear touches the floor. Raise your body by extending your arms and repeat.

Figure 12.3 Dip.

4. Dumbbell one-arm rows. Place your left knee and left hand on a bench. Position your right foot slightly back to the side. Grasp a dumbbell in your right hand. Pull the dumbbell straight up until it makes contact with your ribs or until your upper arm is just beyond horizontal (figure 12.4). Lower the weight until your arm

Figure 12.4 Dumbbell one-arm row.

is fully extended and your shoulder is stretched forward. Repeat and then change sides to continue with the opposite arm.

5. Bridges or bent-knee sit-ups (crunches). For the bridge, lie on your back with your knees bent, feet flat on the floor. Lift your hips off the floor until your knees and hips are in line with your shoulders (figure 12.5) or as high as you can. Hold for 5 seconds and slowly return to the starting position. For crunches, lie on your back with your knees bent and your feet on the floor. Cross your arms at your waist. Contract your abs and flex at your waist to raise your upper torso until your elbows touch your knees. Your feet should always remain in contact with the floor. Lower your torso until the backs of your shoulders contact the mat. Repeat.

Figure 12.5 Bridge.

Session B

1. Split squats or step-ups. For the split squat, stand with your feet shoulder-width apart and your hands on your hips. Use dumbbells for greater resistance. Take an exaggerated step forward with your left leg while your right leg remains straight. Keep your head up and slowly lower your body by bending both knees (figure 12.6). Make sure your left knee does not extend over your toes (step is too short) and your right knee does not touch the ground (squat is too deep). Return to the starting position by pushing off with your lead leg. Repeat the exercise and then change legs. For step-ups, stand facing the side of a bench with your hands on your hips. Hold dumbbells to the sides for greater resistance. Place your right foot on the bench. Stand on the bench by extending through your right hip and knee and simultaneously pushing off with your left foot. Bring your left foot up onto the bench alongside your right foot, feet hip-width apart. Step down with the left leg by flexing the hip and knee. Repeat using the same leg on the bench and then change leg positions and continue. The height of the bench should require no more than a 90-degree knee bend. Keep your torso upright during the exercise. Your lead knee should point in the same direction as your foot throughout the movement.

Figure 12.6 Split squat.

2. Ball back extensions. Lie facedown on an exercise ball with your arms out in front of you and your feet stable on the floor behind you. Slowly raise your upper body off the ball (figure 12.7). Your hips maintain contact with the ball for support. Keep your arms in front of you for extra weight. Once your upper body is fully extended (hips and shoulders are in line), hold your position, breathe out and then slowly lower your body and repeat. You may want to add dumbbells to increase the resistance.

Figure 12.7 Ball back extension.

3. Push-ups. Lie facedown on the ground with your hands in line with your chest and slightly wider than shoulder width. Feet are shoulder-width apart. With your arms slightly bent, push your torso up by extending your arms (figure 12.8). Your legs remain straight with your weight through your palms. Your feet act as a pivot. Keep your head up. Breathe out on the way up and in on the way down. Ensure that your shoulders, hips and knees are straight. No sagging. For knee push-ups, start in a kneeling position with your feet crossed and off the floor. Place your hands parallel with your shoulders a bit wider than shoulder width. Extend your arms and raise your torso. Pause; then lower your body until your chest is close to the ground. Repeat.

Figure 12.8 Push-up.

4. Chins. Grasp an overhead bar with your hands wider than shoulder width. You may use an underhanded or overhanded grip. Cross your legs and bend your knees to 90 degrees to prevent body sway. Pull up your body by retracting your shoulder blades (figure 12.9). Pull them

Figure 12.9 Chin.

down and in. Flex your arms until your chin is just above the bar. Slowly lower your body until your arms and shoulders are fully extended. Repeat. For assisted chins, assume the same start position, but have an assistant gently push your body up from the knees to help you raise your body. Lower your body without support from the assistant.

5. Ball side crunches or twisting sit-ups. For ball side crunches, lie sideways over an exercise ball. Stagger your legs front to back for stability. Put your hands over your head, if you can, or cross them over your chest. While completely relaxed, pull up with your abdominal and oblique muscles until you cannot go any further (figure 12.10) and return to a full stretch. For twisting sit-ups, lie on your back with your knees bent at 90 degrees and your hands by your sides or crossed at your waist. Slowly lift your torso, bringing one elbow and shoulder towards the opposite knee. Keep your head and shoulders aligned. Slowly return to the starting position. Repeat to the other side.

Figure 12.10   Ball side crunch.

Sets and repetitions

Week 1: 3 sets of 8 reps per set

Week 2: 3 sets of 10 reps per set

Week 3: 3 sets of 12 reps per set

Week 4: 12 reps the first set, 10 reps the second set, 8 reps the third set

10-Minute Lower-Body Stretch

1. Gastrocnemius stretch. Stand facing a wall with your feet staggered. Bend your front leg and stretch your back leg, keeping your heel on the floor (figure 12.11). Stretch your arms forward to support yourself against the wall. Straighten your back and carefully lean forward until you feel the stretch. Switch legs and repeat.

Figure 12.11   Gastrocnemius stretch.

2. Soleus leg stretch. Stand facing a wall with your feet staggered. Bend both knees, keeping your heels on the ground (figure 12.12). Use your hands to support yourself against the wall. Carefully lean forward until you feel the stretch. Switch legs and repeat.

3. Hamstring stretch. Sit with one leg straight and the other leg bent to the side. Place your foot along the inner thigh of the straight leg. Lean forwards over the stretched leg and grasp the ankle or foot with your hands until you feel the stretch (figure 12.13). Repeat the stretch on the opposite leg.

4. Quad stretch. Lie on your abdomen with one leg straight and one leg bent. Grasp the foot of the bent leg and pull your thighs together. Carefully pull the foot down towards your buttock until you feel the stretch (figure 12.14). Repeat the stretch on the opposite leg.

Figure 12.12   Soleus leg stretch.

Figure 12.13   Hamstring stretch.

Figure 12.14   Quad stretch.

5. Inner thigh stretch. Stand with your feet spread wide apart. Bend one knee and straighten the other leg to the side (figure 12.15). Bend the knee to an approximately 90-degree angle. To deepen the stretch, turn the stretched leg so the toes point up towards the ceiling. Let the foot slide farther to the side and bend the opposite

Figure 12.15   Inner thigh stretch.

leg until you feel the stretch. Repeat the stretch on the opposite leg.

6. Iliotibial band stretch. Lie on your back with your hands to your sides or behind your neck and legs bent. Put one foot on the opposite knee. Use the foot to press the knee towards the floor until you feel the stretch (figure 12.16). Repeat the stretch on the opposite leg.

Figure 12.16   Iliotibial band stretch.

7. Prone hip flexor stretch. Lie flat on the floor. Bend one knee and pull your foot up to one side. Hold your foot with your hand and carefully lower your knee towards the floor until you feel the stretch (figure 12.17). Repeat the stretch on the opposite leg.

Figure 12.17   Prone hip flexor stretch.

8. Runner's hip flexor stretch. Stand with feet spread far apart and staggered. Bend the knee of the front leg and stretch the back leg, keeping your instep against the floor (figure 12.18). Support yourself by placing your hands on the floor in front of you. Stretch the back leg farther back and push the hip downwards until you feel the stretch. Hold the stretch for 15 to 20 seconds. Repeat the exercise with the opposite leg in front.

Figure 12.18 Runner's hip flexor stretch.

9. Glute stretch. Lie on your back with one leg bent and off the ground. Grasp your knee with your opposite arm. Carefully pull your knee down towards the ground until you feel the stretch (figure 12.19). Repeat the stretch on the opposite leg.

Figure 12.19 Glute stretch.

10. Back stretch. Stand with feet together and hands together above your head, arms stretched. Bend your torso to the side, without turning your hip, until you feel the stretch (figure 12.20). Repeat the stretch to the opposite side.

Figure 12.20 Back stretch.

11. Seated back stretch. Sit in a chair or on a bench with your legs shoulder-width apart. Lean forwards and stretch your arms backwards until you feel the stretch (figure 12.21).

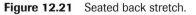

Figure 12.21 Seated back stretch.

12. Lower back stretch. Lie on your back with your legs together and knees bent. Put your hands behind your neck. Rotate your hip, without turning your upper body and lower your knees towards the floor to one side (figure 12.22). Repeat the stretch to the opposite side.

Figure 12.22 Lower back stretch.

6-Minute Upper-Body Stretch

1. Upper trapezius stretch. Stand with your back straight and look straight ahead. Place one arm behind your back and grasp your wrist with the other hand. Carefully pull your arm down and tip your head towards your shoulder in the same direction until you feel the stretch (figure 12.23). Repeat the stretch to the other side.

Figure 12.23   Upper trapezius stretch.

2. Lower trapezius stretch. Stand with your feet hip-width apart facing a wall. Place your hands on the wall to support yourself and bend your upper body forwards. Lower your chest down towards the floor until you feel the stretch (figure 12.24).

Figure 12.24   Lower trapezius stretch.

3. Shoulder stretch. Stand with your back straight and clasp your hands behind you. Stretch your arms and turn your elbows backwards until you feel the stretch (figure 12.25).

Figure 12.25   Shoulder stretch.

4. Rotator cuff stretch. Sit on your knees with your back straight. Bend one arm behind your neck as far down as possible. Bend the opposite arm up behind your back with palm outwards and let your fingers meet behind your back (figure 12.26). Fold your hands together until you feel the stretch. Release, relax and switch arms.

Figure 12.26   Rotator cuff stretch.

5. Chest stretch. Stand with your side against a wall or door frame. Hold your forearm against the wall in a vertical position while the upper arm is horizontal. Stretch your chest muscle by turning the chest away from the wall (figure 12.27). Repeat the stretch with the opposite arm.

Figure 12.27 Chest stretch.

6. Triceps stretch. Bend one arm and hold the elbow behind your neck. Use the other hand to pull the arm behind your neck until you feel the stretch (figure 12.28). Repeat the stretch with the opposite arm.

Figure 12.28 Triceps stretch.

Sprint and Agility Development

Objective: Introduce acceleration and agility drills

Frequency: Three times per week

Duration: 30 minutes, not including the warm-up

Notes

- Begin with 10 minutes of an active warm-up. It is essential to be fully warmed up prior to sprint drills to maximise the session and avoid injury.
- For variety, mix up the order of the exercises.
- Focus on body lean (leaning forward at the ankles, trunk not bent at waist), fast feet, arm drive, head and eyes level. Master one cue at a time. Initially focus on strong arm drive, then body lean, then fast feet.
- Remember that your feet will follow the rhythm of your arms. Slow arm swings mean slow feet. Fast arm pumping means fast feet.

Session A

1. Jog for 600 to 800 metres (3 to 4 minutes).
2. Sidestep for 30 metres, followed by 10 straight-leg swings across the body (left and right legs).
3. Run backwards for 30 metres, followed by 10 straight-leg swings forward and back.
4. Do walking lunges for 30 metres (walk in a straight line, hands on hips, alternately lunging forward off each leg; stay balanced and upright, bend at the knees, keep your head and eyes level) followed by three tuck jumps.
5. Do walking side lunges for 30 metres (similar to the walking lunge but take large sideways steps, stay low, keep your body upright) followed by three sit-ups.
6. Carioca for 30 metres (run laterally while crossing your feet alternately).

7. Skip for 30 metres followed by three push-ups.

8. Run backwards for 30 metres.

Session B: Sprint Technique Drills

Perform each drill for 5 minutes (for a total of 20 minutes). Choose four drills per session.

1. Plyometric Star Jumps, 3 sets of 8 or 10 reps. Jump high and fully extend, with minimal ground time after landing. Rest for 30 seconds between sets.

2. Plyometric Two-Footed Forward Hops, 3 sets of 8 or 10 reps. Hop forward on two feet, with minimal ground time after landing. Rest for 30 seconds between sets.

3. Quickfoot Ladder, 4 to 6 reps. Quickly move forward through the ladder with fast feet and minimal ground time. Both feet must touch in each square. Keep your head up and look up. Land and take off on the ball of your foot, not on your toes. Pump your arms quickly to create a rhythm.

4. Run-Throughs, 8 or 10 reps of 50 metres. Start with a jog for 10 metres (70 percent maximal heart rate). Change to a run for 10 metres (80 percent), then sprint at 90 percent for 10 metres. Run for 10 metres (80 percent), then sprint 10 metres again (90 percent). Gradually decelerate to a stop over 20 metres. Walk back to recover. Focus on technique—powerful arm drive; fast feet; back, shoulders, hips and knees in line in front of the ankle; body lean of 30 to 45 degrees.

5. Stair Sprints, 4 sets of 15 to 20 steps. Move your feet as fast as possible, lean forward, pump your arms, land and take off on the balls of your feet, and actively push off each step through your glutes. For the first and third sets, use both feet on each step. For the second and fourth sets, alternate feet on each step.

6. Stop 'n' Go, 4 to 6 reps for 30 metres (requires two players). Player A stands at the 30-metre mark and randomly calls "Stop" or "Go" as player B runs. The object of the exercise is for the running player to accelerate or decelerate rapidly on each call.

Session C: Agility Drills

1. Plyometric Two-Footed Lateral Hops, 3 sets of 8 or 10 reps. Hop laterally on two feet with minimal ground time.

2. Plyometric Two-Footed Zigzag Hops, 3 sets of 5 or 6 reps. Zigzag off both legs with minimal ground time.

3. Quickfoot Ladder, 4 to 6 reps. Quickly move sideways through the ladder with fast feet (short ground time). Both feet must touch in each square. Keep looking up. Land and take off on the ball of your foot, not on your toes. Move your arms quickly to create a rhythm.

4. Dodge Run-Throughs, 5 reps of 50 metres, 90 to 100 percent efforts, soft starts. Gradually accelerate over 10 metres. Dodge 2 metres left and right. Sprint at 100 percent for 10 metres. Back off to a 90 percent pace for 10 metres. Dodge 2 metres left and right. Sprint at a 100 percent pace for 10 metres, then decelerate gradually.

5. 5-0-5 Up-and-Back drill, 4 to 6 reps. Place three markers 5 metres apart in a line. Start in the centre. Sprint forward, touch the marker, shuffle back to the centre, turn 180 degrees, sprint to touch the other marker, shuffle back to the centre and turn 180 degrees (1 rep).

6. 5-0-5 Left-and-Right drill, 4 to 6 reps. Place three markers 5 metres apart in a line. Start in the centre. Sprint left, touch the marker, slide back to the centre, turn right 90 degrees, sprint to touch the other marker, slide left to the centre (1 rep).

Advanced Athletes

When undertaking any new programme, make sure that you gradually build the workload, particularly if you are coming from a fairly low base. Your body has to adapt to the increased demands now being placed on it. Racing into a programme and overtraining results in injuries. The body simply can't cope, so it breaks down. If you plan well, you can avoid this.

Your programme should be periodised to take into account the four training periods that make up the year for netball players: off-season, preseason, in-season and active rest.

Use the off-season training phase to begin a structured training plan for the next netball season. Concentrate on the development of aerobic and muscular endurance while laying the foundations for sprint speed and agility and stability and flexibility. Use this phase to build a solid foundation so you can build the components of fitness more successfully as the year unfolds.

Use preseason training to develop fitness components that are more specific to the game of netball, including strength, speed, power, anaerobic endurance, agility and flexibility.

The in-season training phase is game oriented. It focuses on the development and enhancement of netball-specific skills and fitness. The in-season phase includes power, speed and agility training; anaerobic conditioning; and skill-based sessions, emphasising technique for landing, jumping and turning in the air. The in-season training phase also focuses on maintaining the fitness components previously developed, such as flexibility, core strength, aerobic conditioning and muscular endurance.

During the active rest phase you take a break from the physical demands of netball. This will give your muscles, joints and supporting structure a rest from the wear and tear that has occurred throughout the season. Try other sports casually, swim, cycle or row, and attend to any injuries.

Following is an example of some early season work that will give you an excellent base on which to build your season.

Senior Netball Strength and Conditioning Training Programme: Early Off-Season

Aerobic Endurance

Objective: Develop aerobic base

Frequency: Two moderate runs and one easy run or cross-training session per week

Duration: 30 to 40 minutes

Notes

- Warm up with a 5-minute run (65 to 75 percent maximal heart rate).

- The easy run (65 to 75 percent maximal heart rate) can be replaced with other aerobic activity such as swimming, using a stepper or rower or riding a bike.

- Cool down with a 5-minute run (65 to 75 percent maximal heart rate). Follow with 10 minutes of lower-body stretches for the calves, hamstrings, quads, groin, iliotibial band, hip flexors, glutes and lower back (flexion and rotation), spending 1 minute on each area (2 sets of 3 reps of 10 seconds, 30 seconds each side).

Volume and Intensity

Week 1: Two 30-minute runs at 75 to 80 percent maximal heart rate and one 30-minute run at 65 to 75 percent maximal heart rate

Week 2: Two 35-minute runs at 75 to 80 percent maximal heart rate and one 30-minute run at 65 to 75 percent maximal heart rate

Week 3: Two 40-minute runs at 75 to 80 percent maximal heart rate and one 30-minute run at 65 to 75 percent maximal heart rate

Week 4: Two 30-minute runs at 75 to 80 percent maximal heart rate and one 30-minute run at 65 to 75 percent maximal heart rate

Sprint and Agility Development

Objective: Develop good sprint technique, introduce acceleration and agility drills

Frequency: Three sessions per week

Duration: 30 minutes, not including the warm-up

Notes

- Begin with 10 minutes of an active warm-up. It is essential to be fully warmed up prior to sprint drills to maximise the session and avoid injury.

- For variety, mix up the order of the exercises.

- Focus on body lean (leaning forward at ankles, trunk not bent at waist), fast feet, arm drive, head and eyes level. Master one cue at a time. Focus initially on strong arm drive, then body lean, then fast feet.

Session A

1. Jog for 600 to 800 metres (3 to 4 minutes).

2. Sidestep for 60 metres followed by three star jumps.

3. Run backwards for 60 metres followed by 20 straight-leg swings (10 forward and back, 10 across the body).

4. Do walking lunges for 30 metres (walk in a straight line, hands on hips, alternately lunging forward off each leg). Stay balanced and upright, bend at the knees and keep your head and eyes level.

5. Do walking side lunges for 30 metres (similar to walking lunges but take large sideways steps) Stay low; keep your body upright.

6. Carioca for 60 metres (run laterally while crossing your feet alternately) followed five star jumps.

7. Power skip for 60 metres (jump off every third skip) followed by 10 two-footed lateral hops.

8. Run backwards for 60 metres followed by 5 two-footed forward hops.

9. Do acceleration runs (ins and outs)—3 sets of 50 metres, with a soft start. Gradually accelerate for 10 metres (80 percent maximal heart rate), stride out for 10 metres (90 percent), then sprint at 100 percent for 10 metres. Stride out for 10 metres (90 percent), sprint for 10 metres (100 percent), then gradually decelerate and stop. Walk back to recover.

Session B: Sprint Technique Drills

Perform each drill for 5 minutes (total of 30 minutes). Choose six drills per session.

1. Plyometric Cone Jumps, 3 sets of 8 or 10 reps. Quickly jump sideways over a cone with minimal ground time. Rest for 30 seconds between sets.

2. Plyometric One-Footed Forward Hops, 4 sets of 8 or 10 reps. Hop forward on one foot. Change legs each set. Rest for 30 seconds between sets.

3. Wall drill, 2 sets of 3, 5, 7, and 9 reps each leg. Place your hands at approximately eye height on a wall. Step back one large stride and lean on the wall (30 to 45 degree body lean), keeping your body and arms straight (no sagging or piking through the midriff). Drive your right knee up to the high knee position and hold. Check your body alignment; then quickly change legs, driving your right leg down and back as if sprinting, pushing the wall and lifting your left leg. Check your position again. Maintain a smooth rhythm and sound technique as you progress. Use a mirror or partner for feedback.

4. Arm Action, 5 sets of 10 reps or 10 seconds. This can be done standing or seated. Alternate arm swings. Start slowly and build up your speed with rhythm. Your elbows should be bent at 90 degrees, and your fists should be lightly closed. Drive your elbow back past your midline. Your hands should travel in line with your body, not across, to eye level.

5. Quickfoot Ladder, 4 to 6 reps. Quickly move forward through the ladder with fast feet and minimal ground time. Both feet must touch in each square. Keep your head up and look up. Land and take off on the ball of your foot, not on your toes. Pump your arms quickly to create a rhythm.

6. Lean, Fall and Run, 5 sets of 10 metres. Lean forward from the ankles with your body straight until you must step forward to catch yourself; then sprint.

7. Push-Push drill, 5 sets of 10 metres (requires two players). Lean forward 30 to 45 degrees (same body position as the wall drill). Your partner stands in front of you, partially bracing your body weight at your shoulders. Drive forward by pushing back with fast force as your partner lightly resists for the first three paces. Then your partner lets go and you sprint forward, maintaining fast feet, body lean and a straight trunk. Your partner's support allows you to maintain the correct body lean while driving forward. Your partner

should provide just enough support so you don't fall.

8. Run-Throughs, 8 or 10 reps of 50 metres. Start with a jog for 10 metres (70 percent maximal heart rate). Change to a run for 10 metres (80 percent); then sprint at 90 percent for 10 metres. Run for 10 metres (80 percent); then sprint 10 metres again (90 percent). Gradually decelerate to a stop over 20 metres. Walk back to recover. Focus on technique—powerful arm drive, fast feet, back and hips in front of feet, body lean of 30 to 45 degrees.

Session C: Agility Drills.

Drills 3, 4 and 5 can be set up as relays, with two groups competing against each other.

1. Plyometric Two-Footed Forward Hops, 3 sets of 5 or 6 reps. Hop forward on two feet with minimal ground time.

2. Plyometric One-Footed Zigzag Hops, 3 sets of 8 to 10 reps. Zigzag off each leg with minimal ground time.

3. Quickfoot Ladder, 4 reps. Quickly move sideways through the ladder with fast feet (short ground time). Both feet must touch in each square. Look up and land and take off on the balls of your feet, not on your toes. Pump your arms fast to create a rhythm.

4. 5-0-5 Up-and-Back drill, 5 to 8 reps. Place three markers 5 metres apart in a line. Start in the centre. Sprint forward, touch the marker, shuffle back to the centre, turn 180 degrees, sprint, shuffle back to the centre and turn 180 degrees (1 rep).

5. 5-0-5 Left-and-Right drill, 5 to 8 reps. Place three markers 5 metres apart in a line. Start in the centre. Sprint left, touch the marker, slide back to the centre, turn 90 degrees to the right, sprint, slide back to the centre (1 rep).

6. Shadows or Agility Belt, 6 reps of 10 seconds (3 reps per player as lead, 50 seconds recovery between each rep; requires two players). Use four cones to set up a 10-metre by 10-metre square. Stand within the square. Your partner lines up within an arm's reach of you.

Dart within the square, trying to evade your partner. Your partner shadows your moves, remaining within an arm's reach. You can attach an agility belt if you wish. Try to outmanoeuvre your partner and break the weak link on the belt.

7. In-and-out Sprints, 6 to 8 reps with 1 minute of recovery between reps. Lay 10 cones 5 metres apart as shown in figure 12.29. Sprint forwards and sideways through the cones. Give 100 percent efforts with sharp turns.

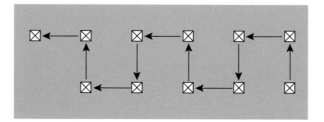

Figure 12.29 Cone setup and action for In-and-Out Sprints.

8. Double Triangles, 6 to 8 reps with 1 minute of recovery between reps. Place seven cones 5 metres apart as shown in figure 12.30. Sprint and slide around the cones. The sequence of sliding and sprinting can be changed for variety and challenge.

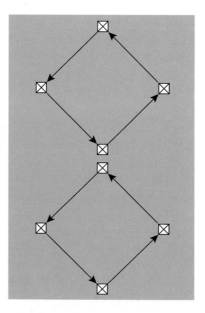

Figure 12.30 Cone setup and action for Double Triangles.

Stability and Flexibility

Objective: Develop stability and flexibility in the shoulders, trunk and hips

Frequency: Three sessions per week, alternating between sessions A and B

Duration: 75 minutes, including 16 minutes of stretching on completion

Notes

- Commence the workout with a proper warm-up. Spend 5 minutes jogging, skipping, rowing, riding a bike or using a stepper.

- Be sure to use the correct technique to maximise the benefit of the exercise. Do the exercises slowly and under control with good technique. See your coach for technical feedback and correct load.

- Increase the weight used each week. Use progressively heavier dumbbells, or select a more advanced exercise when the exercise becomes easier.

- Complete a full stretch for the upper and lower body on completion (approximately 15 stretches for 15 minutes). Stretch for 3 reps of 10 seconds on each side and try to increase the stretch on the second and third repetitions. You will spend 1 minute on each area. Complete a 10-minute lower-body stretch that stretches the calves (soleus and gastrocnemius), hamstrings, quads, groin, iliotibial band, hip flexors, glutes and lower back (flexion and rotation), doing two sets for each part. Complete a 6-minute upper-body stretch of the upper and lower trapezius, shoulders (rotator cuff), chest (pectorals), biceps and triceps.

Session A

1. Step-ups Stand facing the side of a bench with your hands on your hips (use dumbells for greater resistance). Place your right foot on the bench stand on bench by extending through your right hip and knee simutaneously pushing off with your left foot. Bring your left foot up onto the bench alongside your right foot (hip width apart) step down with left leg by flexing the hip and knee. Repeat using the same leg on the bench and then change leg positions and continue. Use a bench height that requires no more than a 90 degree knee bend. Keep your torso upright during the exercise. Your lead knee should point in the same direction as your foot throughout the movement.

2. Side lunges (see description on page 175)

3. Wood Chopper. Use a cable machine or an exercise band. Stand with feet shoulder-width apart. Reach over your shoulder for the handle on the cable machine or exercise band. Bring the handle down and across your body to the other side as far as you can (figure 12.31). Return to the starting position, using your abdominal muscles. In lieu of a cable machine or exercise band, you can use a medicine ball.

Figure 12.31   Wood Chopper.

4. Dips (see description on page 176)

5. Dumbbell one-arm rows (see description on page 176)

6. Dumbbell side raises. Grasp the dumbbells in front of your thighs. Bend at your hips slightly with your knees bent, feet shoulder-width apart. Raise your arms to the sides until the dumbbells are at shoulder height (figure 12.32). Lower and repeat. Maintain a fixed elbow position (10- to 30-degree angle) throughout the exercise.

Figure 12.32   Dumbbell side raises.

7. **Bridges** (see description on page 176)

8. **Back and hip extension** (see description on page 177)

Session B

1. **Split squats** (see description on page 177)

2. **Barbell full squats.** Use a wide grip to hold a barbell over your shoulders. Keep your shoulders back and your chest out. Stand with your feet shoulder-width apart, knees slightly bent and back straight. Lower your body until your thighs are just past parallel to the floor (figure 12.33). Pause; then extend your hips and knees

Figure 12.33   Dumbbell full squats.

(push your feet through the floor) until you are upright. Repeat. Keep your head and eyes level, chest out, back straight and feet flat on the floor. Equally distribute your weight through your forefoot and heel. Your knees should point in the same direction as your feet throughout the movement. You can use dumbbells instead of a barbell if you wish.

3. **Opposite arm and leg extensions** (see description on page 175)

4. **Push-ups** (see description on page 177)

5. **Chins** (see description on page 177)

6. **Dumbbell front shoulder raises.** Grasp the dumbbells in both hands. Raise both dumbbells with elbows fixed in a 10- to 30-degree angle throughout until your upper arms are parallel to the floor (figure 12.34). Lower your arms and repeat.

Figure 12.34   Dumbbell front shoulder raise.

7. **Rear raises.** Hold dumbbells down at your sides. Bend your knees and with a straight back bend over until your hips are at a 30-degrees angle to the floor. Raise both arms to the sides until your elbows are at shoulder height (figure 12.35). Keep a fixed elbow position (10- to 30-degree angle) throughout the exercise. Lower and repeat.

Figure 12.35 Rear raise.

8. Ball bridges. Lie on top of an exercise ball. Bend your knees at 90 degrees and keep your feet firmly in contact with the floor. Contract your abdominal muscles to maintain a stable trunk position parallel to the floor. Raise one leg off the floor, maintaining the stable trunk position, and extend the knee (figure 12.36). Return to the starting position and repeat with the other leg.

Figure 12.36 Ball bridge.

9. Ball crunches. Lie back on an exercise ball with your shoulder blades and hips on the ball and arms crossed at your waist or behind your head (advanced). Bend your knees to 90 degrees and keep your feet firmly in contact with the ground. Slowly curl up by contracting your abdominal muscles (figure 12.37). Slowly return to the starting position.

Figure 12.37 Ball crunch.

10. Side crunches or twisting sit-ups (see description on page 178)

Sets and Repetitions

Week 1: 3 or 4 sets of 12 reps per set

Week 2: 3 or 4 sets of 10 reps per set

Week 3: 3 or 4 sets of 10 reps per set

Week 4: 12 reps the first set, 10 reps the second set, 8 reps the third set

SUMMARY OF THE FIT TEAM

Improving your level of fitness will help you maintain the intensity of your game throughout the match. Achieving a high level of fitness will require dedication and commitment to the extra work that is required.

Work with your coach to design a year-round programme that relates to your training experience, your position and the competitive season. Consulting experts is very helpful, but be sure they understand the requirements of the game.

Fitness programmes should be enjoyable, challenging and specific to netball. The needs of young athletes are quite different from those of the senior players, and your programme should reflect this. Make sure that training loads are appropriate because the risk of injury rises when the body is overloaded.

Congratulations. You are now ready to step onto the netball court and enjoy this great game. You have the skills and the strategies, you know how a successful team operates and you also know the fitness that you will need to win—so step out with confidence. Don't forget to try a few positions before you decide just where your talent is best suited. Become a thinking player right from the start. Challenge yourself to see just how good you can be. Remember to keep polishing those basics, like great champions do, and then add your own flair and creativity. Use this book as your good companion as you make your way in the netball world.

Glossary

attack—When a team or individual in possession of the ball attempts to move it down court to the shooters.

baulk (fake or feint)—The action players use when they appear to be about to release a pass but do not let go of the ball.

blocking or channelling—Defending the ground in front of an opponent to force her wide and hold up her down-court drive.

centre circle—A circle 0.9 metres (3 ft) in diameter that marks the centre of the court.

centre pass—The pass that starts and restarts play after each goal is scored or after an interval.

clearing run—A wide, arcing movement that attempts to draw the defence away from critical space.

cushioning the impact of the landing—Bending the knees and lowering the body weight to reduce the jarring forces generated by landing.

defence—The actions of a team or individual resisting an attack. A team defends when it does not have possession of the ball.

front and back half of the circle—When the goal circle is divided in two by drawing a line parallel with the baseline through the midpoint of the circle, the front half is farthest from the goalpost and the back half is nearest the goalpost.

goal circle—A semicircle with a radius of 4.9 metres (16 ft) that radiates from the goalpost. The shooters must have possession of the ball and be wholly within the goal circle before they can shoot for goal.

grounded, or landed, foot—The foot that first makes contact with the ground when a player who has possession of the ball lands. If both feet land simultaneously, the player can choose which foot will be the landing foot.

intercepting—Cutting off a pass from the opposing team.

long ball—A ball that travels the length or width of a third.

obstruction—Any attempt to defend a player who has possession of the ball from less than the correct distance of 0.9 metres (3 ft). Obstruction is also defending a player who does not have possession of the ball with outstretched arms in less than the correct distance. Making intimidating movements to a player with or without the ball is also regarded as obstruction.

offer—A player's first attacking move; also called a lead.

preliminary move—A move used to clear space before offering an attacking move. The fake and roll are often used in this context.

recovery step—The step a defender takes to clear to the correct distance (0.9 m or 3 ft) when the first attempt to defend has been unsuccessful.

regrounding the landed foot—Replacing the landed foot onto the ground while still in possession of the ball. This is an infringement of the footwork rule.

re-offer—When the lead, or offer, is not used and the player makes another move.

shooter (goaler)—The goal shooter or goal attack; one of the team's two players who can score goals.

shuffle—A technique used to move quickly across a short space. The feet push and slide quickly with the weight down.

specialist session—A training session that focuses on the specific third of the court—defence, centre or attack—that the player works in.

stepping—Infringing the footwork rule.

stepping on—Taking full advantage of the footwork rule to take a step and three quarters before disposing of the ball.

substitution—Replacing a team member during the game.

throw-in—A move used to restart play when the ball has been thrown out of court. A throw-in is awarded against the team that last had contact with the ball.

timing—Knowing just when to make a move. Players often use on-court cues (e.g., a teammate's catch) to time their movements.

toss-up—A contest between two players in which the first player to catch a ball thrown into the air is the winner for the team. The ball is put into play from a toss-up when two players infringe simultaneously or when the umpire is unsure about who was last to contact a ball that has gone out of court. Both players face each other and their own goals. The umpire releases the ball between them, and both players quickly attempt to gain possession.

transverse line—A line that divides the court into three equal parts: a centre third and two goal thirds. There are two transverse lines on the netball court.

turnover—When the defending team takes possession of the ball from the attacking team.

About the Authors

Wilma Shakespear was the director of Queensland Academy of Sport and has recently retired as the director of the English Institute of Sport. Before overseeing the delivery of support to elite athletes, Wilma played and coached for the Australian netball team. In fact, Wilma was the world's first professional coach of an elite netball programme, and at 26 she was the youngest national coach ever appointed by Australia.

Margaret Caldow, BEM (British Empire Medal) recipient, was a player on the Australian netball team for 10 years and was the captain for 8 years. She played on three winning World Championship teams. She has been involved with netball coaching since 1980. Her various coaching roles have included coach at the Australian Institute of Sport, specialist shooting coach of the Australian National team, head coach of the Victorian Institute of Sport and head coach of the Melbourne Kestrels. From 2004 to 2008 Margaret was employed by England Netball as the national head coach. During this time she led England to a bronze medal in the 2006 Commonwealth Games and a fourth-place finish at the 2007 World Championships, and on the new world rankings that commenced in January 2008, she took England to a third-place world ranking. In 1988, Caldow was inducted into the Sport Australia Hall of Fame.

In 2005, Sport Australia Hall of Fame honoured both Margaret and Wilma as members of the 1963 Australian netball team for winning the first world netball championships in England.

STEPS TO SUCCESS SPORTS SERIES

The *Steps to Success Sports Series* is the most extensively researched and carefully developed set of books ever published for teaching and learning sports skills.

Each of the books offers a complete progression of skills, concepts and strategies that are carefully sequenced to optimise learning for students, teaching for sport-specific instructors and instructional program design techniques for future teachers.

The *Steps to Success Sports Series* includes:

ADVANCED SWIMMING — Steps to Success

Archery — STEPS TO SUCCESS — Third Edition — Kathleen Haywood • Catherine Lewis

Australian Football — STEPS TO SUCCESS — Second Edition — Andrew McLeod • Trevor Jaques

Badminton — STEPS TO SUCCESS — Second Edition — Tony Grice

Basketball — STEPS TO SUCCESS — Hal Wissel

Bowling — STEPS TO SUCCESS — Doug Wiedman

FENCING — Steps to Success — ELAINE CHERIS

Field Hockey — STEPS TO SUCCESS — Second Edition — Elizabeth Anders with Sue Myers

Golf — STEPS TO SUCCESS — Paul G. Schempp • Peter Mattsson

ICE SKATING — Steps to Success — KARIN KÜNZLE-WATSON • STEPHEN J. DeARMOND

Netball — STEPS TO SUCCESS — Wilma Shakespear / Margaret Caldow

Racquetball — STEPS TO SUCCESS — Dennis Fisher

Rifle — STEPS TO SUCCESS — Launi Meili

RUGBY — Steps to Success — TONY BISCOMBE • PETER DREWETT

Self-Defense — STEPS TO SURVIVAL — A proven plan for personal protection — Katy Mattingly

Soccer — STEPS TO SUCCESS — Second Edition — Joseph A. Luxbacher

SOCIAL DANCE — Steps to Success — Second Edition — JUDY PATTERSON WRIGHT

Softball — STEPS TO SUCCESS — Third Edition — Diane L. Potter / Lynn V. Johnson

SQUASH — Steps to Success — PHILIP YARROW

Swimming — STEPS TO SUCCESS — Third Edition — David Thomas

TABLE TENNIS — Steps to Success — LARRY HODGES

TEAM HANDBALL — Steps to Success — REITA E. CLANTON / MARY PHYL DWIGHT

Tennis — STEPS TO SUCCESS — Third Edition — Jim Brown

Volleyball — STEPS TO SUCCESS — Bonnie Kenny / Cindy Gregory

Weight Training — STEPS TO SUCCESS — Third Edition — Thomas R. Baechle • Roger W. Earle

To place your order, U.S. customers call
TOLL FREE 1-800-747-4457
In Canada call 1-800-465-7301
In Australia call 08 8372 0999
In Europe call +44 (0) 113 255 5665
In New Zealand call 0064 9 448 1207
or visit **www.HumanKinetics.com**

HUMAN KINETICS
The Premier Publisher for Sports & Fitness
P.O. Box 5076, Champaign, IL 61825-5076